COLLECTIVE ILLUSIONS

COLLECTIVE ILLUSIONS

CONFORMITY, COMPLICITY,

and the SCIENCE *of* WHY

WE MAKE BAD DECISIONS

TODD ROSE

NEW YORK

Hachette Books
Hachette Book Group
1290 Avenue of the Americas
New York, NY 10104
HachetteBooks.com
Facebook.com/HachetteBooks
Instagram.com/HachetteBooks

First Edition: February 2022

Published by Hachette Books, an imprint of Perseus Books, LLC, a subsidiary of Hachette Book Group, Inc. The Hachette Books name and logo is a trademark of the Hachette Book Group.

The publisher is not responsible for websites (or their content) that are not owned by the publisher.

Print book interior design by Six Red Marbles

Library of Congress Control Number: 2021947540

ISBNs: 9780306925689 (hardcover), 9780306925702 (ebook)

Printed in the United States of America

LSC-C

Printing 1, 2021

To Parisa Rouhani—the most congruent person I know

CONTENTS

CONTENTS

The real question is whether the brighter future is really always so distant. What if, on the contrary, it has been here for a long time already, and only our own blindness and weakness has prevented us from seeing it around us and within us, and kept us from developing it?

—VÁCLAV HAVEL

INTRODUCTION

The Secret of Elm Hollow

We suffer more often in imagination than in reality.

—SENECA

THE CHARMING FAKE lighthouse attached to the post office in Eaton, New York, is a remnant of once-upon-a-time days when the building was the Tower Gas Station. Painted with an eye-catching red-and-white helix that recalls a barber's pole, the two-story tower peers out over a small town of a few thousand people, set deep in the green belly button of New York State. Almost a century ago, it stood silent witness to one of the most important public opinion studies that you've never heard of.

In 1928, a doctoral student from Syracuse University named Richard Schanck came to live in this village. One of the very first researchers in the brand-new field of social psychology, Schanck sought to conduct a study of how people, as individuals, form their opinions. He chose Eaton (in his 128-page PhD dissertation, he called it "Elm Hollow") because it was a small, tight-knit religious community, remote from the complexities of city life, where everyone knew everyone. As in all tiny towns, neighbors in Elm

Hollow scrutinized each other zealously. The gossips kept careful tabs on everyone. If a child walking home from school picked an apple from a neighbor's tree or a man stumbled on a root while hurrying home late at night, someone was bound to notice.

The people of Elm Hollow understood that Schanck was there to study their social behavior, but it didn't take long for them to treat the big-city academic and his wife as their own. In the course of their three years in the village, the Schancks came to befriend Elm Hollow's residents, embedding themselves into the community. Since the couple attended church every Sunday, they were invited to baptisms, weddings, and funerals, as well as into people's homes for intimate dinners.

Schanck wrote down his observations of the townspeople's behavior in a notebook he carried around with him. He queried them about proper public comportment—particularly their views on the various social prohibitions issued from the pulpit. "Should baptism be done by immersion or sprinkling?" he inquired. "Is it acceptable to go to the theater on Sundays?" "Is it okay to play games with face cards?" (a prohibition originating from a Puritan hatred of British royalty and its dirty penchant for gambling). Publicly, the response was nearly unanimous: the vast majority of those he surveyed agreed that even playing games with face cards, such as bridge, was off limits.

But after his first year in Elm Hollow, Schanck realized that Elm Hollowites weren't quite the same people they pretended to be at church and elsewhere. For example, despite what they professed in public, Schanck reported that he'd personally drank, smoked, and played face card games with most adults in Elm Hollow...in the privacy of their own homes. This hypocrisy puzzled Schanck: Why in the world would most people in a community say they disapprove of things that they clearly had no problem doing?

In his private discussions with them, Schanck pressed his new friends to level with him. Attempting to understand the cause of this disconnect, he asked them a question whose answer would forever change how we think about public opinion—one that would lead directly to this book.

"What," he asked, "do you think *most people* in this community would say about smoking, drinking, and bridge playing?"

"Most people," came the reply, "would say that those are very sinful activities."[1]

For instance, a whopping 77 percent of Elm Hollowites told Schanck that while they themselves had no problem playing with face cards, they believed most people in their community were in favor of the strict prohibition against doing so.[2] But they had no idea that they were actually members of a silent majority. Nearly three-quarters of them indulged in the exact same "vices," but they all kept it secret. Even Mr. Fagson, a young, outspoken Baptist minister who pushed a strong fundamentalist position in public, was in fact a staunch, bridge-playing liberal in private.

Similar schisms emerged when Schanck asked the villagers about a range of other religious and secular issues, including whether or not they should build a new high school with the neighboring community (a particularly heated debate that led to fisticuffs). Puzzling over these weird gaps between public and private opinion, Schanck concluded that the people adopted just enough of the majority stance to be seen as acceptable members of the town. But why would they adhere to norms that they individually and collectively disliked? And how could the people of this small town be so utterly wrong about each other?

That's when he learned about the cultural grip of a dowager widow named Mrs. Salt. Because her father had previously presided as the minister of young Mr. Fagson's church, Mrs. Salt claimed to embody that institution's history and ethics. Since she was also its largest donor, Mr. Fagson depended on her for a paycheck.

Mrs. Salt managed to hold the townspeople in her iron grip for a full generation. Through the sheer strength of her personality, she dictated what one did and did not say in public. "Inasmuch as Mrs. Salt is a vigorous woman and in the habit of giving her views on a subject considerable public expression," Schanck wrote, "people frequently [hear] this oracle of the church expound her opinions [and] accept her views as typical of the group without critical enumeration of just how many believe as she."[3]

When the old woman passed away, however, things started to change. One night shortly afterward, the seemingly fundamentalist minister and his wife participated in a bridge party where they publicly played with face cards. This phenomenon kicked off a wave of gossip that spread through Elm Hollow like wildfire. If the minister played bridge, who else did? As they talked, people confessed to one another that they too were okay with playing with face cards, which led them to wonder out loud what else they had been wrong about. And with that, the spell was broken.

Richard Schanck concluded that the residents of Elm Hollow had willingly surrendered to Mrs. Salt because they believed (incorrectly) that she spoke for the majority. Schanck showed how, even in a tiny town, people don't necessarily know each other as well as they think they do. He demonstrated how easily a small, highly vocal minority—in this case, one single person—can misrepresent and mislead the rest of the group. And so he gave us the first true, research-driven peek at the subject of this book.

———

DR. SCHANCK WAS one of the first scholars to explore what I call "collective illusions."[*,4] Simply put, collective illusions are social

———

* Historically, scholars have referred to this as "pluralistic ignorance," but I find that term inadequate and confusing. The problem for an individual under a collective illusion is not that she is ignorant of what the group thinks; rather, she believes she knows, but she is wrong. That is not ignorance; it is an illusion.

lies. They occur in situations where a majority of individuals in a group privately reject a particular opinion, but they go along with it because they (incorrectly) assume that most other people accept it. When individuals conform to what they think the group wants, they can end up doing what nobody wants. That is the collective illusion's dark magic.

The most famous illustration of a collective illusion is Hans Christian Andersen's "The Emperor's New Clothes," published in 1837. You know the story: two con men convince a vain emperor that they are weaving fine clothes for him. They claim that the clothes are exceptionally beautiful but visible only to intelligent people. Of course no one wants to be seen as stupid, so everyone goes along with the con, even though the clothes don't actually exist. As the emperor parades through town, proud and nearly buck naked, the spell breaks when a small boy speaks up, outing the truth.[5]

If collective illusions were limited to the realm of fairy tales or religious expression, they wouldn't seem terribly important, and there would be no need for this book. Unfortunately, this is not the case. In society today, collective illusions are both ubiquitous and increasingly dangerous.

MODERN MISUNDERSTANDING

If I asked how you personally define a successful life, which of these answers would you choose?

- A. A person is successful if they have followed their own interests and talents to become the best they can be at what they care about most.
- B. A person is successful if they are rich, have a high-profile career, or are well-known.

Now, which one do you think *most* people would choose?

If you chose option A for yourself but thought that most people would choose option B, you are living under a collective illusion.

This question came from a 2019 study of more than fifty-two hundred people that my think tank, Populace, conducted on the ways the American public defines success. The result was that 97 percent chose A for themselves, but 92 percent thought that most others would choose B.

This finding was just the beginning. Using methods that get around the effects of social pressure to reveal authentic private trade-off priorities, we learned that a large majority of people felt that the most important attributes for success in their own lives were qualities such as character, good relationships, and education. But those same people believed that most others prioritized comparative attributes such as wealth, status, and power.

To put a finer point on it, consider the attribute of fame. In this study, out of seventy-six possible options, respondents told us that they believed "being famous" was the single most important priority for other Americans in their definition of success. But on a personal level, fame ranked dead last.

That's right: in private, most Americans do not care about being famous. However, they think it's the North Star for pretty much everyone else in America.[6] The takeaway from this Populace study was clear: the vast majority of us want to pursue lives of meaning and purpose; yet we simultaneously believe that the majority doesn't share our same values. As a result, we keep twisting ourselves into pretzels, trying to conform to what we falsely believe everyone else expects of us.

Personal success is not the only place where Populace has found collective illusions. In the span of a few short years, my organization has drawn attention to massive collective illusions that affect everything from the lives we want to live, to the kind of country we want to live in, to the trustworthiness of other people and even our views on the purpose of institutions like criminal justice, education, and health care. We have found that collective illusions flourish in just about every important area of social life in America.

Populace is not alone in this research. In recent years, scholars have unearthed collective illusions in just about every corner of the world and in all aspects of society. Collective illusions color everything from our views on war and climate change to our politics. They affect our attitudes regarding everything from gender bias to mental health and what constitutes physical attractiveness. They influence our ethical behavior and even our choice of foods.[7]

In the United States, for example, most people value and want to use the family-friendly benefits their employers provide (e.g., flexible work arrangements, resource referral programs, child care subsidies, and so on). Yet they also believe most other people do not.[8] As a result, all the people suffering from this illusion are less likely to actually use the benefits, even though they personally would like to.

Unfortunately, stereotypes tend to become supersized by collective illusions. Thus, in China, people perceive other Chinese people as holding more negative views of Japanese people than they actually do, driving them to express a more anti-Japanese public attitude.[9] In Japan, most men want to take paternity leave, but they believe most other men in their country do not. As a result, those who want to take paternity leave are significantly less likely to do so.[10] In California, both Democrats and Republicans assume the other side holds more extreme views than they actually do, creating a self-fulfilling misperception of political polarization.[11] Most American student athletes have positive views about academic achievement, but their notion that most other student-athletes do not drives them to act like they don't care about grades, damaging their own academic performance and reinforcing a collective illusion.[12]

In just the past twenty years, the rate and impact of collective illusions has accelerated to such an extent that they have become a defining feature of our modern society. And make no mistake: the consequences are profound. Take, for example, the issue of gender representation in politics. Despite the fact that they comprise more than half of our nation's population, women are profoundly underrepresented in American politics. And the easy answer—sexism—only partially explains the problem. Indeed, private opinion research conducted by Populace found that 79 percent of respondents agreed with the statement "A woman is equally capable as a man of being a good president of the United States."[13] Moreover, when they get to a general election—whether at the local, state, or national level—women actually win at the same rate as men.[14]

But the moment you ask, "Is a woman as *electable* as a man?" everything changes. Because, at the most fundamental level, electability is about what you think other people think, not which candidate you believe is the most capable. For instance, the political scientist Regina Bateson found that most people didn't personally care about a candidate's gender. However, once they learned that a competing candidate with the same qualifications was a white male, they overwhelmingly deemed him the most electable.[15]

Given the structure of our winner-take-all politics, voters regularly play "who-can-win" games that highlight our societal biases. So they think, "I'm not sexist, but other people are, so I'm going to vote for the white man because I want my party to win." This is exactly the problem with collective illusions. You may, in fact, be the least sexist person on the planet, but nevertheless your misreading of other people may lead you to become part of the problem without realizing it.

This problem isn't just hypothetical: we actually saw it play out in the 2020 presidential election. In a poll conducted prior to the Democratic convention, Avalanche Insights asked Democratic voters whom they would choose if the election were held that day. They responded (1) Joe Biden, (2) Bernie Sanders, and (3) Elizabeth Warren. However, when asked whom they would choose if they could just wave a magic wand and that person would automatically become president, respondents selected Elizabeth Warren as the winner, hands down.[16]

Bateson calls this phenomenon "strategic discrimination." As she explains, the problem here "is not animus toward the candidate. In contrast to direct bias, strategic discrimination is motivated by the belief that a candidate's identity will cause other people not to donate, volunteer, or vote for him or her." Thus, "Americans consider white male candidates more electable than equally qualified Black women and white women and, to a lesser extent, Black men."[17]

Unfortunately, the consequences of collective illusions aren't limited to politics. They strike at the heart of just about everything that matters in our social lives. Name anything that truly matters to you, and I'll wager that you are flat-out wrong about what the majority of people really think about at least half of them. And that's being generous.

Given their destructive power, we clearly have to get a handle on collective illusions. But we cannot do that if we do not understand *why* they exist in the first place.

WIRED TO EACH OTHER

Do you wash your hands after using the toilet?

This question was actually the centerpiece of a 1989 study of fifty-nine college women who used the library restroom at their school. In one instance a researcher served as an observer and was visibly present in the restroom while thirty-one students used the toilet; in another experimental condition, twenty-eight other subjects couldn't see her. The researcher found that while 77 percent of the women washed their hands when they thought they were being observed, just 39 percent did so when they believed they were alone.[18]

Silly as this experiment sounds, it tells us a lot about the underlying cause of collective illusions. We humans are so profoundly social that just our awareness of others can shift our behavior. This desire to be aligned with other people—what social scientists call our "conformity bias"—isn't optional: it's a hardwired part of our biology.

For example, in 2016, researchers used functional magnetic resonance imaging (fMRI) to scan the brains of subjects while they looked at 150 images of different foods, ranging from nutritious items like broccoli to junk foods like candy. Immediately after seeing an image, the subjects were asked to rate it in terms of personal preference on a scale of one (dislike) to eight (like).

Next, after rating a given item, subjects were shown the average score from two hundred prior participants, and if the subjects' personal rating was the same as the group, the word "agree" appeared. Otherwise, a number showed the difference between the group rating and their own. Finally, after finishing all of their own ratings and getting feedback on what the group had chosen, the participants were asked to rate the foods a second time.

As you can probably guess, on their second ratings participants fell into conformity, shifting their own food preferences to be closer to the group average. Interestingly, their behavior wasn't the only thing affected; the part of their brain involved in processing the value of different foods (the ventromedial prefrontal cortex) was also overwritten by the conformity. Once the subjects knew what the group preferred, the fMRI showed that this brain area shifted from tracking the healthiness of different foods to tracking their popularity.

But what the subjects did not know is that the group averages were entirely made up—manipulated by the researchers to make it seem like the participants were going against the group.[19] This is important because it reveals something fundamental about our bias toward conformity: *reality doesn't matter*. More precisely, our brains respond to what we believe about the group, regardless of whether or not that belief is rooted in truth.

Like the relentless tug of Earth's gravity, our yearning to go along with the crowd is an unconscious and largely inescapable part of how we move through the world—even when it's entirely fictional. It's also why we are always at risk of not only misreading others but also conforming to a false notion of what they think or expect. At the most basic level, this bias toward the majority makes us easy prey for collective illusions.

I myself fell for a short-lived one during the Covid-19 pandemic, when I eagerly participated in a toilet paper buying spree. A false rumor, spread via social media, led shoppers like me to empty store shelves of TP, despite the fact that North American manufacturers reported no actual shortage in supply. Once people began running out to buy extra rolls, the race was on.[20]

Even in the midst of this collective illusion, I thought, I know there's no shortage of TP. But it seems like everyone else thinks there is. So I couldn't help myself. Thousands of others like me acted like there was, indeed, a shortage, and so illusion rapidly snowballed. Before we knew it, the entire country was scrambling to stockpile the stuff and apparently with good reason: the shelves *were* empty! And before I knew it the collective illusion had become a reality.

A key principle from sociology neatly captures what happens when we buy into collective illusions. Developed by sociologist William Isaac Thomas and his wife Dorothy in 1928, the Thomas theorem says, "If [people] define situations as real, they are real in their consequences."[21] In other words, if you and I both truly think that people with freckles who hop on one foot are witches or that there will be no toilet paper left to buy during a pandemic, the *consequences* of that conviction are absolutely real, regardless of whether or not the belief itself is grounded in reality.

Because of our conformity bias, we all collude with collective illusions, both small and large, in our daily lives; but we don't realize that everyone else is playing exactly the same game. Our internal drive to follow others is so powerful that, if we are not careful, we end up tossing our own private judgment out the window. And so we all tumble together into Elm Hollow–ish misunderstandings.

AT THE DAWN of the social media age, Facebook CEO Mark Zuckerberg argued that new technologies would usher in an era of pluralism and free speech. "Those early years shaped my belief that giving everyone a voice empowers the powerless and pushes society to be better over time," Zuckerberg observed in an October 2019 speech.[22] By that logic, because more people have a voice, collective illusions should have gone extinct by now. Of course, this is not what happened. Ever since Prometheus stole fire from the gods, the story of new technology has always been entwined with unintended consequences.

Today, collective illusions have been turbocharged on a global scale—thanks, in part, to the wonders of platforms like Facebook and Twitter. Under the right conditions, anyone with a smartphone can do something that was impossible back in the days of Mrs. Salt. For Elm Hollowites, the tug of old religious traditions and local history were the source of misunderstandings. Today, by contrast, social media facilitates rapid shifts in perceived consensus, allowing fringe actors to manufacture illusions by creating the impression of majorities that don't exist in reality.

Imagine hundreds of thousands of Mrs. Salts on Twitter, and you can already guess how this story ends. By making us doubt our own judgment and causing us to believe that we're out of step with the majority, the loud fringe can effectively drive us into silence, exacerbating collective illusions and making us complicit in them.

On a national scale, these collective illusions have fed a deep, unsettling sense that something is wrong with our society. The past several years, we've felt as if we're all stuck in some weird *Twilight*

Zone nightmare where we are constantly, relentlessly gaslit. Up is down, left is right, right is wrong. It feels as if the values of our society have changed almost overnight. We feel disoriented, frustrated, disaffected, and distrustful of each other. We ask ourselves whether we've gone crazy, or the world has, or both. No wonder people in the United States are waging a kind of war on trust, building elaborate castles of suspicion that imperil our personal happiness and national prosperity.

All around the world, democracy is now under strain due in part to social problems that cannot be solved through legislation or technology. In a very real sense, collective illusions do the most damage in free societies, precisely because they depend on shared reality, common values, and the willingness to engage with different viewpoints in order to function, let alone flourish. That is why I see collective illusions as an existential threat.

The bad news is that we are all responsible for what is happening. And yet that is also the good news, because it means we have the power, individually and together, to solve the problem. The best news of all is that, as powerful as collective illusions are, they are also fragile because they are rooted in lies and can be dismantled through individual actions. With the right tools and some wise guidance, we can dismantle them.

I think I know just the guide.

WHEN IN ROME

First-century Rome was dragged down from its pedestal as a proud republic and into a cynical dictatorship under a series of selfish and debauched emperors. Pressed beneath the muscled thumbs of their first autocratic—if not outright crazy—emperors, Roman citizens found that there was no rule of law except that of obedience to the ruler. Saying the wrong thing could, and regularly did, cost people their livelihoods (and in many cases their lives). And so the name of the game became self-censorship—that is, live your private life how you wish, but don't say what you really think in public. I imagine the citizens of first-century Rome may have felt much the same way we do today.

Enter the great Roman statesman, dramatist, and philosopher Seneca (aka Lucius Annaeus Seneca the Younger). Born in 4 BC under the autocratic first Roman emperor, Augustus, Seneca witnessed at very close hand the tyranny of Tiberius, the paranoia of Claudius, the perversions of Caligula, and the narcissism of Nero. He recognized all of them as emperors with no clothes. While he dared not criticize them to their faces, he did write plays, essays, and speeches that served as a kind of antidote to the awful behavior that everyone around those rulers enabled, colluded with, or conformed to.

Seneca is one of those people in history with whom I would love to have dinner. I find him endlessly intriguing, in part because he was a bundle of contradictions. He was an educated man who preached the ascetic life despite being one of the richest men in Rome, a sage who was not above palace intrigue, an elitist who condemned his peers for their out-of-control lifestyles, and a utilitarian who studied human passions (and felt them too).

Seneca is most famous for writing about Stoicism, a philosophy many people dismiss as a simple commitment to keeping a stiff upper lip and repressing one's emotions. (We usually call someone "stoic" when they don't get upset by trying circumstances.) But Seneca's brand of Stoicism was much richer, more profound, and far more practical than that.

Like all Stoics, Seneca believed that the solution to our misery lay not in the external world but rather within each one of us. He thought that if you wanted to lead a satisfying life, you should not repress your emotions but instead claim personal responsibility for them (he called the work of doing this "self-shaping"[23]). Most importantly, he showed that we have far more personal power and autonomy than we realize.

Seneca also demonstrated how surrendering to fear, resentment, envy, lust, and other emotions at the moment they occur is self-destructive—an insight made more salient by the many impulsive Roman emperors he knew who had wrecked so many lives.[24] To this end, he offered his followers a practical program of knowledge and simple, actionable tips to help anyone, in any circumstance, to control their passions. In this way, he reasoned, their passions would not control them.

For example, he said that people who are afraid of losing their money should try giving some of their material goods away to see, on reflection, that they can live perfectly well without them. He also had gentle tips for self-correction. Instead of beating yourself up over your out-of-control emotions, Seneca would suggest lying in bed at the end of the day and thinking over moments when you had let a negative passion like anger or fear overcome you. Then he would ask you to forgive yourself in the knowledge that, having reflected on the moment that triggered you, you can be more in command of yourself next time it happens.[25]

Nearly two thousand years later, Seneca is still relevant. In fact, his approach is exactly how I want you to think about conformity and collective illusions. If we swap his word "passion" for "social influence," you have the same thing. Like our passions, our social nature is a built-in feature of who we are. Surrendering blindly to either one can be dangerous and damaging. But what Seneca did to tame passion, you and I can do to tackle social influence.

While our social nature is part of our biology, our reaction to our social instincts is within our control. When we're armed with the right knowledge and skills, we don't have to choose between being a maverick or being a lemming. This book aims to give you the tools you need to truly understand why and how we conform, how conformity leads directly to collective illusions, and how you can learn to control social influence so that it doesn't control you.

To that end, the book is organized into three parts.

You're probably familiar with the "first law of holes," credited to the British chancellor of the exchequer Denis Healy: when you're in a hole, stop digging. As a society, we've dug ourselves into a substantial hole, and the shovel is our systematic misunderstanding of one another. Part I, "The Conformity Traps," is about how we easily fall into holes of blind conformity—the collective situations where we are most likely to stop thinking for ourselves and surrender to the group's collective illusions. The three traps I describe here are the places where you're likely to make bad decisions that run contrary to your own preferences or values and that can harm other people. By learning to recognize these traps and applying a few simple solutions, you can begin to free yourself from the worst effects of social influence.

Nevertheless, collective illusions still exist everywhere. In Part II, "Our Social Dilemma," I show how the biological limits of our brains bend us toward them in the first place. To truly get a handle on collective illusions, you need to comprehend how they form and how we all become complicit in them. Specifically, the building blocks of our social nature, imitation and comparison, can trick us into following outdated norms and mistaking the loudest people on the fringe—the Mrs. Salts of the world—for the majority. By the end of this section, you'll be armed with the knowledge you need to battle collective illusions on a broader scale.

Parts I and II contain the information you can use in your personal life. Part III goes broader and has implications for all of us as a society. "Reclaiming Our Power" shows how you and I can contribute to a world free of collective illusions by taming social influence, once and for all. We can do this by committing to two things: regaining our personal congruence and restoring social trust. By doing this, we can help to create the kind of cultural inoculation needed to ensure that collective illusions get swept into the dustbin of history.

We live in challenging times: there is enormous pressure to go along to get along, to stay silent, or to lie about our private beliefs in order to belong. But blind conformity is never good for anyone—it robs us of happiness and keeps us from fulfilling our potential, individually and collectively. With the help of this book, you can step around the conformity traps that lead to illusions. You can make better decisions. You can build better relationships. You can have a more meaningful life, lived on your own terms—one that promises greater fulfillment and ultimately contributes to a better life for everyone.

Part I

THE CONFORMITY TRAPS

Once conform, once do what other people do because they do it, and a lethargy steals over all the finer nerves and faculties of the soul. She becomes all outer show and inward emptiness.

—VIRGINIA WOOLF

CHAPTER 1

NAKED EMPERORS

Trust yourself. Think for yourself. Act for yourself.
Speak for yourself. Be yourself.

—MARVA COLLINS

WHEN TIM MCCABE showed up at his local hospital with signs of congestive heart failure in 2009, doctors found a dangerous buildup of fluid around his heart and lungs. Five years before, Tim's wife, Christina, had donated one of her own kidneys so that he could go on living.[1] Now, suddenly, his body was rejecting the new kidney wholesale, and his heart was in trouble. The doctors put him on dialysis to keep him alive while he waited for another kidney.

So Tim waited. And waited.

Tim is a tall guy with close-cropped brown hair, piercing light-blue eyes, and a cleft chin. He has a thick, no-nonsense New York accent. When a telemarketer called in the middle of his dialysis in the mid-2010s, he smirked ever so slightly as he flipped to speakerphone. He had apparently won a "free cruise to the Bahamas!"

Before his illness, Tim loved to be outside, coaching his elder son in baseball, football, and basketball: "I was out there constantly with him, day and night, as soon as I'd get home from work." But with his younger son, this was harder. "I just don't have the strength," Tim told *The Atlantic*. "They shouldn't have to deal with this, and I feel bad sometimes that they do." On dialysis, his quality of life was "just shot." He couldn't do much and quickly became weak after any physical activity.

Each day, Tim waited by the phone, hoping for that one call to say, "Come in, we have it for you now." "And that sucks," Tim said. "Every time a phone rings you're thinking it's gonna be something good for you."[2]

Each year, one hundred thousand Americans like Tim wait for kidneys in a market of just over twenty-one thousand available donors.[3] One in four die within a year.[4] When you zoom out and look at transplant wait-lists in general, things only get worse. On average, seventeen people die every day waiting for a transplant, and a new patient is added to the wait-list every nine minutes.[5]

This might seem like a classic supply-and-demand problem, until you realize that almost one in five donated kidneys is actually *thrown away*.[6]

Why does this happen? It has to do with how the wait-list is structured and how we make inferences about the choices of others. When a donated kidney becomes available in the United States, it's evaluated for matches and then offered on a first-come, first-served basis to the matched individuals on the wait-list. This means that, when a person at the top of the queue rejects a kidney, others in line then have to decide—on the basis of little information and with precious little time—whether to accept that same, previously rejected kidney. Like a house that's sat on the market too long, the longer a kidney sits on the wait-list, the lower its perceived quality. If you are number twenty on the wait-list, you suspect that the other nineteen people before you had good reasons to reject that kidney, and so more than 10 percent of perfectly healthy kidneys from deceased donors are discarded due to repeated refusals.[7]

Those nineteen people, waiting for a cure that could save their lives, are falling into what I call "the copycat trap." In the absence of more information, they simply assume that the people ahead of them on the wait-list had good reasons for rejecting the organ, and therefore they should pass on the kidney. In reality, their refusal may have little to do with the kidney itself and instead reflect logistical issues or concerns about the closeness of the match.[8]

You and I get caught in this kind of trap more often than we realize. For example, when we observe others passing on a house for sale that looks good to us, we assume there must be something we can't see: ghosts in the attic, flooding in the basement, or some serious deferred-maintenance issues. If you're in line to wash your hands in a public restroom and nobody appears to be using one of the sinks, you believe, as others before you did, that there must be something wrong with the plumbing. And if you're unemployed, the longer you go without a job, the less likely you are to get a new one because potential employers wonder why another employer hasn't snapped you up. There must be something wrong with you.

The copycat trap captures us when we defer to others because we don't believe that we have enough solid information of our own or we don't trust our personal judgment. As our brains subconsciously seek to verify what we are seeing, they take cues from people who appear to have better knowledge than we do, especially when we are uncertain. Because we can never be totally sure that our private views and knowledge are correct, we often fill in the gaps by copying the behavior of others.

As humans, we are particularly susceptible to the copycat trap for two reasons. First, we have a built-in need to be accurate about our world. As toddlers, we wonder, "Is the stove hot?" and if we'd rather not find out on our own, we look to a nearby adult for verification. This kind of social learning is incredibly valuable to us at every age, as it keeps us from having to learn everything the hard way. Second, we have a profound fear of social embarrassment that makes us reluctant to speak up, interfering with the impulse to blurt out that the emperor is, in fact, butt naked. Combine these two motives, and you end up with a situation in which uncertainty frequently drives us to surrender our own private knowledge in favor of what we observe the "crowd" doing.[9]

As with flocks of snow geese or schools of sardines, our emotional and behavioral connections to others make it difficult to resist the impulse to conform. If we think someone is more expert, influential, or prestigious than we are, this becomes even more difficult. It's like fighting a flood with a single sandbag. And the copycat trap is the first place where we are likely to stumble into collective illusions, particularly when we worry about sticking out.

THE MIMES OF BOGOTÁ

Imagine that you're sitting alone in a waiting room, filling out a survey, when you begin to smell smoke. Looking around, you see gray clouds billowing from a wall vent. You go take a closer look, grab your stuff, and quickly report the problem to the secretary down the hall. That's what any sane person would do, right?

Now, conjure another scenario in which you're with several other people in the same room, and everyone is filling out surveys together. You smell smoke and see it pouring out of the vent, but nobody else seems terribly bothered. A few people start to wave their hands in front of their faces to push the smoke away as if it were a bothersome fly, but they don't otherwise appear to register that anything is amiss.

At the end of four minutes, the smoke starts hurting your eyes. You're having trouble breathing, and you start to cough. You ask the person sitting next to you whether the smoke is getting to him, but all he does is shrug and go back to his survey. "What's going on here?" you wonder. "Am I nuts?"

In the 1960s, social psychologists John Darley and Bibb Latané ran this exact experiment with a group of Columbia University students. In the first (solo) condition, 75 percent of the students left their seats to report the problem. But in the second (group) condition, the students were accompanied by research confederates who had secretly been instructed not to react to the smoke. Only 38 percent of these students got up to report the problem.[10] Why?

The simple answer is that we often conform because we're afraid of being embarrassed. Our stress levels rise at the thought of being mocked or viewed as incompetent, and when that happens, the fear-based part of the brain takes over.[11] Confused and unsure of ourselves, we surrender to the crowd because doing so relieves our stress. Caving to the majority opinion also diffuses our personal responsibility for our decisions, making it easier to bear mistakes. When you find yourself making a decision on your own, it can feel isolating, and the personal responsibility can be intimidating. Indeed, whether our actions are right or wrong, they always feel better if we take them together with others.

In the late 1990s, Antanas Mockus, a former mathematics professor and then the mayor of Bogotá, Colombia, found a clever way to make the fear of social embarrassment work for the public good. When Mockus first came to office, Bogotá had one of the highest traffic-fatality rates in Colombia, and deaths from motor vehicle crashes had risen by 22 percent between 1991 and 1995.[12] Jaywalking, in particular, was a problem: from 1996 to 2000, pedestrians accounted for over half of all Colombia's road traffic deaths in urban areas.[13] At the time, Mockus described the city's traffic as "chaotic and dangerous," a situation only aggravated by the city's corrupt traffic police. So he decided to take a radical step. He did away with the traffic cops and replaced them with a troop of mimes.

Dressed in brightly colored, baggy pants and bowties, twenty professional mimes silently applauded pedestrians who followed the street-crossing rules and mocked those who did not.[14] They also ambled around busy intersections making fun of drivers whose bumpers stuck out into the crosswalk. With their exaggerated gestures and expressive, white-painted faces, they exhorted motorcyclists to tighten their helmets and stay in their lanes.[15] By making a public show out of people's transgressions, the mimes poked at our natural aversion to being singled out. Mockus reasoned that this public discomfort might prove even more compelling than the traffic fines people paid privately.[16] He was right.

Given the choice between a solo spotlight of shame and going with the crowd, the vast majority of Bogotanos picked the crowd. Soon, some former traffic cops were being retrained as traffic mimes. A huge success, the program ballooned to four hundred clowns. "With neither words nor weapons, the mimes were double unarmed," Mockus commented. Their power lay in their ability to mobilize social influence to change popular, unsafe behaviors.[17] Used in tandem with other programs aimed at improving traffic safety, the mimes performed a true magic trick. In the space of ten years, Bogotá's traffic fatalities dropped by more than 50 percent.[18]

It would be one thing if we fell for the copycat trap and the social information were more accurate than what we know privately. But unfortunately, this is often not the case. It's also terribly easy to misread the behavior of the group.

THIS MANY PEOPLE CAN'T BE WRONG

One August afternoon in 2010, a small turboprop airplane carried twenty people, including the British pilot and one flight attendant, into the hot blue sky above Kinshasa, the capital city of the Democratic Republic of the Congo. The plane was on a routine round-robin flight to Bandundu, 160 miles away, with stops in between. As it approached Bandundu airport, the flight attendant noticed something rustling around in the rear of the passenger compartment and went to take a look.

She found a live crocodile grinning up at her.

The terrified attendant rushed toward the cockpit, presumably to inform the pilot. One alarmed passenger, seeing her fear, jumped up and hurried after her toward the front of the plane. In short order, the other passengers did the same. Their combined weight destabilized the turboprop and, despite the pilot's efforts, forced it nose-down into a house a few miles from the airport. All but one passenger, who witnessed what happened, died in the crash.

Oh, and the crocodile survived.[19]

Tragic as it is, this story sounds like something out of a Mel Brooks movie. We wonder how the passengers on that plane could have been so quickly compelled into playing follow the leader. The answer lies in how shared actions tend to cascade. The flight attendant was spooked by the crocodile, and the first person to follow her naturally inferred that something terrible was happening in the rear of the plane. But what about the people in the other rows? They were all copying those in front of them. They could not see what was wrong, so when one person after another ran after the flight attendant, the remaining passengers felt compelled to do likewise. Assuming that so many people couldn't be wrong, the frantic passengers surrendered their private judgment to the authority of the crowd.

Modeling our own actions on those of others can also be a matter of survival, particularly when we are under time pressure or in situations of uncertainty or ambiguity. And most of the time, filling in missing information from social cues works pretty well. If you are playing in the waves on Cape Cod and suddenly see everyone around you rushing to get out of the water, it's probably a good idea to assume there may be a great white shark nearby and hurry onto the beach too. Assumptions like this one are perfectly logical, given the information you have and what your brain is able to process.

And the truth is that there are times when the crowd can be right. In the long-running game show *Who Wants to Be a Millionaire?*, contestants try to win a top prize of $1 million by answering a series of multiple-choice questions, each worth a specific amount of money. In one format called "Ask the Audience," live audience members can vote on the answer they believe is correct using a handheld device, in real time. (Those at home can use instant messaging to send in their own guesses.) Amazingly, 91 percent of the time, the audience members together choose the correct answer.[20] In this case, the crowd truly is wise.

Unfortunately, real life rarely works like this, because the wisdom of the crowd requires that each individual make his or her own private decision. If people can see one another's choices, and if they are merely copying each other, wisdom becomes stupidity in a hurry.

In doubting our own judgment and defaulting to conformity, we transform ourselves from individuals into members of the herd. And before we know it, this seed of error can become a copying cascade that devours all other knowledge and leaves a collective illusion in its wake.

It's terrifyingly easy to start a copying cascade. Models developed by the economist Abhijit Banerjee suggest that the first person in a sequence always follows whatever private knowledge she has, and so does the second. But the third person is more likely to simply copy those who went before, especially if the first two do the same thing.[21] Banerjee observes that it's rational for individuals, having seen the behavior of other people ahead of them, to copy that behavior and abandon their own private judgment. This is because, as with the kidney, we aren't 100 percent sure about our own knowledge—we don't "know" that the kidney is good. We have information that suggests it is, but we weigh that against the social information we have. If we see dozens of other people doing the same thing, it's tempting to just assume that they know something we do not.

But once it begins, the copying cascade is both dangerous and counterproductive. It can swiftly lead to error on a massive scale, such as discarding healthy kidneys that would have saved lives.

And make no mistake, no one is immune to this trap—even people who should know better.

THE MANIAS

In 1841, the Scottish journalist Charles Mackay published a book about copying cascades titled *Memoirs of Extraordinary Popular Delusions and the Madness of Crowds*. His thesis was that "men think in herds" and "go mad in herds, while they only recover their senses slowly, and one by one."[22] One fad he explored was the famous "tulip mania" of 1634, when Holland's elite decided that having one's own unique collection of the spring-flowering bulbs was an absolute necessity. Despite the flower's lack of any intrinsic value, "the rage for possessing them soon caught the middle classes of society, merchants and shopkeepers, even of moderate means," he wrote.[23] As one modern scholar observed, at the height of tulip mania in 1635, "the average price of a tulip bulb exceeded its weight in gold, and a single rare bulb might easily trade for more than $50,000 in today's money."[24]

When prices began to waver and then fall, Mackay reported how "confidence was destroyed, and a universal panic seized upon the dealers." The great tulip boom was followed by a colossal tulip bust. Acknowledging the grip of temporary insanity, the government declared that "all contracts made in the height of the mania... should be declared null and void."[25]

Yet Mackay himself soon fell victim to this very trap.

A few years after he published his book, investors began rushing to buy shares in Britain's new railway system, expecting to earn 10 percent dividends at a time when stable companies were expected to pay about 4 percent. Some of the leading intellectuals of the day joined in, including Charles Darwin, John Stuart Mill, and the Brontë sisters. Charles Mackay, too, became a vocal supporter, asserting that the railway system would reach far beyond one hundred thousand miles. At its peak in 1847, railway construction employed almost twice as many men as the British army.

Mackay had all the information he needed to recognize this trend as a speculation frenzy. Instead, he got swept up in the excitement. He championed the railways in a string of newspaper articles; even as shares began to decline, he continued to reassure his readers. A steadfast supporter of technology, free markets, and economic progress, he slipped easily into the mania's central delusion that, as he wrote, "a huge expansion of the railway network could be carried out with profit to both the nation and investors."[26]

But the costs ran high, and instead of the anticipated 10 percent, railway shares ended up averaging a mere 2.8 percent. In reality, it turned out Parliament had approved the construction of just eight thousand miles of new lines. As a result, thousands of investors were ruined.[27]

Three years after the railway mania ended, in 1849, Mackay published the second edition of his book with substantial revisions. But he chose not to mention his own involvement in the British railway craze. Like the majority of his compatriots, Mackay was reluctant to acknowledge his own blindness and vulnerability to the mania, even years afterward.

If this kind of cascade sounds familiar, it's because it is the root cause of most financial upheaval. From irrational stock market leaps (the dot-com craze of the 1990s) to crashes (the collapse of the housing market in 2008), these cascades typically end with burst bubbles. But some will continue on for much longer, creating new norms that can lure us into something even more destructive.

Take bottled water. There's no question that drinking at least eight eight-ounce glasses of water a day is good for you. In recent years, our impulse has been to increasingly reach for plastic water bottles with their shiny, crystalline allure, because we assume that the water in them is safer and cleaner than filtered tap water.

The bottled-water mania first began in the United States back in 1994. The Environmental Protection Agency had issued a safety warning about drinking well water, because well pumps were leaching huge amounts of lead. So the government urged those with wells to start using bottled water until they had upgraded their pumps to stainless steel.[28]

Pretty soon, however, the notion that bottled water was safer than filtered tap water, in general, grew into a perceived consensus. Enterprising soda and bottled-water companies, seeing a huge opportunity, began selling consumers something that's about as free as it gets (it does, after all, fall from the sky), putting out new brands and flavors of water like leaves on an April tree. Today, the world's top two bottled-water brands are worth more than $1 billion each, and the once temporary solution to the well-water problem has become a gigantic and rapidly growing industry whose value is projected to reach $400 billion by 2026.[29]

But is bottled water actually cleaner and safer to drink? Sure it is, if you live in Flint, Michigan, where the tap water was found to be poisonous in 2015. With the exception of anomalies like Flint, however, filtered tap water is just fine. In the United States, 99 percent of filtered tap water is potable, and, in fact, that's exactly what many people are drinking out of bottles.[30] Over half of all bottled water is little more than treated tap water, and the two largest bottled-water brands, Aquafina and Dasani (manufactured by Pepsi and Coca-Cola, respectively), simply filter Detroit's municipal water, stick it in plastic bottles, then turn around and sell it for a massive markup.[31] Each of us buys into this colossal scam every time we opt for bottled water.

Still, we can't seem to get enough. In 2019, Americans drank 42.7 billion gallons of bottled water, surpassing our total consumption of carbonated soft drinks.[32] For those shopping at any old gas station or supermarket, a gallon of regular bottled water (averaging $1.50

per plastic bottle) runs roughly two thousand times what we pay for tap water.[33] And from there, the prices only go up. The finest vintages, supposedly filtered through volcanic rock from sacred, cloud-topped Japanese mountains or culled from the teardrops of angels, start at about $5 for roughly three cups. A bottle of Canada's Aqua Deco will run you $12; if you feel like splurging on a crisp Hawaiian Kona Nigari, it will run you $402. True connoisseurs can drink an Acqua di Critallo Tributo a Modigliani from a twenty-four-karat gold bottle for a mere $60,000.[34]

The bottled-water phenomenon is our contemporary tulip mania. Setting aside the fact that we are spending hundreds of billions of dollars on little more than a tenacious lie, the environmental consequences of generating such a massive amount of plastic are profound. A single cup of bottled water takes two thousand times as much energy to make as the same amount of tap water. Meanwhile, in the United States alone, 70 percent of all plastic water bottles end up as litter that pollutes our land and clogs our waterways.[35] The impact of this cascade is an enormous floating gyre of plastic twice the size of Texas, lurking on the ocean's surface somewhere between California and Hawaii.[36]

Cascades of illusion, like the bottled water mania, are sticky because they draw heavily on our deep-seated emotional connection to others. This fact makes them both deceptively easy to fall for and extremely difficult to dislodge once they are in place.

BEWARE THE CLAQUEURS

In the mid-1990s, the sociologist Nicholas Christakis worked as a hospice doctor at the University of Chicago, where one of his female patients lay dying of dementia. Her daughter, who had spent years caring for her mother, was bone weary and burned out, while her husband was exhausted from the effort of supporting his overworked and emotionally drained wife. One day a friend of the husband called Christakis, saying he was worried about his buddy. Like the creeping shadows of dusk, the emotional weight of this one woman's illness had spread.

The extent of the contagion set Christakis wondering. At the time he had been researching the notion that people could die of a broken heart. The "widower effect" is the very old idea that if someone's beloved dies, their own chances of dying within a year double. In his subsequent research, Christakis went deeper and found that human emotion and behavior actually clusters, coalescing into groups whose members conduct themselves in a similar way. In other words, birds of a feather do, in fact, flock together.

Researchers have shown how this social influence operates in subconscious ways. For example, Christakis discovered that if one person is obese, there is a 57 percent chance that someone in that person's cluster will likewise become obese. And vice versa: nonobese people who cluster together have a better-than-average chance of staying trim. Voting behavior, smoking, drinking, divorces, and altruism also spread in clusters.[37] This means that we can easily get swept up in imitative waves of behaviors and lifestyle choices that have nothing to do with information or reason.[38]

These waves, in turn, suck us into collective illusions that can be manipulated and supersized.

A fun illustration of this phenomenon is the "claque." (*Claque*, pronounced "clack," is the French word for "clap.") According to the classicist Mary Francis Gyles, the Roman emperor Nero (the man who forced Seneca to commit suicide) was an insecure fellow who sang, played the lyre (not the fiddle), and fancied himself a world-class actor, which he wasn't. To salve his delicate ego, he often entered singing competitions—which he always won because he was, well, the emperor. Wherever he competed, Nero brought along throngs of people to lead the crowd's applause, creating the false impression that he truly was a god of song.[39]

In sixteenth-century France, a playwright named Jean Daurat picked up on this idea and roped some friends, whom he called "claquers," into cheering at performances in exchange for tickets. Just as the clapping contagion spread throughout the theater, Daurat's idea caught on, and eventually claquing became a real source of income for wannabe actors. A theater or opera manager would order up some claquers for a performance, each with their own specialty: *pleureurs* (weepers) pretended to cry, *rieurs* (laughers) feigned hilarity at the right moments, and plain old *bisseurs* just clapped. Sometimes women were even hired to sit in the front row and pretend to faint so that male claquers could rush to their rescue—all as a kind of quasi-audition for the hiring manager.[40]

The beauty of claquing lies in the ability to invite copying, and claquers themselves understood something important about the way we humans relate to one another. Our propensity to copy others—whether in yawning, laughing, or cheering at a theater performance—springs from our deep connection. And because we connect, we fall into cascades.

Cascades affect all types of decisions, from how we vote and where we invest to what we wear, where we eat, and what school we choose to attend. Cascades also reveal a fundamental flaw in our tendency to copy others. Individually we may think we're acting reasonably and in our own self-interest, when in fact we're falling into the copycat trap.

Sometimes these cascades, like most fads, are relatively benign; other times, as with bottled water and the kidney wait-list, they have real and even deadly consequences. In the case of the kidney transplants, even if you believe you have nineteen pieces of evidence that the available kidney is bad, in truth you only know that the first person on the list made an independent choice to refuse it. Their reason for rejecting it might have been as simple as not having access to transportation on that particular day, but without that information the second person in line thought there might be something wrong; after that, the rest of the people on the list just copied those before them.[41] The resulting illusion affects not just your choice but everyone else's.

Unfortunately, we're not always just passive victims of cascades. In playing follow the leader—particularly if you're the first follower—you can also unknowingly create these illusions and cement them in place.

FOOL'S GOLD

As a doctoral student, I was once invited to a summer wine and cheese party by one of my fellow graduate students. I got dressed up and picked out one of my own particular wine favorites, a grapefruity Marlborough sauvignon blanc. At the party, the scent of blooming wisteria drifted through the garden, and a fountain tinkled in the background. Everyone was enjoying conversation and politely sampling the decorative spread of wines and cheeses, when a familiar voice burst out, "Hey, everybody! I'm here!"

"Oh, shoot," I thought. "Here he comes."

Into the garden swanned Ambrose—dreadful Ambrose, whose last name was followed by the Roman numeral III—whose demeanor seemed to confirm, in the flesh, all of the worst Ivy League stereotypes. This guy wasn't just wealthy and cultured; he knew it, and he made sure everyone else knew it, too. He wore a navy-blue tailored suit with a crisp white pocket handkerchief, topped off with his usual bow tie.

It wasn't long before Ambrose pinged his wine glass with a cocktail fork to call for our attention. "Hi, everyone!" he announced cheerily. "Just wait until you taste this! It's a rare vintage from a family friend's vineyard in Sonoma. I recommend getting a fresh glass."[42]

Ambrose waited while we all complied. Then, with a flourish, he tipped a few ounces of the ruby-red wine he'd brought into each glass. "Don't drink it," he instructed. "Just swirl it around in the glass and look at the streaks. And sniff it."

I dutifully obeyed.

"Now take a sip and swirl it around in your mouth before swallowing," our guide continued.

"Mmmm," somebody said, looking Ambrose in the eye. "Delicious!"

I took a sip and looked at the others, all of whom were nodding their approval. I couldn't believe it. The wine tasted like vinegar. Was something wrong with my palate? I wondered whether I might be coming down with a cold, which could be interfering with my tastebuds. Or maybe my palate wasn't refined enough to appreciate what was apparently an acquired taste.

Then one of our professors—I'll call her "Dr. Smith"—arrived. We'd all taken her statistics class. We knew she was a true wine aficionado because she'd given us an assignment asking us to identify the most undervalued wine region in France, using a statistical method called "multiple regression." (The answer, in case you were wondering, turned out to be Languedoc.) I wondered what she'd think of this stuff.

"Oh, Dr. Smith! Please join us!" Ambrose cried, pouring her a bit of wine. "This is something special that I brought."

Dr. Smith took a taste and immediately spewed it out onto the grass. "This is corked wine," she stated flatly. ("Corked" wine is tainted with a molecule that sommeliers know as 2,3,6-trichloroanisole, or TCA, which makes it smell like anything from a wet dog to a dirty restroom.[43]) I suppressed a smile.

Clearly, either my fellow students were insensitive to the smell and taste or they just fell for Ambrose's sales job. But until Dr. Smith spoke the truth, everyone behaved as if Ambrose knew exactly what he was talking about.

We frequently fall in line behind people who we assume know more than we do. Indeed, though we may not be inclined to believe "the world is ending" if we hear it from a sixth grader, if a doctor or scientist utters the same words, they carry significantly more weight.[44] If the weatherman, a trained meteorologist, tells you that there's a 75 percent chance of a thunderstorm in your area this afternoon, you grab a raincoat before you leave the house.

But that still doesn't explain Ambrose, who never once told us he was an expert; we simply assumed that he knew a lot about wine. If wealthy, cultured Ambrose sails into your group with his perfectly manicured nails and bow tie and your peers give him attention or deference, you are equally likely to accept him as some kind of an expert, even though he isn't.[45]

Why do we do this? It turns out that expertise is really hard to sniff out. So we rely on the correlates of expertise instead—in Ambrose's case, we fell for his fancy clothes and his boarding school accent. Under the spell of what scientists call the "prestige bias," we accept mere signals of prestige such as wealth, job title, beauty, clothing, and possessions as indicators of true expertise (never mind that they are largely unrelated).[46] So we might decide to become a loyal Goop customer just because we aspire to be like Gwyneth Paltrow.

We are particularly duped by the visible symbols of authority. In one 1984 study, a young man pretended to be looking for change to feed a parking meter, while a second, older man approached passersby and told them to help the younger man by giving him a dime. The older man dressed up first as a homeless person, then as a well-dressed "businessman," and finally as a "fireman in uniform": 45 percent of subjects obeyed the homeless person, 50 percent obeyed the businessman, and 82 percent obeyed the fireman.[47]

Like our natural tendency to follow the crowd, this deference to perceived prestige and authority runs deep. Indeed, something as simple as a title can easily fool us into prestige bias. In 1966, a team of researchers tested this theory by having an unfamiliar "doctor" instruct nurses, over the phone, to administer an "obviously excessive dose" of an unauthorized medicine. A staggering 95 percent of the nurses complied, illustrating the enormous power of perceived authority and the title of physician, even when that title was not confirmed.[48]

It gets worse. We are so bad at detecting genuine expertise that we will even defer to people simply because they display self-assurance. When someone seems confident, their affect suggests that they know something we don't.[49] In mid-nineteenth-century New York City, a nicely dressed scammer named Samuel Thompson conned his marks by pretending that he knew them. Once he gained their trust, he would ask them to lend him money or their watches, after which he disappeared. A reporter for the *New York Herald* called Thompson a "confidence man," and the nickname stuck.[50] Confidence and illusion are, and always have been, cozy bedfellows.

Fortunately, once we have the factual information we need (i.e., the wine is corked; the tulip bulb isn't worth $50,000), most cascades tend to self-correct. But this is not always true. When we are emotionally invested in an outcome, and especially when our reputations are on the line, the goal posts shift. Like Charles Mackay, we may not *want* to see the truth, and so we do everything we can to avoid looking it in the face. This snare is both easy to trigger and hard to escape.

A VOYAGE TO LAPUTA

In 1996, New York University physics professor Alan D. Sokal published an academic article titled "Transgressing the Boundaries: Toward a Transformative Hermeneutics of Quantum Gravity" in the postmodern journal *Social Text*. Based on the author's summary, below, what do you think the paper was about?

Here my aim is to carry these deep analyses one step farther, by taking account of recent developments in quantum gravity:

the emerging branch of physics in which Heisenberg's quantum mechanics and Einstein's general relativity are at once synthesized and superseded. In quantum gravity, as we shall see, the space-time manifold ceases to exist as an objective physical reality; geometry becomes relational and contextual; and the foundational conceptual categories of prior science—among them, existence itself—become problematized and relativized. This conceptual revolution, I will argue, has profound implications for the content of a future postmodern and liberatory science.[51]

If you think this is all just confusing, academic gibberish, you're 100 percent correct. Professor Sokal pumped his paper full of jargon and submitted it to the cultural studies journal, whose half dozen editors vetted, accepted, and published it as a serious piece of scholarly work for a special edition on science.

Then Sokal revealed that the whole thing was a hoax. He was just taking pains to make a point about academic publishing, demonstrating how a lot of academics are rewarded for sounding like the inhabitants of Laputa, the floating island in Jonathan Swift's 1726 satire *Gulliver's Travels*. The narrow-minded theoreticians and academics who live in Laputa spend their days conducting useless, impractical research. Of course, the joke is on them because they are completely out of touch with reality.

Like Swift, Sokal made up a lot of ridiculous stuff, heavily salting his essay with popular deconstructionist lingo, such as "contingent," "counterhegemonic," and "epistemological." "I structured the article around the silliest quotes about mathematics and physics from the most prominent academics, and I invented an argument praising them and linking them together," he told the *New York Times*. "All this was very easy to carry off because my argument wasn't obliged to respect any standards of evidence or logic."[52]

While making fun of the kind of gaseous lint picking that fills cultural studies and literary criticism journals, Sokal was also needling the deliberate use of complex terms and concepts that characterizes all kinds of competitive academic cliques. Indeed, this fad often reaches such a pitch that it becomes impossible to discern what the authors really mean to say, even for those within their own disciplines.

The response from the top editor of *Social Text* was pretty sour. "[Dr. Sokal] says we're epistemic relativists," said Stanley Aronowitz, the journal's cofounder and a professor at City University of New York. "We're not. He got it wrong. One of the reasons he got it wrong is he's ill-read and half-educated."[53] "*Social Text*'s acceptance of my article exemplifies the intellectual arrogance of Theory—postmodernist literary theory, that is—carried to its logical extreme," Sokal shot back. "No wonder they didn't bother to consult a physicist." In their world, he added, "incomprehensibility becomes a virtue; allusions, metaphors, and puns substitute for evidence and logic. My own article is, if anything, an extremely modest example of this well-established genre."[54]

White-collar professions such as academia, law, and medicine are particularly susceptible to reputational cascades like this one. When reputation is everything, the voices of those who reside at the top of the professional heap get amplified—not necessarily due to the merits of their arguments but because we expect them to know what they are talking about.[55] The vast majority of other professionals go along with them as a matter of safeguarding their careers.

Take, for example, the tonsillectomy, a once popular surgical procedure. Lacking in scientific justification or results, this medical fad continued for decades based solely on the vagaries of "expert medical opinion." At its height in the twentieth century, tonsillectomies were routinely performed on millions of children, some of whom were injured or even died as a result. Yet, when the procedure at last came under scrutiny, the obvious lack of a scientific basis drove it quickly out of fashion.[56]

When we defer to authority because our reputations have something to gain or lose, our commitment to one particular narrative makes us immune to new information, which makes this sort of cascade very hard to undo. It doesn't really matter whether the story we're colluding with is true or not. To everyone else, however, it looks like we and all the others who are going along can't possibly be wrong.

Solid as they seem, cascades like these are fortunately more like a Jenga tower with one key weak point. Remove that one pivotal brick, and it all comes crashing down.

THE POWER OF "WHY?"

Think back now to the awful problem of the discarded kidneys. Is there any way to fix it?

Believe it or not, there's an exquisitely simple solution—one so simple, in fact, that it was completely overlooked before an MIT researcher named Juanjuan Zhang figured it out. All the people on the wait-list who pass on a kidney have to do is say *why* they are refusing the organ: "I'm traveling out of state," "I have a bad cold," "It's not a close enough match," and so on. With just a little more information, the people on the wait-list can come into line with reality and make a better personal decision. And we can stop sacrificing perfectly good kidneys on the altar of collective illusion.[57]

And this solution doesn't apply only to kidney wait-lists. Asking "Why?" is a handy, general-purpose tool that can keep you out of any kind of cascade. With the power of this one simple question, you can hold onto your own personal knowledge rather than abandoning it in favor of others' opinions. It allows you, instead, to blend your view with that of others as needed, in order to get better information and ultimately make your own determination.

Some people might think that asking "Why?" is bad form. Indeed, the question can feel so obvious that it might seem offensive, but it turns out that people actually *like* to share the reasoning behind their own opinions and preferences. One Harvard study showed that sharing our views is intrinsically rewarding, even on a sensitive question such as "What's your view of abortion?" Simply being asked about and sharing our views makes us like each other more.[58]

Think about your most recent conversation with a close family member or friend. What did you talk about? How did you feel afterward? Statistically speaking, you spent up to 40 percent of the conversation sharing or discussing your personal feelings or experiences, and the other person did the same.[59] Chances are things felt balanced, with neither person hogging the phone. You came away feeling refreshed and happy to have connected.

In fact, the satisfaction we gain from talking about ourselves is on par with other, more objective rewards such as money or food. This helps to explain why a whopping 80 percent of the material posted to social media platforms pertains to people's private (and, let's face it, largely insignificant) thoughts or experiences. Scientists have found that we have an actual neurological drive to disclose personal information; each tidbit shared stimulates the reward system in our brains, giving our bodies a hit of pure pleasure. In other words, we don't just spill our guts because we're nervous or overwrought; we are intrinsically motivated to do so.[60]

This propensity to disclose personal information is part of what makes us human, and it has helped our species survive over time. (It's also been great for Facebook's bottom line.) It makes forming connections and cultivating bonds with others easier. By encouraging the exchange and accumulation of knowledge through shared expertise, it also gives us opportunities to lead, instruct, and learn.[61]

Ultimately, there is no real downside to asking "Why?" while there are plenty of upsides. It not only cultivates social connection but allows you to quickly root out a possible cascade. If someone can't explain their reasons beyond saying, "Because so and so did it," you know you are at risk of following the herd and falling for a collective illusion. Asking "Why?" pulls back the curtain, revealing the truth behind the actions and assertions of others.

In a similar way, this one simple question blocks the creation of cascades by preventing us from relying solely on snap (often incorrect) assumptions. Unlocking the reasoning behind the other person's choice also allows you to assess whether the rationale for their behavior aligns with your own values and priorities and even whether their judgments apply to your own personal situation.

In the end, we can and should strive to be accurate by observing and listening to other people, but we must resist the seductive pull of abandoning our own judgment and blindly following others, regardless of whether it's a whole crowd or someone we view as an authority. Exhausting as it may seem, thinking for ourselves is absolutely essential not only to you and me, as individuals, but to the survival and health of our entire society.

CHAPTER 2

LYING TO BELONG

The individual has always had to struggle to keep from
being overwhelmed by the tribe.

—FRIEDRICH NIETZSCHE

BURIED DEEP IN a South American jungle, the People's Temple
in Jonestown, Guyana, lay six miles from the nearest airstrip, down
a rutted dirt road. Founded on the principles of racial justice and
Soviet communism, this colony of one thousand predominantly
working-class black members—a majority of whom were women—
was led by a charismatic leader named Jim Jones.[1] At its center
was a pavilion with a broad metal roof, where children attended
school and the community gathered for assemblies. Nearby stood
rows of fruit trees and carefully tended farm fields. There was a
sawmill, a library of ten thousand books, and a children's nursery
festooned with mosquito netting. Everyone there had given up
their jobs and personal possessions in order to commit fully to
the Temple community and its Communist ideals. Its members
believed Jonestown was Utopia.

You probably remember what came next: in November 1978,

California congressman Leo Ryan showed up in Guyana to investigate reports of strange happenings at the colony, including reports of sexual abuse and torture. Jones, a paranoid "prophet," told his followers that Ryan and his team would bring violence and ruin to Jonestown. When Ryan left the colony, a handful of Temple defectors went with him, but at the airstrip he and several others were murdered by Jones's henchmen.[2] Back at the compound, Jones informed his followers of the murders and warned of an imminent backlash. Temple members would be severely punished, he said, and their children and elderly would be tortured.[3] Enacting a scenario already rehearsed repeatedly in mock suicide ceremonies known as "White Nights," Jones explained that group suicide was a way to die with "dignity and honor"—a definitive act of protest against fascism and racism.[4]

At least one member, however, disagreed. Most notable among them was Christine Miller, a woman who stood up and asked, "Is it too late [to leave] for Russia?" An older member of the community, Miller had given generously to its various charitable causes before coming to Jonestown. This was not the first time she had stood up to Jones, but it was certainly the most important.

Miller did not want to die that day. Referring to those who had defected with Ryan, she argued that too few people had left the colony that day for the rest of them to give their lives. Quoting one of Jones's own sermons, she added, "As long as there's life, there's hope." As one of those who had joined Jones believing he would help them achieve the greatest version of themselves, she based her appeal on the individual potential of each person and child.[5]

Still, despite the sound logic of Miller's arguments, she was fighting against the faith of a thousand others who not only believed in reincarnation but had been brainwashed to follow Jones's orders straight into the jaws of death.[6] If others had joined her, perhaps she could have broken the spell. But her comments were taken, instead, as an expression of treason. Her pleas were quickly drowned out by the loud voices of Jones's guards and a few others, one of whom proclaimed to Jones, "If you tell us we have to give our lives now, we're ready."[7] Moments later Jones called for the "medication"—cyanide-laced fruit punch in giant vats—and urged his followers to face death courageously.[8] The children went first, and as they were brought forward, music, cheering, and applause mixed with the sounds of agony.

It is unknown how many people willingly drank the poison and how many were forced to drink it or receive it as an injection. Of the more than nine hundred people who died that day, Miller, who was seated at the front of the hall, was probably one of the first adults to step forward.[9]

Christine Miller tried to save herself and others. But in the end, she succumbed to two fundamental characteristics of human nature: the need for acceptance by her in-group and the profound fear of being ostracized from it.

As social creatures, we humans joyfully connect with others wherever we go, from our families to our neighbors, online groups, and workplace colleagues. But when it comes to collective illusions, not all groups are created equal. We care most about the people with whom we feel the deepest connection, whose praise or condemnation matter the most: our in-groups. These close members of our perceived tribes might share our religion, our politics, our nationality, or our family ties. They might be our school or work buddies. They might be fellow fans of our favorite bands or sports teams or belong to one of our Facebook groups. Inclusion in our in-groups makes us feel happier, safer, and more certain of ourselves and our place in the world.[10]

You and I are constantly doing things to solidify our bonds with our closest communities. Everything from our choice of clothing to our public behavior signals our membership in various groups. We instinctively follow the norms of each group because we don't want to feel out of place, and we understand the importance of mediating our own appearance and behavior based on our social surroundings. Every time we do this, we reshape our perception of ourselves around what we believe to be the group ideal.[11]

The satisfaction and security we glean from this process springs largely from our deep desire to feel psychological and emotional coherence with our groups. Not surprisingly, then, as soon as doubt begins to crack our sense of solidarity, illusion follows. We begin to worry that we are the only ones afraid of rejection, and we start second-guessing ourselves and misreading others. The same fear also makes us frighteningly compliant. It also promotes tribal, us-versus-them thinking that can lead us to do unbelievable harm in the name of our group. Indeed, under the right circumstances, the pull of our tribes can be so strong that what I call the "identity trap" can actually push us to lie about our private values and even enforce beliefs we don't personally support, ultimately causing us to hurt others who are secretly like us.

Not only does this identity trap create and sustain collective illusions, as we saw at Jonestown, but it can also destroy the group itself.

US VERSUS THEM

The moment immediately after birth, when we connect with our mothers, is absolutely fundamental to our well-being. If babies don't bond with their caregivers, they can "fail to thrive" and literally die. Attachment disorder explains why so many orphans rejected in their earliest years go on to experience immense psychological and behavioral problems. From an evolutionary perspective, this craving for belonging has helped our species survive by encouraging people to cooperate and protect each other. By competing for limited resources in groups rather than as individuals, we have been able to more easily reap the benefits of strength in numbers. As a matter of survival, our bodies have evolved to make this an actual neurochemical need.[12]

When we feel connected to others, our brains release oxytocin, the bonding hormone that increases feelings of love for those in our community, beginning with our families. Oxytocin also pushes us to prioritize our groups' interests over our own and, if necessary, to defend our in-groups against threats from others. In one 2015 study, participants who were given oxytocin were more likely to adopt the mistaken views of their in-group members than subjects who did not receive the hormone. The authors of this study concluded that giving a person oxytocin "increases in-group favoritism, lying for one's team, costly contributions to in-group welfare, conformity to in-group preferences, and aggressive protection against threatening outsiders."[13]

In other words, oxytocin increases our likelihood of complying with or temporarily supporting a position we may personally dislike. In search of this happy hormonal reward, we tend to prioritize behaviors that benefit our relationships. We look for affinity even when the basis for doing so is tenuous or trivial. We yearn to do more of what our community expects just so we can enjoy that sunny feeling of being included or admired by those we care about.

John Hughes's classic 1985 film *The Breakfast Club* offers some insight into this kind of bonding and the sacrifices it often entails. The film opens with a motley collection of teenagers arriving at their high school to suffer through a day of detention. After taking their seats in the drab library, they are told to write an essay describing "who you think you are."

At this point in the film, we've already been introduced to the five protagonists' familiar stereotypes: a brain, an athlete, a basket case, a princess, and a criminal. But over the course of the movie, in a series of comedic and occasionally dark exchanges, each student challenges these characterizations to some extent. The athlete confesses to feelings of weakness, the princess swears she hates her life, the basket case opens up, and the brain admits that he recently attempted suicide. The criminal ends up saving the day by stuffing his weed down the brain's pants. In the seminal bonding moment, they all smoke pot together and forget themselves, dancing and laughing around the smoke-filled library. The resulting "Breakfast Club" decides to continue meeting for detention every Saturday from then on and writes a defiant group essay proclaiming, "We think you're crazy to make us write this essay telling you who we think we are. What do you care? You see us as you want to see us, in the simplest terms and the most convenient definitions."[14]

In our American culture, young people are often encouraged to "find themselves" in order to maximize their unique contribution to society. Personal drive, confidence, and independence are seen as critical to success and personal happiness. Yet *The Breakfast Club* satire gets at a deeper, somewhat painful truth about our identities and humanity in general. The answer to the question "Who are you?" is not only about your distinctiveness as an individual. It's about the groups to which you belong.[15]

We naturally gravitate toward people whose views and beliefs are similar to our own, seeking what the eighteenth-century moral philosopher Adam Smith called "a certain harmony of minds."[16] Spending time with people who share our opinions reinforces our group identity, strengthening trust, cooperation, equality, and productivity. Our shared reality grounds us not just in our common perceptions but in similar feelings and worldviews. This helps to preserve our core values and beliefs about ourselves. It also provides us with meaning and a feeling of self-worth. And with each decision or interaction that confirms our tribe's common experience, we get rewarded with the hormonal happiness we crave.[17]

Our perception of ourselves is a mixture of our own unique characteristics and our sense of belonging to our in-groups. In fact, our personal identity is so closely intertwined with our social identity that our brains can't tell them apart. If I put you in a scanner and ask to you talk about yourself and then about the groups to which you feel the closest affinity, it will activate the same neural networks in your brain.[18] This helps to explain why all of us have such an irresistible need to belong—but that's not all.

When we feel an emotional attachment to certain views even before we've had a chance to form them for ourselves based on our own private experiences, confirmation bias easily sets in. We end up using whatever proof we find to simply reinforce the preestablished conclusions of our in-group.[19] And the stronger this shared feeling becomes, the more we want to conform with what we view as our in-group ideals. Particularly when we have already invested time, energy, and faith in an in-group—when membership in it becomes a part of our identity—we become protective of its worldview, which we have taken pains to reinforce. We can also become more hostile toward people who are not in the group.[20]

Indeed, neuroscience confirms that we actually feel pleasure when we see the rivals of our in-group lose. In an experiment conducted by researchers from Princeton, avid fans of the Boston Red Sox and New York Yankees underwent fMRI testing while watching their teams make plays. Seeing a player from their favorite team make a successful play triggered the reward system in participants' brains, which was not surprising. But the same neurological response also occurred when subjects saw a player from the rival team miss a play. One potentially sinister side-effect of belonging to an in-group, then, is how much enjoyment we find in watching members of a competing group lose.[21]

As powerful as this pull of belonging from our in-group can be, there is one thing that is even stronger, and that's our fear of ostracism. Because our social identity is so tied up with our tribes, getting expelled from them can feel like the kiss of death. And if we aren't careful, this fear can lead us to fall for, and become complicit in, some of the worst forms of collective illusions.

AND STAY OUT

The verb "ostracize" comes from the word "ostracon," a type of ballot used by the ancient Greeks to vote politicians, blowhards, the dishonest, and the generally obnoxious out of Athens. In the fifth century, long before the painful process of impeachment was invented, Athenian voters inscribed the names of their least-favorite fellow citizens on broken pieces of pottery (ostraca) in order to banish the unwanted from their midst.

Every year, the voters lined up in the market square to toss their inscribed ostraca into pots, after which their votes were dutifully counted. Whoever received the most votes that year got the boot. The ostracized man had about ten days to pack up and leave the city, and he was not allowed to come back until a full decade had passed. Once the ten years were up, however, he could return and resume his Athenian life and career. As part of the deal, his old property in the city remained perfectly safe and intact.

One fellow named Megakles got kicked out because people didn't like his bossy mother and the fact that he spent too much money on horses. But famous men got kicked out too, including Aristotle and the hero Pericles.

My favorite story about the ostracon vote concerns the states-man Aristides, whom the historian Herodotus called "the best and most honorable man in Athens." It's said that during one voting session, an illiterate man asked a favor of Aristides, whom he didn't recognize. I imagine their conversation went something like this:

"Sir, will you please write the name of Aristides on my ostracon?"

The statesman frowned. "I suppose so, but what's your beef with him? Do you know him personally?"

"Well, no, I don't know him at all," said the man, "but everyone in Athens calls him 'Aristides the Just,' and I find that annoying."

Aristides then inscribed his own name on the ostracon, and the man tossed it in the pot.[22]

While it's highly unlikely that you and I would ever get booted out of the country for ten years, we still fear rejection all the time. An entire area of our brain (the anterior cingulate cortex, which is involved in aspects of both physical and social distress) is constantly on the lookout for even the smallest hint of negative judgment. Interestingly, real-time scans using fMRI have shown how the same neural mechanisms respond to both social rejection and physical pain.[23] In a variety of studies, ostracized people exhibit elevated blood pressure and increased levels of the stress hormone cortisol.[24] Regardless of whether we feel a social or a physical injury, our brains sound the same alarm.[25] Indeed, the pain of social rejection has been likened to chronic back pain and even childbirth.[26] A wounded heart, it would seem, can hurt just as much as a broken leg.

It doesn't take much for us to experience this social pain. Indeed, psychological research on ostracism suggests that even the mildest snub can cause distress. Worse still, it appears that we experience it on a regular—sometimes daily—basis. In one study, forty participants kept a daily diary to reflect on the little acts of ostracism they experienced in their community. Some of the more than seven hundred acts they recorded were mundane (such as not being greeted on a bus or a train by a stranger or not getting a quick response after sending an email to a friend), while others were more serious (such as receiving the silent treatment from a partner). After being ostracized, especially by friends or relatives, the participants reported feeling lower levels of belonging, control, and self-esteem. They also felt their existence was less meaningful.[27]

Our internal sensors are so attuned to rejection that we feel pain even when it is remote and clearly artificial. Cyberostracism, or the feeling of being ignored or excluded online, can be triggered more easily than an in-person rejection; yet it produces a similar physical and emotional response. The problem is, in a world of likes, instant gratification, and thousands of virtual "friends," it's easy to feel ignored. For example, something as minor as having to wait for a response to a status update can prompt feelings of ostracism. People suffering from cyberostracism lose the precious feeling of belonging, as well as their self-esteem.[28] Our biological response to social disconnection has apparently been outpaced by our technological propensity for connection.

Regardless of the magnitude of the perceived rejection, once it's switched on, our ostracism alarm only appears to have one setting: full blast.[29] Even brief exposures to social rejection can trigger life-threatening stress.[30] For example, in one often-repeated experiment, the subject is put in a room with two other people who initially include him or her in their game of ball tossing. Then the two others suddenly start excluding the subject from their game, for no apparent reason. Thousands of people from around the world have participated in an online version of this test, known as Cyberball. Both versions reveal the same pattern: just two or three minutes of social ostracism produces "strongly negative feelings," especially sadness and anger.[31] Thus, when thrown together with strangers under arbitrary conditions or even when playing versions of the game in which the computer throws the ball, participants still feel both excluded and upset.[32]

Even the simple act of witnessing someone *else* being ostracized can make us feel bad, as if we were the ones being excluded. To the extent that it indicates some deeper, essential component of what it means to be human, this instinctive empathy is reassuring. But the fact that our own sensations of social pain are similar to those of the actual target also reveals a potential weakness in our neural response to ostracism.[33] Like an oversensitive mouse trap, it appears incapable of moderation, too touchy for its own good.

In fact, our automatic response to social ostracism is so powerful that when we are threatened with ejection from our community, the otherwise influential in-group/out-group boundaries dissolve. Overwhelmed by fear, self-doubt, and emotional pain, we forget whether those excluding us are friends or enemies and lose sight of the actual situation at hand. In one study from 2006, for example, Australian subjects were asked to play Cyberball with people they believed to be members of the Ku Klux Klan. Imagining yourself in their shoes, you might guess that being ostracized by mega-racists would feel okay. But even in this case, the people who were excluded still felt hurt.[34]

In addition to the psychological costs, there is another reason to fear ostracism. Groups will use it without compunction to assert their will and achieve their ends.

WHAT SHOULD WE DO WITH JOHNNY?

Born and raised in the slums of a midwestern city back in the 1930s, juvenile delinquent Johnny Rocco described himself as someone "here today and gone tomorrow." The second to last of eleven children, Johnny was constantly beaten and ignored. His father was a violent drunk and a gambler who couldn't keep a steady job. His mother was constantly ill and thus unavailable. When he was five, Johnny watched his father die after a drunken brawl with a friend. Meanwhile, his brothers got in bloody fistfights. Food was scarce. The rent was barely paid, if at all.

In a world where the entire Rocco family was already branded as "chiselers, thieves, and trouble-makers," Johnny's deck was stacked against him from birth. Growing up, he found it hard to fit in. "I never belonged anyplace. I never found anybody that liked me a lot, and that I liked, and could trust," he noted. His family kept moving around the slums, and Johnny attended seven different schools in his first seven years of education. One of his teachers wrote, "He is the most difficult boy I have ever had. Does not belong in a classroom." Johnny's classmates actively shut him out, excluding him from birthday parties and refusing to give him a Valentine.

When he was twelve, Johnny enrolled in an educational clinic and a private Catholic school with the help of a counselor. He finally learned to read and advanced several grades. He made a concerted effort to behave, but still he fluctuated between trying hard and acting out. After he had exposed himself to a roomful of Girl Scouts, vandalized a community space, and roused a group of kids to attack a house with bricks and rocks, Johnny was sent back to public school. But not everyone had lost faith in him. The sister superior at his old school urged his counselor not to "give this boy up" because "he is trying a lot harder than we know sometimes. Often it seems he just can't help doing some of the things he does."

Unfortunately, like his brothers before him, Johnny soon ran up a police record. Any time something went wrong in the neighborhood, the cops assumed he must be involved. Then one summer night, Johnny and two friends broke into a house and stole jewelry worth $50. Johnny confessed that they'd immediately sold the jewelry to a widow, Mrs. Hatfield, whose son was a local gang leader.

At his trial, Johnny's counselor pleaded on his behalf. A local policeman even testified in his favor, noting how much his behavior had improved in recent months. Ultimately, however, the judge had to answer the question "What should we do with Johnny?"[35]

———————

IN THE LATE 1940s Stanley Schachter, a doctoral student in social psychology at the University of Michigan, asked groups of experimental subjects to read Johnny's story and give their own opinion about what should be done with him. Schachter's goal was to discover how people handle differences of opinion in social settings. He asked his subjects to pick one of four types of social clubs and arranged a forty-five-minute meeting for each club of eight to ten people. Schachter didn't tell the students, however, that each of the clubs secretly contained three confederates who were paid to play a specific role.[36]

He then instructed the groups to discuss Johnny's story. Should Johnny be sent to a school for juvenile delinquents or a state-supervised foster home? Or should he receive some other form of punishment? Participants could answer these questions on a scale ranging from one (all love for Johnny, no punishment) to seven (all punishment for Johnny).

Finally, each club member shared his number with the others. The three paid members went last, and each one selected a pre-assigned position: the "deviate" picked and stuck to the extreme opposite of what the club majority had chosen, the "mode" selected and stayed with the most popular view, and the "slider" started out extreme but afterward allowed himself to be pulled over to the majority view.

Most club members were sympathetic to Johnny's story and selected positions ranging from two to four. The deviate (I'll call him "Tom") always picked seven (extreme discipline), and the reaction was striking. In every case, the beginning of the discussion focused intensely on Tom, as the other club members tried to persuade him to change his mind. But after a while, people started giving up. They stopped talking to Tom, and when asked afterward to evaluate fellow members, they rated him as less likeable than others in the club. They also identified Tom as the least competent club member, incapable of handling the most important tasks.

Schachter found that the more someone goes against the group, the less fellow members like them.[37] He also discovered something decidedly unsettling about how we approach differences and achieve solidarity in social settings. The most cohesive groups were the most likely to reject and ostracize the deviate more quickly: 75 percent of these groups cut off all communications with Tom after thirty-five minutes.[38] Schachter concluded that the more connected the group, the more likely it was to reject those whose opinions differed from the popular view of things.[39]

In other words, groups use ostracism as a tool to discipline and minimize deviance. Not surprisingly, being at odds with their in-group is something most people would rather avoid altogether. But such clashes do happen; in fact, if you are truly thinking for yourself, they are inevitable. So, what if you privately object to what your in-group is promoting?

SUSAN'S DILEMMA

A friend of mine named Susan called me not long ago to talk about a problem she was facing at work. She had recently returned from maternity leave to her job as a senior researcher for a large consulting firm whose blue-ribbon clients included big corporations in the technology, finance, and energy sectors.

When Susan was hired fresh out of graduate school, she told me that she'd found her "dream job." The consulting firm was well known, and the pay and benefits were excellent. She loved the work and her colleagues. She felt that she'd found a really meaningful vocation at a company that would help her to be successful. She believed in the company's mission to make the world a better place, including its stated commitment to sustainable energy.

The job quickly became an essential part of her identity. In her first two years with the company, she showed herself to be an exemplary employee. When she took maternity leave to have her first baby, she was eager to prove that she could go back to work with as much gusto as she had shown before she became a mother.

But when she returned to work, Susan was disappointed to learn that senior management had abruptly reassigned her from the technology unit to a new client in the energy industry, under a boss she'd never met.

Her first big assignment was to produce a rosy white paper about the practice and process of fracking. When she called to tell me about it, she was practically beside herself. "First they move me to a new department without consulting me, and then they put me on this awful assignment with a really bad company," she said. "I mean, it's supposed to be about the benefits of freaking *fracking*!"

I knew that Susan was a frequent donor to environmental protection organizations like 350.org and the Natural Resources Defense Council, so I wasn't surprised by her reaction. She was probably the last person I would have tapped to sing the praises of fossil fuel extraction.

"So did you talk to your manager about it?" I asked.

"Of course," she said, "but I probably shouldn't have."

"Why?"

"Well, I told him that working with this client would look bad for the firm. This company has broken all sorts of environmental laws, but they've only gotten slaps on the wrist. Meanwhile they're poisoning groundwater in Pennsylvania and Missouri and puking pollution into the air. And it's contrary to what we say we stand for—there's that bit about sustainability in our mission statement. Doing their bidding would look like guilt-by-association PR for us."

"What did he say to that argument?"

"He practically laughed in my face. He said the contract with them was already signed, so it was unprofessional of me to even question it. And he said he expected the deliverable as scheduled."

"Okay then," I said. "How about asking to move to a different department?"

"I would, but that would take time, and in the meantime I have to produce this damned paper. I mean, Todd, I'd be doing something to promote a practice I don't believe in. How would I live with myself? I'd have nightmares every night. And the baby will barely let me sleep as it is!"

We were both silent for a while.

"So..." I said slowly, "Are you thinking of..."

"Quitting? Sure. But I can't, at least not right now. It would take a while to find another position, and we need the money."

I felt terrible for Susan. What were her choices? We'd basically walked through them all.

Most of us can relate to Susan's problem. We have all felt boxed in like this at one time or another. In the end, she overrode her personal ethical views for the sake of her job, wrote the paper, signed her name to it, and stayed with the firm until she found a new job with a company whose values aligned more with hers.

It doesn't matter how you get there, whether through pragmatism or a fundamental reckoning with your identity. When your personal values conflict with those of your tribe, you face three choices: You can challenge the group and risk being ejected from it. You can decide to leave, which is basically self-ostracism. Or you can go with the third option: simply surrender to what the group wants, even though you privately disagree.

Though it's not ideal and often makes you feel rotten, this third option—what the economist Timur Kuran calls "preference falsification"—can look in the moment like a reasonable and even practical choice.[40] The problem is, taking this route has unintended consequences far more lasting and profound than most of us realize or even imagine. Once you are willing to mislead others about your true beliefs in order to belong, you can easily end up feeding collective illusions by enforcing things you don't really want.

FAKE IT 'TIL YOU MAKE IT

When our beliefs and behavior are misaligned, we feel thrown off kilter. The social psychologist Leon Festinger called this sensation "cognitive dissonance." The unpleasantness of this feeling motivates us to bring things back into alignment. We can either change or justify our behavior, and we usually do the latter.

For example, one of Festinger's studies looked at what happens when a person is paid to tell a lie. After participating in a long and boring experiment, college students were asked to tell the next participant how fun and exciting it was. Some were paid $1 to lie, while others were paid $20. When asked to share their private opinions of the experiment afterward, both the control group and the participants who received $20 said it was boring. Those who had been paid $1, however, viewed the experience more positively.

Festinger explained that the subjects who were paid $20 could easily conclude that they'd agreed to lie for the money. But those who had told the same lie for only $1 had little justification for why they had lied. The resulting cognitive dissonance prompted them to alter their personal opinion in order to provide the missing justification: Why else could they have said it was fun, if not from personal conviction? So even though they knew the experiment was actually boring, they recalibrated their reality to reflect the lie they had told.[41]

This is the first risk that comes with lying about our private beliefs: if we aren't careful, we can come to believe our own lies. But it gets worse. One reason it's so hard to lie is that when we aren't telling the truth, we get a nagging feeling that other people know it, even though that's not really the case.[42] Thomas Gilovich, the Cornell psychologist who pioneered research on this effect, calls it the "illusion of transparency."[43] This illusion makes us *feel* like terrible liars, even when we are not.

Who hasn't pretended to like a gift in order to avoid offending the kind gift giver? It's common courtesy to answer kindness with kindness. But when that same philosophy leads us into telling more consequential lies, we inevitably worry about being found out. So we overcompensate by believing that others can read our minds a lot better than they actually can. Especially when it comes to strong internal emotions such as anxiety, shame, or disgust, we assume others can see right through us.

In one study, subjects were instructed to maintain a neutral expression as they drank a red liquid out of fifteen small cups.

Ten of these cups contained a drink with a pleasant taste, while the liquid in a random five had a distinctly unpleasant taste. The entire experiment was filmed, and each subject was asked how many subsequent viewers of the film, out of ten, would be able to tell which drinks were actually disgusting. The subjects estimated that roughly half of the observers would correctly identify the yucky drinks. In reality, only about a third of the viewers were able to pick up on their disgust.[44]

This same tendency to exaggerate our own transparency pops up everywhere. We overestimate how well other people can detect lies, read compassion, or discern personal preferences.[45] And if you think other people will figure out that you're lying, it creates a whole new set of choices.

Say you choose to lie in order to go along with what you think your group believes, and then someone confronts you about it in the presence of everyone. You can disavow your own lie (but you're in the thick of it now, and it's embarrassing to look like a hypocrite). Or you can double-down on your lie in order to stay in your group; only that means maintaining the illusion that you are a true believer, despite what you may really think. And the more you feel you need to convince others of your loyalty and throw them off your scent, the more you will escalate your position in the group by, for example, becoming a dedicated enforcer of the group's view (which you privately oppose).

This kind of effort to deflect attention from one's lie is all too common. Consider the case of Ted Haggard, a good-looking, born-again evangelical Christian who decided to become a pastor after receiving the call of God in college. The New Life Church, which he founded in Colorado Springs, Colorado, in the mid-1980s, grew rapidly from a handful of people in a basement to eleven thousand members in 2005, when it was dubbed America's most powerful megachurch.[46] At its height in the early 2000s, New Life had an annual budget of $12 million, and Haggard had risen to become president of the National Association of Evangelicals (NAE), an organization representing forty-five thousand churches throughout America.[47]

Like most evangelical pastors, Haggard opposed gay marriage. But he didn't just decry it: he went so far as to try to enshrine its prohibition in Colorado's state constitution. "We don't have to debate about what we should think about homosexual activity," he declared. "It's written in the Bible."[48] Unfortunately for Haggard and his followers, everything came crashing down in 2006. Late that year, a male prostitute and personal trainer named Mike Jones outed Haggard. "It made me angry that here's someone preaching against gay marriage and going behind the scenes having gay sex," Jones told the *Rocky Mountain News*.[49] "I had to expose the hypocrisy. He's in a position of influence of millions of followers, and he's preaching against gay marriage. But behind everyone's back he's doing what he's preached against."[50] Following the scandal, Haggard was fired from his job as senior pastor of his own church and resigned from his leadership role at the NAE.[51]

In my opinion, Haggard's decision to lie and enforce antigay dogma didn't just hurt him, his family, and his evangelical followers; it also hurt gay men, the group to which he secretly belonged. Because he was so famous and had so much power, the country as a whole paid a terrible price for this one man's cognitive dissonance.

Compromising your personal integrity for the sake of belonging quietly wears away at your self-esteem and has been shown to negatively affect personal health in both the short and the long term.[52] Certainly, if your in-group really does hold a view you dislike and you choose to conform to the group anyway, that's your decision. But what if you've misread others and they privately don't like the view either? If you do make this mistake and then lie about what you really want or who you are in order to fit in, you become complicit in creating and sustaining an illusion. And this is where things scale up—because your decision to deceive others can have profound collective consequences, feeding a shared misunderstanding that can bring social progress to a halt.

The history of efforts to desegregate the South offers an interesting example. Despite the laws and court rulings meant to end segregation, change was particularly slow based on one specific, very peculiar reason: whites thought *other* whites opposed it. In the 1960s and 1970s, a professor of sociology at Wesleyan named Hubert O'Gorman found that those who advocated for segregation were the most likely to believe that those around them also supported segregation. On the other hand, those advocating change from the status quo were much more likely to think that they were alone, even though they were not. "The closer whites came to endorsing the value of strict racial segregation," O'Gorman observed, "the more apt they were to assume that the majority of whites in their areas agreed with them."[53] By misreading others and keeping quiet about their true views, people thus damaged their own integrity and the greater cause they privately hoped would advance.[54]

This misinterpretation of others' opinions on racial justice reappeared again and again, in study after study. Researchers found that white department store managers didn't hire African American salesclerks because they falsely believed their customers wouldn't approve. In 1969, a survey found that over 75 percent of white Detroit residents supported playdates between black and white children, yet simultaneously believed only a third of other residents shared their opinion. These misperceptions supported existing forms of systemic racism such as housing covenants and zoning and residential restrictions that blocked generations of African Americans and other minorities from access to quality health care, education, homeownership, and other opportunities.[55] They also reinforced stereotypes that continue to dictate how some people behave, consciously and unconsciously, toward others today.

Writing in 1976, O'Gorman seemed to speak directly to our times when he noted,

Even members of small and relatively cohesive groups frequently misjudge the values and attitudes of other members. In larger and more impersonal contexts, this form of ignorance, involving known and unknown others with similar social identities, is even more apt to occur, and in [a] time of accelerated social change it tends to become extensive. Under these circumstances, moral principles with relatively little popular support may exert considerable influence because they are mistakenly thought to represent the views of the majority.[56]

The result is a pernicious, self-fulfilling prophecy. By making blind and ultimately false assumptions about the opinions of those around us and worrying that we are in the minority, we become more likely to perpetuate the very views we and others do not hold. Worse, because the very same people who disagree with the status quo are the ones enforcing it, it becomes all but impossible to dismantle the illusion. This is how the identity trap weaponizes our need to belong, making us complicit in harming others and holding back social progress.

EXPANDING YOUR SOCIAL PORTFOLIO

When Jim Jones seduced Christine Miller and others into his cult, he made sure his followers were utterly dependent on him. Even before isolating them in a deep jungle, he demanded that they sacrifice their possessions, their homes, and even, in some cases, custody of their children to his cause. Once in Jonestown, members had their passports and medications taken away from them, and all their communications with the outside world were censored.[57] Lacking any other social connections and policed incessantly by Jones's armed guards, Miller and the others in Jonestown were out of options.

Their story illustrates how a single group can gain cultlike power over you if you're not careful. If you believe your groups and your fellow members are largely homogeneous, then your social identity becomes simplified, less flexible, and less receptive to social difference. Conforming to your tribe becomes tangled up with your sense of self, and so you do so at all costs. You also grow suspicious of anyone who doesn't seem to fit.[58]

When stuck in this kind of identity trap, we find reasons to draw boundaries and exclude those who are "not like us." We become less tolerant of diverse, cross-pollinating groups, and we embrace stereotypes. We seek comfort and assurance by drawing our social worlds in black and white.[59] Writing in 2005, psychologists Marilynn Brewer and her colleague Kathleen Pierce predicted that "when individuals, or social systems, are threatened by psychological, economic, or political loss," social identities will be defined based on more exclusive and less complex categories that simplify the world, driven by a desperate need to reduce uncertainty. The result is increased discrimination and resistance to change.[60]

So how do we avoid falling into this trap? In this case, the answer is simple, and it is a proactive measure. If you want to avoid the identity trap, you must increase your identity complexity. That is, rather than investing everything in one single group, as cult members must, you can avoid this identity trap by belonging to a variety of groups, which also means you have a healthy, diversified portfolio of social identities. It doesn't really matter what affinity groups you choose to join. They just need to hold some positive, personal significance to you. You can join a sports or music fan group; a book club, game night, or study group; a garage band or a choir; or just about anything else that engages you and is sure to make you feel happy on a regular basis. My wife, for example, joined a group of senior dog walkers twice her age and, to her surprise, found herself gaining a whole new, devoted cluster of friends.

A larger social portfolio doesn't just lead you safely past the single-group quicksand to dispel the age-old "us versus them" curse; it directly benefits you, me, and all of society. Research has shown how, if one of your social identities feels rejected or inferior, you can shore up your self-esteem by putting more energy into another one. In one experiment, Euro-American women who initially said they identified equally with their ethnicity and their gender were told that an Asian American woman had scored better on a test than they had. The Euro-Americans responded by placing greater emphasis on their ethnic identity, as opposed to their gender.

In this way, having multiple identities allows us to subtly recast exactly who we are, shielding our sense of self-worth and neutralizing the impact of otherwise withering social comparisons.[61] We also get a nice little reward signal each time we feel approved of by our tribes, which means we can maximize our chances of happiness by joining more of them (to a point, of course).[62]

But the benefits of identity complexity go further. In the early 2000s, Sonia Roccas and Marilynn Brewer discovered something else about belonging to multiple tribes. They found that the more diverse you believe your groups to be, the more resilient you are, and the more tolerant, inclusive, and nuanced your overall worldview will be.[63] Interacting with a greater diversity of people also provides you with better information and a well-rounded perspective that makes you less likely to fall for the illusions of a single group.[64]

In this way, expanding our social identity portfolios is one of the most valuable things we can do for ourselves. But here's the thing: identity complexity is also good for our groups. Just as we need to build up our immune systems by exposing ourselves to various germs, our groups can only survive and thrive by adapting to change. The greater diversity of understanding and ideas strengthens us all.

CHAPTER 3

THE SOUND OF SILENCE

There comes a time when silence is betrayal.

—MARTIN LUTHER KING JR.

IMAGINE THAT YOU are a college student in the Netherlands in the late 2000s. Passing through the social sciences building on your way to class one day, you see a flyer seeking participants for a study. The social psychology experiment "Seeing Beauty," it says, will explore how people perceive facial attractiveness. You enjoy leafing through fashion magazines and consider yourself a relatively discerning judge of beauty. According to the ad, the project is simultaneously taking place in France and Italy. "Cool," you think and sign yourself up.

A few days later, you fill out a questionnaire on your health history—including whether you tend to be claustrophobic—and schedule your visit to the lab. The experiment seems simple enough: you merely need to rate the attractiveness of various women's faces while having your brain scanned. You're excited to be able to contribute to science by basically doing the equivalent of spending an hour on Tinder.

On the day of the experiment, an assistant in a white lab coat walks you into a room with a narrow bed, one end of which sits inside what looks like a gigantic white plastic donut. The hole in the donut is a tube just large enough to fit the bed and a human body. "This," she tells you, "is the fMRI machine." You lie down, and she gives you two controllers, each with four buttons. "You will use these to rate each picture you see on a scale from one (very unattractive) to eight (very attractive)," she says, pointing to the appropriate buttons. "You will have three to five seconds to respond." Then she covers your ears with headphones and clicks something around your head to keep them stable. Just inches from your eyes, a small mirror shows a screen that is set up at the other end of the donut hole.

"How do you feel?" the assistant's voice comes through the headphones.

"Fine," you reply, though you're actually feeling jittery and kind of cold.

She reminds you to keep as still as possible. Then you feel the bed sliding backward, straight into the donut hole. A minute later the screen in the mirror lights up, briefly showing you a picture of a woman's face. She's wearing heavy eye makeup and a half smile. Her hair looks greasy. The screen goes black except for the rating numbers at the bottom, and you give the picture a six. A few seconds later, a box appears around the number eight with a "+2" above it. Apparently the "average European female participant from Milan and Paris" rated the same face two points higher than you did.

"Huh," you think. "That's strange. Did I miss something?"

As the next image pops up, you try to ignore the loud buzzing and banging of the fMRI machine in the background. You continue rating faces, one after another, for fifty minutes.

Afterward, you're hanging out in a recovery room when another assistant unexpectedly enters. He explains that they need you to rate the images again, this time without the fMRI machine. He leads you into a different room, makes sure you are comfortable, and then shows you the same images again, but in a different order. This time the European "average" does not appear after each of your ratings. You can also move along at your own pace since your responses aren't timed.

Following a short interview about the experience, you leave the lab, happy to have contributed to scientific knowledge.

Indeed, you did contribute to science, but perhaps not in the ways you expect. As it turns out, the entire premise of the experiment, as presented to you, was a complete lie. Its actual goal was to observe how your opinion about a set of faces changed in response to how other people rated them. The pan-European "average" ratings were totally fictional, engineered to reflect extreme judgments that differed from your own opinions in predetermined ways. So much for France and Italy. But the findings themselves are fascinating.

The fMRI scans showed, in real time, how learning that we've deviated from the group actually triggers an error response in our brains. At a neurological level, this is the same reaction we have when we encounter an outcome that is different from what we'd expected. Typically, then, we register this kind of prediction failure as a mistake. Our brains make a note of the error and direct us to change our behavior the next time we are in danger of repeating it. If we're driving a car or downhill skiing, this makes perfect sense. But in group social settings, the same response means that our brains treat differences of opinion as errors to be corrected. In other words, we have a subconscious drive to conform to what appears to be the consensus of the group.

Thus, findings from the second round of the experiment revealed a change in subjects' ratings: they slid closer to the pan-European "average." But think about what this finding really means. The subjects were not pressured by an in-group in which their identity was on the line; rather, they were simply told what the average was for a group of women across two other countries in Europe. And yet, even when this group was absent and anonymous (not to mention fictitious), its opinion was enough to push participants toward conformity.[1]

The truth is, we care about being in the numerical majority even when we don't necessarily care about the group and even when the group opinion is merely an illusion. Acting on instinct, in social situations our brains don't actually bother to make the distinction between appearance and reality.

When this happens, we can fall into what I call the "consensus trap." This trap creates its own breed of collective illusions—one rooted not in lies but in silence that spreads until the fog of misunderstanding envelops us all. Silent consensus is extremely pernicious because it doesn't feel like we're doing anything wrong. We aren't blindly copying the group, and we aren't lying about our views. But going silent in response to the consensus trap can cause as much, if not more, damage to society than the other two traps. And worst of all, we do this all the time.

CLINGING TO CONSENSUS

Just as fish have an instinct to swim toward the center of their schools to avoid being picked off by predators, we stick close to the majority in order to hedge our bets on survival.[2] Indeed, being out of step with what we think is the crowd—even if, as in the beauty study, it is completely fictional—makes us feel incredibly vulnerable.[3] This bias toward the majority manifests itself in humans at a very early age. Indeed, studies with infants demonstrate that at as early as nineteen months, babies who have no experience with certain toys look to the numerical majority of adults to learn which ones they should like best.[4] Even in the absence of intentional pressure or incentives, we like to go along with what we think is the consensus because, quite simply, we're biologically wired to do so.

Just as we harbor deep anxiety about ostracism, we have a biological fear of social isolation. Considerably subtler and more insidious than ostracism, isolation is truly damaging to humans both psychologically and physically. Among other things, social isolation can lead to poor cognitive performance and dementia, as well as elevated stress, fragmented sleep, depression, and increased vigilance surrounding potential threats.[5]

By contrast, when we're part of a large group, we feel connected to a network that's stronger than any one individual. This is a mutually beneficial arrangement: the majority's power protects us and feels more like our own, while our motivation to conform grows over time, reinforcing the influence and reach of the group. Thus, being part of the majority confers a sense of control that grows with the power of the group. This is the idea that, due to your shared beliefs and norms, you tend to think "if they are in control, then I am, too." Because this feeling of power stimulates our reward system, our brains latch onto it hungrily, like a baby to its pacifier. The numerical advantage of the majority also gives us the satisfaction of apparent supremacy and influence. Our citadel is fortified.

The problem is that this particular combination—our fear of isolation plus the benefits of being in the majority—heavily incentivizes us to go with whatever we perceive to be the consensus. Thus, when we're in fluid social decisions where competing ideas (often just two) jockey to define the majority view, most of us will wait to see which way the numbers are going. Once that direction is clear, we join the larger number of fish and reap the benefits: we avoid isolation, and we share in all the rewards of membership in the most popular group.[6]

One example of this phenomenon unfolded in Germany in 1965. For most of that year, the country's two major parties—the Christian Democratic Union (CDU) and the opposing Social Democratic Party (SDP)—were tied, 45–45. The deadlock went on for months. But something shifted in the final few weeks before the election, when the CDU suddenly gained ten percentage points. When the election finally happened, the CDU won by nine points.

Nobody understood why this had happened; at first, people thought the polling was faulty. But in her study of the six months leading up to the vote, a German survey and communications researcher named Elisabeth Noelle-Neumann suspected the shift had to do with a specific event that pushed undecided voters to climb off their fences. She hypothesized that it might be related to Queen Elizabeth II's visit to Germany around the same time, in May 1965. Accompanied by the German chancellor, CDU party member Ludwig Erhard, the visiting queen raised the moods of CDU supporters and inspired them to voice their support for the party more openly. Discouraged SDP supporters, meanwhile, grew reticent and exceptionally quiet. Because the CDU supporters were more vocal about their party's possibilities, it gave the impression that they were more likely to win; as a result, undecided voters jumped on the CDU bandwagon.[7]

Though Noelle-Neumann was the first person to describe this "bandwagon effect," it actually happens all the time, particularly in politics. In pre-election polls, people with heavier exposure to news coverage of poll results are often more likely to change their vote in favor of the projected leader over the course of a campaign.

In the spring of 2019, for example, Joe Biden was getting clobbered in the race for the Democratic nomination by his chief rivals, Bernie Sanders and Elizabeth Warren. While Sanders and Warren were beloved by the Left and the younger flank of the party, moderate and older voters weren't as smitten with them. Then, one cold February day in South Carolina, Biden gave a speech at a high school gym. His words highlighted his empathetic connection with African American voters, who comprise a large proportion of the Democratic Party in the state, and this message was amplified in the news and over social media. When South Carolina's primary votes were tallied, Biden carried the support of 64 percent of African American voters. Overnight, the race changed, and Biden won state after state. Once the momentum was behind him, the game was pretty much over.[8]

Now imagine being an enthusiastic supporter of Amy Klobuchar (one of the candidates who dropped out after South Carolina). Would you continue pushing the core elements of her platform to friends and family, or would you simply settle for Biden, as the apparent best Democratic candidate?

Once we start to feel the bandwagon rolling, we don't necessarily falsify our preferences, but we're unlikely to continue to be vocal about the candidate who isn't in the lead. In other words, the bandwagon effect makes us less willing to voice unpopular opinions. In the end, our shared tendency to support whichever party appears more popular has taken a heavy toll on our national politics, giving both the polls and the media an enormous, undue influence on our democracy and its ability to function.[9]

Of course, the bandwagon effect isn't just about politics. The slight preference to go silent if we are unsure of our side, or if we think the tide is turning in the other direction, plays out over and over in our own lives. The more our judgment becomes distorted by fear of isolation and our desire to be in the majority (or, in this case, our absolute terror of political defeat), the less we speak out. In contrast, as part of the majority, we feel we can share our views publicly with very little risk, confident that most others "out there" agree with us.[10]

PLAYING IT SAFE

Let's say you're a newly elected member of a city council, and you are being mentored by the chairman. You're excited to be participating in city government and working on issues you care about.

At your very first meeting, the council is presented with a quandary. The housing authority has raised alarms about rising crime and drug use in its high-demand apartments. There is a long waiting list of qualified candidates for these subsidized dwellings, including senior citizens and people with disabilities. The housing authority is therefore hoping to evict tenants who have been arrested for drug-related crimes to make room for those who are less likely to commit them.

The plan seems reasonable enough, especially if the evicted tenants are single people living alone. But then you learn that most of those charged with drug crimes are teenagers under the age of eighteen. Now you and other city officials are confronted with tough questions: Should you separate a family by evicting, say, a juvenile drug dealer or evict an entire family just because of one kid's actions? And won't failure to mete out some kind of punishment only encourage adult dealers to use minors as couriers?

Personally, you would like to see more city money spent on helping families and rehabilitating offenders, and you assume that most of your council colleagues agree with you. You at least expect a nuanced conversation about the pros and cons. But then your mentor, the council chair, comes right out and says, "If the kids are dealing drugs, they have already been separated from their families," adding that he would evict children as young as twelve if they have been arrested. "Actually, if I had my way, they wouldn't be separated. The whole family would be out," he adds.[11]

You are a bit surprised by his strong and unequivocal stance. And looking around the room, you find it hard to read people's thoughts. Now you aren't so sure whether the other council members really do agree with you. "Maybe people actually agree with him," you think. And since housing is not your area of expertise, it's not the hill you are willing to die on. "It's not going to matter if I speak up," you think. "My opinion is not going to change the vote, and I don't want to risk being seen as a contrarian right off the bat."

So you say nothing.

We sink into this uneasy silence far more often than we would like to admit. In particular, we do it when we have unspoken incentives that we're reluctant to share. If your kid is vying to get on a particular sports team, win a competition, or get into an elite college and the same town council chairman also sits on the high school board of directors, you're thinking about how to pick your battles. Other times, not saying anything can be valuable professionally. If getting a promotion is important to you, it may not feel like a great idea to challenge the boss when he makes an inappropriate joke.

Here you may say, "Okay, I get it. But is there really anything wrong with just maintaining silence and seeing where things go? Sure, I'm not speaking what I feel is the truth yet. But shutting up is a crime of omission, not commission. So where's the real harm?"

There *is* real harm, and it comes in multiple flavors. In the short term, we hurt ourselves by going along with a lie. We also damage our groups by cutting them off from learning new and important information and by reinforcing orthodox norms, however harmful they may be to us and others. And in the long term, our silence becomes a driving force that creates and sustains illusions.

THE BYSTANDER'S PREDICAMENT

Dr. Ivan Beltrami was a handsome young man with a big, toothy smile. A French doctor in the early 1940s, he hated Nazis and the Vichy government that collaborated with them. He was also a Catholic friend of many Jews, some of whom he hid in his Marseilles apartment and at the hospital where he worked as a medical intern. He risked his life transmitting messages among members of the Resistance and warning Jews about raids and roundups. He even rescued them from deportation. When his brother was captured by the Nazis and sent to the Buchenwald concentration camp, Beltrami took command of an underground task force charged with killing Vichy collaborators and members of the Gestapo.[12]

Now, imagine that you are Dr. Beltrami in 1942. And you are watching a local Marseilles policeman—someone you know personally—round up Jewish prisoners. You and other witnesses can see that the policeman's cheeks are wet with tears as he yells at them. He is clearly conflicted, yet he continues forcing frantic people onto the cattle cars.

"How does Monsieur Charon live with himself?" you wonder. "Why doesn't he fight back against this horror? He could join the Resistance, like me. Does he truly believe in what he is doing to these people, or does he just feel like he has no choice?" Other questions only come later, as things begin to sink in. "What about everyone who was watching? Do they really agree with this treatment of Jews? They're probably wondering the same thing about me. But if I had said anything they would have arrested me right then and there. I could never endanger the Resistance that way."

This is, of course, an extreme case. But just think back to all the people who chose not to speak up in a smoke-filled, potentially burning room just to avoid embarrassment. We tend to retreat into silence and the apparent security it promises, even when the potential cost of voicing our opinions is negligible or nonexistent. This habit becomes truly destructive, however, when we decide to zip our mouths shut in the face of actual threats to ourselves and others.

We regularly enable minor but decidedly bad behaviors in our own lives. We often fail to speak out against the occasional evils we witness—say, a child being slapped, an animal being abused, financial fraud, racial or sexual harassment, or oppressive employment practices. Afterward, our lives go on as usual, but our collective silence does spectacular damage. It hurts not only the direct victims of the harm we see but everyone else who witnesses it. Beyond that, our society as a whole suffers because we all end up sending the message, through silence, that we're okay with the wrongdoing. Since we humans copy each other, the effect of this behavior is exponential: when "everyone else" appears to be doing the same thing we are, we assume that they, too, must think the bad behavior is acceptable.

As in Nazi-occupied France, stark power imbalances, and inequality more generally, tend to drive silence. We avoid speaking out against those who hold power over us as a matter of self-preservation, terrified of the consequences. We quietly hope that someone more courageous will say something first, making it easier for us to follow. Anyone who's sat around a conference table with a dominating CEO knows that only those who are in his or her favor or have a higher risk threshold will dare say anything contradictory. Everyone else busily checks their cell phones. Under the threat of potential criticism from an authority figure, it's always easiest to just shut up. After all, that's what we're trained to do, as children. But in the corporate world, where peer pressure runs high and speaking truth to power can be tricky, silence is a dangerous norm. In one study of corporate silence, 85 percent of respondents reported at least one occasion when they felt unable to raise an important concern with their bosses. In another, 93 percent said their organizations risked some major problem or accident because people were either unwilling or unable to speak up.[13]

The literature on organizational behavior is rife with stories about what happens when employees are afraid to mention wrongs or alert top managers to potential accidents.[14] At NASA, engineers too cowed by their higher-ups failed to share their concerns about the potential for leaking O-rings on the space shuttle *Challenger*. On the chilly morning of its launch on January 28, 1986, this vital flaw caused the shuttle to explode just seventy-three seconds after takeoff, killing everyone aboard and shocking the world.[15] At Volkswagen, an allegedly oppressive, authoritarian culture led engineers to build diesel engines with fraudulent emissions controls for their cars. The exposure of the truth led to billions of dollars in fines and a severely damaged reputation for the company.[16] Even in Silicon Valley companies, where speaking up is supposed to be a corporate value, people tend to get fired if they go too far. This is how Timnit Gebru, an African American woman and former Google research scientist, found herself without a job after publishing a research paper that happened to be critical of the company's technology.[17]

Speaking the truth to power can be excruciating, particularly in workplaces where your income, reputation, and corporate profits are on the line. One such case was that of Kimberly Jackson. In the midst of the Covid-19 pandemic, Jackson noticed a jump in the number of elderly and disabled Medicaid patients being discharged from nursing homes to the psychiatric hospital where she worked. "The homes seem to be purposely taking symptoms of dementia as evidence of psychosis," she said. Her observations matched a broader pattern of nursing home evictions: across the country, largely for-profit elder care companies had been using claims of psychosis to dispatch their patients to hospitals, then bar them from returning. Known as "patient dumping," this practice is against the law.[18] But when Jackson spoke up about what she'd seen to the *New York Times*, her employer, the NeuroBehavioral Hospital of Crown Point, Indiana, promptly fired her for violating its media policy. Jackson's response was refreshingly simple: "I saw something that was wrong, and I called it out."[19] Doing that took enormous courage, and we would all benefit enormously from following her lead.

Another example comes from mining country. Since 1970, the federal government has offered free chest X-rays and other screenings to miners under the Coal Workers' Health Surveillance Program. Still, only a third of coal miners are getting tested. In an epidemic of black lung, young workers in particular should be getting tested in order to catch the illness early. In reality, most of those coming in for tests are older workers nearing the end of their careers. Why?

In public comments submitted to the government, mineworkers shared concerns about confidentiality and the likelihood of retaliation by their employers. Firing an employee for health reasons is technically illegal, but employers can easily find other reasons to discriminate against someone or terminate a contract. As one union worker noted, "The last thing that a company wants is somebody... who can later prove that they contracted black lung at their mine."[20] When asked if they felt they could report health or safety hazards without fear of retaliation, only 20 percent of miners said yes. By contrast, 95 percent of their supervisors believed their workers could freely speak up about potential dangers.[21] Like numbness from the cold in the body's limbs, this breakdown of communication can prove fatal to individuals and organizations alike.

Since time immemorial, those with the greatest authority have deployed pressure and threats to keep people in line, cultivating silence. But in recent years social media has changed the equation, democratizing information and inaugurating an entirely new kind of strong-arming—one that is often more perfidious and certainly more widespread than the old-fashioned version.

SILENCE LIKE A CANCER GROWS

Dr. Laurie Forest, a small-town family dentist, neatly tucks her long, straight auburn hair away under a soft blue medical cap and pulls a face shield down over a pair of kind, intelligent green eyes. Cloaked in the pastel scrubs and pasty rubber gloves that so many dread, she smiles and speaks in a calm, confident voice as she sets to work, maintaining and repairing one of our body's most vital tools: teeth. Each day, she immerses herself in the shadowy swamplands of the human mouth. But by night, she peers into a very different, much more glamorous set of jaws.

Forest writes young adult (YA) fantasy novels. She first encountered the genre at the stubborn urging of her four preteen daughters.

"I'd never really read fantasy before, and they kept handing me Harry Potter," she explains. Then "I finally gave in, and I loved it. I started reading everything they handed me."[22] She became an avid fan and soon began crafting a story of her own, inspired by the prejudice and homophobia she was witnessing in her own life. By early 2017, her first novel—a riveting drama that blends magic, dragons, courage, and romance—was poised for publication. But *The Black Witch* was destined for its own taste of dark sorcery.

Just weeks before its scheduled publication date, a Mrs. Salt–like person in the YA fantasy community posted a scathing review on her blog. "*The Black Witch* is the most dangerous, offensive book I have ever read," she wrote. "It was ultimately written for white people. It was written for the type of white person who considers themselves to be not-racist and thinks that they deserve recognition and praise for treating POC like they are actually human." The racial conflict and discrimination portrayed in the book involves certain groups that exhibit racist beliefs and use terms such as "pure" and "mixed-blood." Pulling these passages out of context, the blogger pasted them directly into her review, as fodder for her ire.[23]

Exhorting her thousands of Twitter followers to retweet her review, this critic soon rallied a YA Twitterverse that prides itself on social justice and sharp, no-holds-barred disapproval. In a matter of days, online hecklers deluged the author and her publisher with demands to cancel the book's publication. Meanwhile, a coordinated sabotage of *The Black Witch* on Goodreads led to a flood of one-star reviews, many of them submitted by people who had not even read the book. As views of the original blog post surged into the tens of thousands, critics swarmed positive reviewers of the book like angry bees armed with the sting of "How dare you?" and drove many of them into silence. At their worst, the insults escalated to include accusations of bigotry and sympathy with Nazi and white supremacist ideals.[24]

As a first-time author who explicitly sought to send an antiprejudice, antiracist message, Forest was shocked and deeply disturbed by these attacks. After thinking about the problem, however, she decided to do what her critics were unwilling to afford her. She actually listened to what they had to say.[25] Forest found enormous solace in the voices of people who had actually read the book, whose conclusions differed starkly from the bulk of online criticisms. Ultimately, she decided to go ahead with publication.

As of this writing, *The Black Witch* garners 4.5 stars on Amazon and scores a 4.08 on Goodreads. A user question on Goodreads, posted in 2017, asks why a book "without any critical engagement of the racist purity mythology embedded" in its descriptions could be "published in 2017, especially for a young audience." The twenty-seven responses are a chorus united around a single theme: "That's the entire substance of the book," and "Read the damn book."[26]

The person who posted the original question never responded. Perhaps they in turn were shamed into silence? A community review of four stars, posted by Emily May in 2017, has 1,971 likes and reads, in part, "*The Black Witch* is, in my opinion, a thoughtful consideration of the prejudices people hold." She adds, "The author clearly presents all the races as complex and sympathetic," which no doubt helps to explain the global success of the entire six-book Black Witch Chronicles series, now translated into multiple languages.[27]

Forest's story demonstrates how mindless silencing feeds on itself and burns everything it touches. (Even one of her detractors had the same thing happen to him.) This cautionary tale also shows that our willingness to self-silence is quite often a response not to the actual majority but rather to a vocal minority that convinces us it is the majority.

But it also shows that we can maintain our voice and stand up to bullying without being equally offensive.

IN THE DAYS before digital technology, fringe ideas had a relatively hard time gaining traction because their supporters had to persuade others of their value. Today, all you need is a social media account.

Social media platforms allow anyone who's got an axe to grind to pull a digital power play, exerting direct control over the perceived majority and scaring all dissenters into silence with their unfiltered vehemence. This is exactly what happened to Forest and countless others. Intensified by social media, online bullying drives both silence and a retaliatory backlash, ultimately feeding the very things we seek to avoid: social condemnation, polarization, and fear.

There's no question that using social media to hold sexual predators like Harvey Weinstein accountable for their behavior is an unambiguous public good. But whereas in the past men in positions of power caused harm by flexing the muscles of authority, today's social media has democratized bullying. With the simple tap of a finger, online bullies can use social media to trigger massive landslides of judgment and hate.[28]

Leftist author and academic Mark Fisher fought brilliantly against cancel culture, calling it "The Vampire Castle." He argued that the "open savagery" and harsh condemnations of Twitter storms entrap people by overstepping the mark, incessantly hounding and personally vilifying public figures in a "drip-feed of abuse" (conjuring the haunting image of an ailing patient stuck to a sweaty hospital bed, tethered to an IV). Whether or not someone has done something wrong, this particular form of online attack leaves, in his words, a "horrible residue: the stench of bad conscience and witch-hunting moralism," a noxious cloud that sows fear and enables bullying.[29]

To make matters worse, the kind of strictly curated, remote interaction that occurs on social media creates a particularly fertile ground for snap judgments and the denial of individuals as full and complex human beings. When all you can see of a person is comments, photographs, and a few video clips, their entire identity crowds into a neat little box whose sides are brightly decorated with fanciful stereotypes. The resulting, heavily simplified idea of someone splits away from who they are in reality, creating a cyber cushion that shields and emboldens those who bully even as it callously shatters the defenses of their victims. This is how, as Fisher pointed out, whole people become "defined by one ill-judged remark or behavioral slip."[30]

As if online bullying by real people weren't bad enough, the past few years have added a new player to the mix. Social bots are online robots that can easily be weaponized to amplify fringe views and take advantage of our bias toward the majority. Like funhouse mirrors, they distort even what we think the majority *is*, causing us to fit the evidence to our belief and substitute numbers for real individuals. For example, when a well-known "Never Trump" Republican friend of mine voiced his negative opinion about the former president on his Twitter feed, he was met with a tsunami of hateful responses. "I get that all these retweets were from just a few thousand people," he told me, "but it felt like everyone on the planet was after me." After that, he stopped using Twitter.

These fake, automated social media accounts are designed to mimic certain human behaviors online, including liking, sharing, and posting content to social networks. Depending on their programming, they can flood legitimate debates with their own arguments and soundbites or generate the illusion of popularity by increasing the number of likes a person or post receives (also known as "manufacturing consensus"). As one researcher observes, "Bots massively multiply the ability of one person to attempt to manipulate people. Picture your annoying friend on Facebook, who's always picking political fights. If they had an army of 5,000 bots, that would be a lot worse, right?"[31] That, in effect, is exactly what social bots do.

The illusory majority created by social bots can also mobilize false information to trigger a "spiral of silence," a term first used by Noelle-Neumann to describe what happens when you become stifled by your own self-censorship.[32] Russia has been using bots for years to drown out all criticism of Vladimir Putin and his policies. Other leaders, like Venezuela's president Nicolás Maduro, have recognized their political potential too. On October 31, 2013, Twitter unexpectedly shut down more than six thousand social bot accounts that had been programmed to retweet content directly from Maduro. The bots likely violated Twitter's use rules, which forbid "inauthentic engagements that attempt to make accounts or content appear more popular or active than they are."[33] Despite their representing a mere 0.5 percent of all Maduro's followers, after the bot accounts were terminated the president's average number of retweets plummeted by 81 percent.[34]

An economist named Juan Morales studied this event to better understand how bots affect our perceptions of popularity online. Using more than two hundred thousand tweets sent over six months, he found that the drop in automated publicity for Maduro correlated with an increase in both criticisms of the president and support for the opposition. In other words, the artificial, inflated majority created by the bots had imposed a spiral of silence on political discussion in Venezuela. When this bubble popped, the president instantly lost a large chunk of his perceived support, allowing popular opinion to recalibrate based on reality rather than the bot-generated illusion. This realignment also seems to have decreased Venezuelans' fear of sharing their true views, even when they appear to be in the minority.[35]

Few people realize it, but a chilling 19 percent of interactions on social media are already between humans and bots, not humans and humans. Studies based on statistical modeling of social media networks have found that these bots only need to represent 5 to 10 percent of the participants in a discussion to manipulate public opinion in their favor, making their view the dominant one, held by more than two-thirds of all participants.[36]

When those on the powerful fringe—the Mrs. Salts of the world—enforce a position that doesn't reflect reality, join together with general ignorance, or harness the silent support of all those waiting around to see which way the wind will blow, they can rapidly solidify into a distorted, hurricane-strength social force. Wielding the influence of a majority with the true support of a meager few, the resulting collective illusion harnesses crowd power to entrap us in a dangerous spiral of silence.

CAUGHT IN THE SPIRAL

Back in Germany in 1965, the SDP supporters didn't realize their silence was contributing to the illusion that the CDU was winning. The resulting spiral of silence inspired Noelle-Neumann to reflect on the hidden, dangerous complicity in keeping quiet.[37]

Indeed, the more we think our ideas could get us into trouble with proponents of the status quo—particularly with our family, friends, and neighbors—the more warped our shared perceptions become.[38] The truth becomes a massive, putrefying secret, just like the emperor's nakedness. Too often, however, no one is courageous enough to call it out, so nobody says anything. And by choosing silence, we make it more likely that the emperor's benighted sycophants (a minority) will become the apparent majority.

We've all been in situations where it just seems easier to avoid the question and the inevitable conflict, and to keep quiet. But what we excuse as a matter of relevance or convenience is actually an added boost to bullies everywhere. Not telling Uncle Bill that he's espousing racist beliefs at Thanksgiving, failing to question your boss's unfair treatment of a colleague, or refusing to speak out against bad decisions made by your mayor or congressional representative—all of these little choices help to create an impression of localized uniformity that feeds something much larger and more ominous: massive, widespread illusions.

And make no mistake: you and I are being swept into collective illusions right at this moment. Like so many fish swimming into a transparent net, we are being unwittingly corralled into conformity and self-censorship. Indeed, with the help of social media, our natural propensity to self-censor has metastasized.

Compare what is happening now to the early 1950s, when Wisconsin senator Joseph McCarthy famously accused hundreds of Americans of being Communists guilty of subversion and, in some cases, treason. The resulting "Red Scare" unleashed paranoid fears of a "Communist menace" that poisoned every watering hole in America, seeping into the very foundations of our society. McCarthy's House Un-American Activities Committee became a toxic growth in the heart of our government, victimizing hundreds of innocent people in the State Department, academia, the film industry, and labor unions, ruining many a career as it went. (Homosexuals were also identified as suspect because they supposedly posed a security risk.[39]) The list of the harassed included celebrated actors and directors such as Charlie Chaplin, Orson Welles, Lucille Ball, and Danny Kaye; musicians such as Leonard Bernstein and Pete Seeger; leading scientists, including Albert Einstein; and writers such as Langston Hughes, Bertolt Brecht, and Dalton Trumbo.[40]

Even at the height of the Red Scare, however, Americans weren't particularly worried about speaking their minds. A mere 13 percent of people reported feeling that their voices were more constrained than they had been previously.[41] While McCarthyism left a black stain on our society, and 13 percent is still too many in a democracy, that number was miniscule compared to what's happening in the polarized climate of the United States today.

Currently, we are living through a comparatively dire epidemic of self-censorship. In July 2020, researchers from the Cato Institute asked whether people felt comfortable voicing their private opinions in public. Nearly two-thirds (62 percent) of Americans said no, because they feared others might find their views offensive. A majority of Democrats (52 percent), Independents (59 percent), and Republicans (77 percent) all confessed to feeling this way.[42]

When you think of people who tend to silence themselves, your mind might jump to images of the powerless workers living in fear of reprisal by those in authority. But our modern version of self-silencing is an equal-opportunity destroyer. It can affect anyone, regardless of race, economic status, political orientation, or education.

For example, you might assume that higher education's wide-ranging intellectual thought and commitment to experimentation would lead to more open minds and the protection of diverse minority views. Judging from my own experience in that world, however, the halls of academia are just as rife with self-censorship as anywhere else. Indeed, research from 2019 showed that among those with no high school diploma, 27 percent self-censor; yet among those with a high school diploma or some college, that percentage hits 34 and 45 percent, respectively.[43] (And I'm willing to bet it rises still more among people who hold graduate degrees.)

When we think we're the only ones who fear being in the minority, we tend to misinterpret others' behaviors and assume they agree with the majority. So we stay silent, thinking, "That many people can't be wrong," and this in turn sends the same message to others who either copy or follow in order to belong. Before we know it, we're all playing a giant game of self-censorship for exactly the same reasons, without realizing it. Thus collective illusions are born and grow rapidly, like mythical beasts feasting on silence.

Being silent might be necessary if you are living under an author-itarian regime in which speaking out could cost you your life. But we actively endanger ourselves and others when we stay silent for the sake of a collective illusion. Especially in a democracy whose health and vibrancy depend upon the open sharing of our views regardless of where we stand, this kind of silence is poisonous. It also stymies productive debate, preventing us from having the kinds of conversations we urgently need. For example, researchers have found that people often self-silence around the topic of climate change because they either think others do not share their opinions or fear they won't be perceived as competent in discussing it.[44] The resulting lack of conversation generates a false impression of disinterest that is literally threatening our planet.

Of course, we all have different thresholds for voicing our opinions, and this tipping point can change according to who expresses support for your views and how close you feel to them.[45] Many of us won't speak up until we've already seen public support for our views. Few of us will stick to our guns no matter what, and some need near unanimity before they are willing to voice their opinion. Others want a plurality. Still others keep mum.[46]

Regardless of when you hit your tipping point for speaking up, it's important to remember how each time you decide to keep quiet about your view, you feed the spiral of silence. As it slowly builds, one person at a time, more and more people start equivocating and making excuses, casting their hidden ballots for unethical behavior or obviously repressive, unfair practices and norms. So the spiral grows. And eventually this system of denial becomes so ubiquitous that it becomes normalized. It becomes acceptable. Thus, through our silence, we all become willing collaborators.

SEEDS OF DOUBT

At the conclusion of the Civil War, a freed slave named Lawrence Ware walked from Georgia to South Carolina in search of the wife and family he'd lost under slavery. It was a dangerous journey with terrible odds. Even if he did make it to where they were supposed to be, in the postwar tumult they could easily have moved on or been hurt or killed by the time he arrived. "Every time I hear this story," says his great-great-granddaughter, Tarana Burke, "I think to myself, 'How could he do this? Wasn't he afraid that he would be captured and killed by white vigilantes, or he would get there and they would be gone?' And so I asked my grandmother once why she thought that he took this journey up, and she said, 'I guess he had to believe it was possible.' "[47]

Today Burke, too, dreams of breaking up the centuries-long conspiracy of silence around sexual harassment and abuse.[48] She often cites the grim statistics that led her to launch her global "Me Too" movement. For example, one in four girls and one in six boys are sexually assaulted every year. So are the vast majority of trans women. Indigenous women and people with disabilities are likewise affected in disproportionate numbers. Sixty percent of black girls experience sexual violence before the age of eighteen.[49]

Raised in the Bronx, Burke has dedicated nearly thirty years of her career to activism and organizing in support of marginalized young people. "Me Too" got its start when she met a thirteen-year-old girl at the youth camp where she worked in Alabama. One day the girl approached her privately to share her story of having survived sexual violence, and Burke, overwhelmed, froze. "I was not ready," she later explained. She wanted to help, but she could only refer the teen to someone else. The girl never returned to camp, and Burke has always wondered what happened to her. She couldn't shake her feelings of guilt about what had transpired, and she kept asking herself, over and over, "Why couldn't you just say 'me too'?"[50]

In 2006, Burke did just that. She launched a Myspace page for the movement she wanted to create, and it began to grow and garner attention. But the fire was truly lit in October 2017, after the producer Harvey Weinstein was accused of widespread, repeated sexual abuse. That's when #MeToo took off on social media, helped along by a few celebrities.[51] "If all the women who have been sexually harassed or assaulted wrote 'Me too' as a status," tweeted the actress Alyssa Milano, "we might give people a sense of the magnitude of the problem."[52] Soon, millions of people around the world were responding and posting their own #MeToo stories. As Burke has said, "This is a movement about the far-reaching power of empathy."[53]

People who speak out against wrongs have the power to change society for the better, and we often lionize them for their courage. Of course, ideally, we should all act upon the strength of our convictions and never go silent on important issues. But sometimes even the most courageous among us can't risk the physical, economic, or social consequences of speaking up. For instance, many of the women who have spoken out against harassment worried about their personal safety and that of their families. Wendy Walsh, one of the women who came forward with allegations of harassment by Bill O'Reilly, confessed, "I was afraid for my kids, I was afraid of retaliation. I know what men can do when they're angry." Others simply cannot afford to lose their jobs, and so they make the hard decision to "go along to get along."[54]

But this doesn't mean that silence is the only option. Far from it.

One simple thing you can do to escape the consensus trap is to nudge what appears to be the consensus opinion with a little doubt. Even the smallest seed of doubt is enough to help you discern whether or not the apparent majority is real and correct. For example, you can say something like, "I haven't made up my mind yet" or "On the one hand, I can see the value of x, but on the other..." You can also suggest other options by saying things like "I have a friend who..." or "I read somewhere that..." Doing this gives you plausible deniability while retaining your sense of control. It also offers an escape hatch for others who have been afraid to speak up. Often all it takes is a single spark of ambivalence or mixed opinion. Once you crack open the door, others can gain the courage to follow.

It's also important to remind yourself that raising a contrary view may not necessarily bring the fury of the group down upon your head. In fact, the opposite is more likely to be true. As you remember from the experiment involving the story of Johnny Rocco, the majority didn't immediately expel "Tom." Instead, they tried to persuade him away from his beliefs. Sharing a contrary view, then, is an excellent way to discover what others really think. If you hear strong opinions heavily favoring one side, you can be fairly sure that they represent the group's genuine view. (Of course, this doesn't necessarily mean that you should go along with the majority point of view, but it does tell you that it's less likely to be an illusion.) By contrast, if you see lots of other people engaging with or supporting your opinion, you'll know you've all been stuck in a spiral and it's time to open that escape hatch, wide.

Still, there are a few caveats. When you are planting doubt, it's important to be genuine; it's not helpful to provide a contrary view that you don't really believe in or care about. The point is to help other folks share their own honest views. Like any good debater, you also need to recognize whatever merits there may be in the opposing view. If you think the majority opinion has absolutely no merit and the topic is very important to you, ask yourself why you've felt unwilling to speak up.

If you fear physical or economic coercion, then try to find ways to be anonymous or recruit like-minded others, especially if the issue is of critical importance. Ask yourself whether you've gone silent for all the reasons I've described above and be sensitive to what is motivating your decisions.

Once the seal of silence is broken, you know where the group stands. You know that it was an illusion when people start to use your escape hatch. Then, together, you can all explore the issues more honestly and engage with the truth, a process that can help you sniff out whatever collective illusions may be lurking in the shadows. This discussion can then help you to make an informed personal decision about whether to conform or not. It can also help you to speak truthfully about your views, freeing others to do the same. As individuals, we often feel powerless when we are surrounded by clear majorities. But sometimes all it takes to shatter an illusion, prevent the creation of new ones, and ensure an accurate shared reality is a single person speaking the truth.

Part II

OUR SOCIAL DILEMMA

We cannot live for ourselves alone. Our lives are connected by a thousand invisible threads, and along these sympathetic fibers, our actions run as causes and return to us as results.

—HERMAN MELVILLE

CHAPTER 4

LITTLE CHAMELEONS

We are half ruined by conformity, but we should be
wholly ruined without it.

—CHARLES DUDLEY WARNER

LOOK AT THE image of the two cards below. Which of the lines
on the right-hand card matches the line on the left?

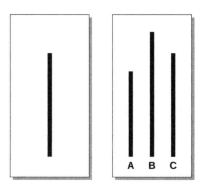

The answer seems immediately clear.

But let's say you are sitting together with seven other people,
and your answer is part of a study. After looking closely at the

cards, you conclude that the length of the line on the first card matches line C on the second card (which is, in fact, correct). But there's a hitch. The seating arrangement in the room is such that everyone expresses their opinion sequentially. And you are the last one in line.

As you wait your turn to speak, one after another of your fellow participants declares, with apparent confidence, that line B matches the length of the line on the first card.

When it's finally your turn, you stare hard at both cards with furrowed brow. What is everyone else seeing that you aren't? Can they all be wrong? You begin to doubt your own senses. You feel lost. Should you insist that your own private view is correct, and everyone else is wrong? Or could line B be the correct answer after all? Do you stick to your guns, or do you deny the evidence of your own eyes and go along with what the others believe?

Of course, as in most psychology experiments, there are a few things you, as the study subject, don't know. First, the seven other people in your group are all so-called confederates, or subjects who are in league with the researchers conducting the study. And second, they have all been instructed to give the same wrong answer and behave as if the obvious right answer (line C) were not, well, obvious.

Is the truth still the truth if you're the only one who sees it? Most of us would say yes: truth bows to no man (or woman). But in the 1950s, a social psychologist named Solomon Asch found otherwise.

He conducted this famous experiment with groups of eight college students. Of the 123 study subjects who were shown a succession of card pairings under the same conditions, a full two-thirds went along with the misleading majority at least once. While some people repeatedly stood by what they saw, despite pressure from the majority, the subjects knowingly gave an incorrect answer roughly 37 percent of the time. Asch concluded that those who gave in thought there must be some "general deficiency in themselves, which at all costs they must hide. On this basis they desperately tried to merge with the majority, not realizing the longer-range consequences to themselves."[1]

Afterwards, all of the participants underestimated how often they had conformed. Even more weirdly, some of those who surrendered to the majority swore up and down that they saw what the larger group told them to see, disbelieving their own eyes. This puzzled Asch. Did they give in knowing that their answers were wrong, or did the power of the group actually change their perceptions? Asch departed this world without ever finding the answer.[2]

Many years later, in 2005, Emory University psychiatrist and neuroscientist Gregory Berns replicated Asch's experiment. The difference this time was that Berns used a tool that didn't exist back in Asch's day: functional magnetic resonance imaging. This then-new technology allowed Berns to see what was happening in participants' brains as they made their decisions. He found that the part of the brain responsible for feelings of reinforcement and reward lit up each time subjects conformed to the group. But if the subjects disagreed with their companions, the amygdala—an area linked to unpleasant emotions—sent subjects an "error signal" that made them feel uncomfortable. Most intriguingly, the brains of those who conformed showed an actual *physical* change in their visual systems, suggesting a shift in what people were actually seeing. Thus, some of the conformists were actually telling the truth as they understood it—a kind of delusion some experts have called "controlled hallucination."[3]

Asch and Berns both confirmed that we humans are hardwired to stick with the group. And they explain why we fall into conformity traps in the first place. As far as we know, we are the most hypersocial of all earthly creatures. This uniquely social disposition has helped us to thrive and achieve a scale of collaboration unknown to any other species. We are so social that we become vulnerable to disbelieving the evidence of our own eyes in order to avoid feeling like an outsider. At a biological level, we are actually programmed to compare ourselves to others and behave as they do, even if we don't want to. This is one of the reasons why we are so highly susceptible to collective illusions. And if we are going to stop falling into conformity traps, we need a deeper understanding of the social instincts that underlie them.

MONKEYS VERSUS TODDLERS

WHICH IS BETTER at using a tool, figuring out which pile of toys is bigger, or locating a reward—a toddler, a grown chimp, or an adult orangutan?

If you guessed the toddler, you're wrong.

In a cross-species study of two-plus-year-olds, chimpanzees, and orangutans, the toddlers and their primate cousins actually scored roughly the same on tests like these, which relate to the physical environment. Yet the toddlers performed at least twice as well on a series of social tests involving communication and one's ability to guess the thoughts of others. The researchers concluded that though we humans aren't necessarily smarter than other primates when it comes to dealing with the physical world, chimps and orangutans don't show anywhere near the same level of observational learning or social orientation that humans do.[4]

How did these social skills evolve? Anthropologists think that about two million years ago, our hunter-gatherer ancestors helped keep each other alive by living in large, cooperative family groups. This arrangement helped them navigate unpredictable environments, ward off predators, and obtain the food and resources they needed to survive.[5] These early humans also developed a sense of time and communicated about it differently than our closest cousins, the chimpanzees. As far as we know, chimps can't chat about how darn hot the weather was last summer or whether it will snow next week.[6]

Once we *Homo sapiens* began forming complex language, things really took off. We could explain, without the need of physical objects or context, that "this berry is safe to eat; this tool works best for skinning a beast; the water is over there; here is the way to start a fire." Not only could we imagine the past and the future, but we began guessing what others thought based on what they were doing. Thus, as our social lives grew more entwined, our brains did too.[7]

In the thousands of generations since, the neurological networks that support our social and communications skills have grown to become three times larger than those of chimps. In addition to evolving more advanced social brains, we also passed on our knowledge to one another and to our progeny.[8] We developed a common understanding of abstract symbols; we drew cave paintings of charging bison and running horses; we began to practice elaborate burial rituals and work together to solve increasingly complex problems. We cultivated cultures and religions that allowed us to bond through a common desire to answer the questions "What is life?" and "Why am I here?" And eventually, through trying to answer these questions together, humans became the planet's most dominant species, with toddlers that get an A+ in social learning.

JUST LIKE YOU

If you've ever watched a video of a baby horse or giraffe being born, you've probably wondered at how quickly after birth the still-wet newborn struggles to its feet. This instinct, encouraged by the mother's licking and nudging, takes hold almost instantly, within an hour of birth. Instructed by its DNA, the baby animal learns to walk and run as quickly as possible, in order to avoid being eaten by a predator.

We humans, on the other hand, are far removed from doing any such thing. At six months most babies begin to crawl, but the majority won't begin walking until around a year. We are the proud record holders for the longest infancy of any animal species, relying wholly on the adults around us for a period longer than our own gestation. This awkward, prolonged year of utter dependence became a necessity when we humans became bipedal, causing a mismatch between the size of our brainy heads and that of our narrow hips. Since the configuration of a human woman's hips won't allow us to spend any more time in the womb, we are essentially born early. In exchange, we've been able to keep and develop unusually large brains with an exceptional capacity to adapt, learn, and survive.

From the moment of birth, a helpless human baby latches onto its caregiver with all its senses, trying to communicate via its cries. It will be weeks before the baby masters the ability to support its own head or voluntarily move its arms and months before it can use anything other than wails to tell its caregiver that it's hungry, wet, or tired. But somehow the cries do their job. If the caregiver is loving, both infant and adult release the precious bonding hormone oxytocin, which makes the adult want to protect the baby and helps the infant feel safe and comforted. Soon enough, the baby begins to recognize the facial expressions of caregivers, and then it starts to mimic them. A smile begets a smile, a wave a wave, and with each exchange an even deeper bond is forged.[9]

This imitative behavior plays an essential role in our conduct as social beings.[10] Indeed, the neurological desire to copy others is so automatic that we do it even when we have no reason, or will, to do so. But why?

The answer may lie in a set of nerve cells in the brain called "mirror neurons," which switch on when we see someone else doing something.[11] Mirror neurons are involved in not only imitation but the ability to understand and empathize with the experiences of others.[12] Thus, our mirror neuron system lets us process what we observe even as it primes our bodies to mimic what we see and hear.[13] At an entirely unconscious level, observing certain movements automatically triggers our brains to prepare our muscles to copy what we have seen, allowing us to rapidly learn from watching others. This impulse to imitate also builds our social connections. Copying is, after all, the sincerest form of flattery.

Andy Meltzoff, a colleague of mine from the University of Washington, has explored this process by looking at how babies learn through imitation. In the experiment, seventy fourteen-month-old infants sat in their mothers' laps while Meltzoff and his team measured their brain activity. In front of each baby sat a researcher, and between them was a toy with a clear plastic dome. When the experimenter touched the dome with her hand or foot, music played and colorful confetti fluttered about inside.

The results showed that when the experimenter touched the toy with her foot, an area connected to the sensory and motor cortex in the center of the baby's brain lit up. If the experimenter touched it with her left or right hand, the left or right side of the infant's brain did the same. In other words, the babies connected the experimenter's hands and feet with their own, mapping the actions of the adult onto their own bodies in preparation for copying. "Babies look at you and see themselves," Meltzoff explained.[14] Such connections between perception and motor control become stronger over time, as the baby grows.[15] Thus, a caregiver's engagement with young children builds a subconscious pattern of reciprocal imitation that supports both familiar, loving relationships and active participation in a shared culture.

This instinctive mimicry isn't something we outgrow. It becomes a part of who we are, a phenomenon so common that it has its own name: the "chameleon effect." Just as chameleons automatically change their color depending on their surroundings, observing someone else makes us more likely to behave the same way they do. This is how we learn to dance, write, throw a ball, use a knife and fork, express ourselves through language, and do countless other things.

Take my friend Jenny, a singer whose "musical ear" has contributed to her knack for picking up foreign sounds (she also speaks several languages). A few years ago, she returned from a week's vacation in Galway, Ireland, sounding like a Galway local, pronouncing the word "Irish" as "oyrish," "earn" as "ayrn," and "Alabama" with a soft *a* (as in "all") and biting down on the *t*s at the ends of words that Americans tend to soften (e.g., "caught").

"What's with the accent?" I asked her.

Jenny laughed. "O yah, I hair't too nah," she replied.

Within a day she'd reclaimed her old American accent. But speaking about it afterward, she confessed, "I noticed a kind of social fracture within myself. When I go to a different country and come back, I wonder whether, and when, I decide which person is the real 'me.'"

Chances are you've either experienced this social fracture or seen it happen. While it's easy to write it off as a part of socializing, friendship, or even finding oneself, in reality we are constantly and automatically changing our behavioral "coloring" depending on our social and physical environment.

One 1999 experiment at New York University showed exactly how the chameleon effect works. Researchers asked two strangers to look at various color photos and describe what they saw. (One student was a confederate; the other was the study subject.) Participants were told that these pictures were going to be used in a psychological test, but the real purpose of the study was to see how much the subjects mirrored the behavior of the confederates.

The experiment began with the confederate sharing his or her interpretation of an image, including the emotions and possible stories about the individuals pictured. For example, "This is a picture of a man holding a chihuahua," he or she would say. "The dog's leg is in a cast, so I guess it's broken... The man looks like a pretty nice guy, so he probably felt sorry for the dog and wanted to help it," and so on. Then it was the participant's turn to describe a different photo. The two took turns doing this until they'd gone through all twelve images together. The same participants engaged in two rounds of the experiment, each with different confederates who occasionally shook their feet or rubbed their faces. In one round, the confederate made minimal eye contact and did not smile at the participant; in the other, he or she made eye contact and smiled.

The two NYU researchers conducting the experiment, Tanya Chartrand and John Bargh, found that participants copied the foot shaking and face rubbing about a third of the time, regardless of whether the confederates were smiling or not. They concluded that we mimic others unconsciously, even when we have no apparent reason to do so.

For chameleons, the purpose of camouflage is obvious: How else would a little lizard ever elude all the fierce predators of the tropical forest? But human mimicry is harder to explain. Chartrand and Bargh hypothesized that our imitation instinct might have an adaptive purpose, similar to the chameleon's ability to change colors. In a second experiment where the confederates copied participants' behaviors, the researchers found that those whose movements were copied felt the interaction was more fluid and comfortable than those whose movements weren't. Basically, we like to be copied. When others emulate us, we feel a more empathic connection with them. Mimicry thus activates a kind of "social glue" that promotes our survival, pulling us into communities regardless of any conscious intention.[16]

Just watch a group of teenagers together—how they use their hands, tilt their heads, and pitch their voices. They're like schools of fish. And as with babies and adults, this behavior is reflexive: if I see you smile, I smile in return. The more this happens, the more we bond and want to protect each other—something every teenager craves. In fact, this instinct is so strong that even being exposed to a very polite person before meeting a stranger makes you more likely to be polite to the stranger.[17]

But there's also a troublesome wrinkle in this instinct: We automatically imitate other people's *desires* as well. And this particular habit can get us into trouble.

I WANT WHAT YOU WANT

Imagine you've just entered a movie theater. As you inch forward toward the snack counter, you smell hot buttered popcorn and begin to salivate just thinking about it. Your eyes absently follow a bowl of nachos as it crosses the counter, the cardboard container brimming with a nest of golden chips and shiny yellow cheese. *Hunh*, you think. Until that instant, you'd been leaning toward a small popcorn and maybe some Twizzlers. But then the next two people in line order nachos. Inching forward, you can't help noticing that just one nacho bowl remains in the brightly lit warming box.

By the time you step up to the counter, your mind is made up. "One nachos and a Twizzlers, please," you say. Passing the clerk your credit card, you can't help smiling as you overhear the cashier at the other end of the counter tell a customer, "Sorry, we just ran out of nachos." In the space of a few moments, a dinky paper bowl of nachos has transformed you into a hard-nosed competitor. How did you come to care so much about something so trivial, a thing you'd barely noticed just moments before?

French historian and philosopher René Girard spent much of his career tracing this kind of longing across humanity's vast history. Such "mimetic desires," as he called them, originate not in ourselves but in our interpretations of others' behavior.

Mimetic desire works like this: due to our neurological wiring, any two people will naturally want to imitate each other. Even when we're looking at meaningless abstract symbols, the brain gives us a reward when we choose one we think is more popular than another.[18] (It's no wonder that people scoop up popular brands like Nike, whose expensive basketball shoes are endorsed by sports stars like Michael Jordan. Each time we spend our money on a brand selected by someone we value, we get a nice little kick in the cranial reward system. And when we put on those high-end shoes, we feel as if we, too, can run a little faster and jump a little higher.) Girard then went a step further, theorizing that merely witnessing someone else's desire for something prompts us to want that same thing, too, *even if we actually don't*. When that happens, our brains automatically refocus on our imagined, yet increasingly real, competitors.

For instance, let's say two people—call them "Harriet" and "Victor"—are in a toy store, shopping for a present for their respective children. When Harriet sees Victor looking at the same stuffed giraffe she has been eyeing at the same moment, she gets worried and hurries to grab the toy first. But her actions indicate a rivalry to Victor, who then acts as if he too really wants the same toy.

In that competitive instant, the illusion of the giraffe's desirability hardens into reality. Whether or not Victor actually wanted the toy in the first place, they both want it now.[19] Thus we end up scrambling for the last nachos or, for that matter, tangled up in love triangles or ridiculous fashion trends, despite our desire to remain true to ourselves and others.

Mimetic desire has two possible outcomes, one good and one bad. The good one leads to better connectedness within a group: as soon as two people pursue the same goal without competing (that is, if the goal they are pursuing is sharable), their common desire spreads.[20] In some cases—most notably, religious belief—shared desire translates into shared understanding and security; we sing our beloved ancient songs, hug one another, release oxytocin, and cultivate love and empathy. We imagine "being in someone else's shoes" and focus on the emotions and desires they must feel. In the best cases, we also recognize our differences and gain insight into diverse perspectives.[21]

The other outcome is much darker. If the wanted object *can't* be shared, competition arises, rivalries form, and violence erupts. Such desires have been taboo across the history of Western civilization, starting with the Ten Commandments (for instance, "Thou shalt not covet"). Other examples abound: Two toddlers fight over one toy. Two divorcing parents fight over the custody of their child or their dog. Two neighbors argue over a piece of land. Two political parties demonize each other. Or two nations go to war over a single, limited resource. Thus, we pit ourselves against one another when the thing we want is in short supply. And the notion of false scarcity these conflicts feed only intensifies the competitive impulse. Among other things, it leads some Americans to believe that their jobs and possessions are part of this zero-sum game, under imminent threat from refugees and immigrants.[22]

Girard observed how, across the course of history, this competitive instinct has been triggered by the simple observation of someone else's apparent desire for something. From birth to death, our social nature drives us to imitate and bond with others even as we compare ourselves to them. In the process, we find ourselves motivated to alter ourselves based not only on our own beliefs or ideas but also on what we see in others.

THE GRASS IS PROBABLY GREENER

When I first entered college in 1996, I jumped from a small pond into a very big one. Weber State University in Ogden, Utah, is nestled beside the Wasatch Mountains north of Salt Lake City. Founded in 1889, it attracts twenty-four thousand students from all over the academic map. Anyone with a high school diploma or a GED can get into Weber State, and the average four-year graduation rate is 12 percent.[23] At the time, the average tuition per student was about

$6,000, pulling it within reach of what I could pay with the meager funds I'd cobbled together with the help of friends and family.

I started out at night school. Foraging a living from an assortment of minimum-wage jobs, I got by on very little sleep. Despite not having done well in high school, I managed through sheer bullheadedness to talk myself into the honors program. My professors of psychology, history, and English always complimented me on my prose writing. This came as a surprise, since I'd never felt that writing was my strong point. Nonetheless, I was flattered, and by the time I graduated I was heartily convinced that I was a decent writer.

And then, wonder of wonders, I was accepted as a graduate student at Harvard. You can imagine the avalanche of "Why me?" moments that flooded my head as I grappled with this shift in circumstances. During our cross-country move, my small family had so little money that we forfeited the option of motel rooms for nights in our minivan. I paid for passage on the toll roads into Massachusetts with $1.50 checks that, of course, bounced. Arriving in Boston with just a few quarters in our pockets, we learned that driving in that city is, quite literally, a form of blood sport. Within a matter of days, we got into a giant accident that totaled our vehicle and left my three-year-old son with a broken femur. Welcome to Boston!

In the new world of Harvard student housing, we had no money, no friends, and a couple of screaming children. I felt utterly lost and perpetually on edge, my nerves jangled. Looking around at the well-dressed students and the ivy-festooned brick walls of that hallowed campus, I experienced a terrible case of imposter syndrome. I felt like a fraud. What the hell was I doing in this place? And worse, what would happen when they found out I didn't belong?

"Well," I told myself, "at least I'm a good writer."

In one of my very first graduate classes, taught by one of the most famous professors at the school, the subject of the first paper was cognitive and symbolic development. I painstakingly researched and wrote that thing over the course of three weeks. On the day it was due, I turned it in proudly, fully convinced that I'd done a good job, and waited for the professor to respond.

When we got our papers back, I was shocked to see I'd received a disappointing C+. At the bottom of the first page, the professor had written bluntly, "Judging by your work here, it is not clear to me that you possess the writing skills to succeed at this level."

I left the class and walked home in tears, my self-esteem pulverized. I felt a blistering shame at having been so wrong, robbed of the one talent I'd believed might save me. I seriously considered dropping out. But in the end I found a writing tutor. A woman who helped undergraduates and looked like she was about fifteen agreed to take me on and stuck with me at every turn. By the end of the semester, I'd redeemed myself with an A in the professor's class.

From this experience I learned (albeit the hard way) one deceptively simple truth: understanding who we are is ultimately an exercise in social comparison. The answer to the question "Am I a good writer?" depends on whom one is comparing oneself to. At Weber, I was comparatively prolific, putting words and paragraphs together in what my professors thought was a decent argument; at Harvard, I was worse than mediocre. Likewise, I am a reasonably solid basketball player compared to middle school kids, but I can't possibly compete with someone like, say, LeBron James. In my teens I was a pretty good pole-vaulter, but compared to my father—a former collegiate champion—I was just passable. You might think you are The World's Most Perfect Person in Every Conceivable Way because your mother told you so, but that's not really an adequate evaluation of your standing in the real world.

How, then, do we figure out where we stand?

In the late 1940s, Leon Festinger—the social psychologist who introduced the idea of cognitive dissonance—launched his career with a study of how we compare ourselves to others. He began by assuming that we are universally motivated to figure out whether our opinions are correct and also what we are capable of doing relative to others. He concluded that though we naturally seek out objective measures of our opinions and our abilities, in the absence of such markers we resort to the next best thing: we use whatever information we can gather from those around us.[24] Thus we instinctively gauge everything from our shoe size, to how we feel, to our own intelligence based on our perceptions of others. And these self-assessments, in turn, guide our behavior and our understanding of the world.

You may be thinking of the times you've consciously compared yourself to others, as I did at school. But such judgments also take place at a neurological level as we instinctively absorb and interpret social information in real time. The way our brains process rewards actually depends upon how we view ourselves in comparison to others. Likewise, our mental predictions about what will happen and what is expected of us grow in part from our own subconscious comparisons of ourselves to others. Whether we like it or not, observing someone whose performance is superior or inferior to our own triggers in us a spontaneous self-comparison. Despite the fact that it is totally unconscious, this whole process has a direct and immediate influence on our reasoning and how we choose to act.[25]

An experiment conducted in 2010 showed exactly how this happens. Subjects who thought they were helping with a study on the movie-viewing experience were told to help themselves to snacks before watching a film. The researchers found that the amount and type of snacks taken by participants tracked closely with their social environment. Thus, when subjects observed another person (a confederate) taking a large number of snacks before them, they took more snacks too. Likewise, if the confederate took fewer snacks, so did the subject. More interesting still: the subject and the confederate ate their snacks in separate rooms, but the subjects consistently ate everything they took, even when the amount was more than twice what they would have taken on their own. In other words, they didn't just take more in the moment because the other person did; their actual desire for snacks shifted in response to witnessing the other person's desire.[26]

Because the comparison instinct makes us particularly sensitive to signals of reward and punishment, it can take us to some pretty dark places. When we feel that we're doing comparatively well, the part of the brain associated with rewards lights up, flooding our brains with dopamine and oxytocin. For instance, the "like" feature on Facebook and other social media acts as a kind of reward, which is why so many people end up compulsively counting and pursuing more likes.[27] To a certain extent, we're all dopamine junkies.

By contrast, when we feel we are doing comparatively badly, our brains release the same opioid chemicals that protect us from physical pain.[28] If we're not careful, this is where the dark side can take over. We will put others down, or even hurt them, in order to feel comparatively better about ourselves. Moreover, feeling like our self-image is under attack makes us much more likely to rate ourselves more highly than someone we view as inferior, triggering not only feelings of superiority, but also the same neurological reward system that gives us a buzz when we win money or a competitive game.[29]

Many people will even sacrifice something they care about in order to feel comparatively superior to others. In February 1995, researchers asked 257 faculty, students, and staff at the Harvard School of Public Health to answer a set of hypothetical questions about which of the two worlds they would rather live in. Here is one of them:

A. Your current yearly income is $50,000; others earn $25,000.

B. Your current yearly income is $100,000; others earn $200,000.

Prices are what they are currently, and prices (therefore the purchasing power of money) are the same in states A and B.

Which one would you choose?

If you answered A, you were in the 56 percent majority. This choice would allow you to earn more than others, even though scenario B would pay you more overall. For most people, then, feeling superior was more important than making more money.[30]

This example reveals the true tragedy of our biological propensity for social comparison. It feeds our worst selfish impulses to the extent that we will do things that harm everyone just to feel better about ourselves. President Lyndon Johnson, who was born and raised in the South, understood this sinister potential and how to use it, with particular reference to racism. In 1963, as his then-young staffer Bill Moyers recalled,

> We were in Tennessee. During the motorcade, [Johnson] spotted some ugly racial epithets scrawled on signs. Late that night in the hotel, when the local dignitaries had finished the last bottles of bourbon and branch water and departed, he started talking about those signs. "I'll tell you what's at the bottom of it," he said. "If you can convince the lowest white man he's better than the best colored man, he won't notice you're picking his pocket. Hell, give him somebody to look down on, and he'll empty his pockets for you."[31]

But this is where it gets strange: We don't just compare ourselves to individuals. We compare ourselves to abstract groups. And this quirk leads us directly into the maw of collective illusions.

———

REMEMBER THE FOOD preferences study from the introduction, when participants changed their own food preferences to be closer to those of the group? The researchers who ran that experiment at Stanford, in 2015, suggested that people shift their personal opinions due to the biological satisfaction triggered in our brains whenever we agree with others.[32] Indeed, the neural reward we get from aligning with our peers, even if we are only imagining they all agree, is so powerful that it can override our personal self-interest.[33] So, when everyone else takes a large helping of mashed turnips at Thanksgiving dinner, you do too, even though you know you'll have to force the stuff down. The truth is that everyone else may also be exchanging the bitter taste of mashed turnip for the neural rewards of social harmony.

Of course, there are many other reasons we might change our views and behaviors to match those of the larger group (a trend also observed by Asch and Berns). Perhaps we want to see whether our interpretations of reality are actually correct. Maybe we're seeking social approval, a requirement our ancestors understood as necessary to their own survival, as individuals in a tribe. Or we may adjust our behavior to maintain our self-esteem. Above all, however, it satisfies a fundamental need to belong. When we compare ourselves against our group and find ourselves aligned, we get a reward response; when we are out of step, the error signal tells us something is wrong and so we make a shift.

The social influence of our groups is so powerful that it can even outweigh common sense and empirical fact. For example, if you live in an area where malaria is common, it makes a lot of sense to use mosquito netting. Sleeping under a mosquito net is a well-known, evidence-based strategy for preventing the spread of malaria. Yet, even in areas where most households have access to free nets, not everyone chooses to protect themselves. In one study of eight villages in rural Uganda, researchers found that willingness to use a net related closely to perceptions of the group consensus. Subjects who believed most people slept under a mosquito net were almost three times more likely to do so themselves than those who did not believe most people used a net. Moreover, 23 percent of subjects believed, incorrectly, that most adults in their community were not using mosquito nets each night. In all, a third of the participants in the study either misinterpreted or were unsure about the norm for mosquito net use in their community.[34]

And yet, recalling the Thomas theorem from the introduction, the consequences of not using nets are real: when nets are deployed, malaria cases drop by nearly 70 percent.[35] Thus, where collective illusions like this one take hold, false perceptions skew the judgment of individuals, and real people get sick and die.

There's something important going on here that is easy to overlook. It's a central insight into what makes collective illusions possible. When we compare ourselves to groups, we can never be sure what most other people really want or believe. Yet our projected notions about these beliefs, however mistaken, can quickly turn into reality.

In the study on facial attractiveness that opened the previous chapter, we learned that even when a numerical majority is chimerical, we still want to be part of the illusion. We've also learned that our personal identity is tightly interlaced with our social identity, to the point that our brains really can't make a distinction between them. And as it turns out, these predilections don't just drive our group conformity right now, in the present; they also allow the ghost of groups past to reach beyond the grave and exert a mighty influence that we almost never notice.

CHAPTER 5

CHASING GHOSTS

I almost think we're all of us Ghosts... It's not only what
we have invited from our father and mother that walks
in us. It's all sorts of dead ideas, and lifeless old beliefs,
and so forth. They have no vitality, but they cling to us
all the same, and we can't get rid of them.

—HENRIK IBSEN

ON A WARM June evening in 1986, I learned to eat peas from
the back of a fork. Why I had to master this particular gustatory
skill made zero sense to me—after all, a spoon has always seemed
more to the point when confronting this particular legume. But I
was required to learn it, and so I did.

That evening, thirty of us sixth-grade farm kids trooped into the
church gymnasium to undergo an annual rite of passage known as
the "Etiquette Dinner." Dressed in our most uncomfortable Sunday
best, we were going to discover the proper way to chow down in
the company of our betters, whether we liked it or not.

The gym had been transformed into a pseudo high-class restaurant: six round folding tables were draped with white tablecloths

and set with floral centerpieces, fake-doily placemats, two kinds of drinking glasses (for water and "wine," or grape juice), white cotton napkins—the works. Taking our seats, we ruffians puzzled over the plates of various sizes and the innumerable pieces of silverware, ranging from tiny appetizer forks to big soup and little dessert spoons, not to mention the various knives for spreading butter, cutting food, and, obviously, pushing peas onto forks.

In the center of the dining space, directly beneath the basketball hoop, sat a woman I'll call "Mrs. Jones," our tutor for the evening. As she waited for us to quiet down, she perched primly on her stool in a bright floral dress, peering at a table of gigglers in center court.

For the first course, the nice ladies who functioned as both serving staff and hawkeyed manners police brought out small bowls of tomato soup and dinner rolls with tiny pats of butter. Since I could barely sit still, let alone wait to eat, I reached for the dinner roll the moment it landed in front of me. Instantly, a light thwack hit the back of my wrist. "We don't begin until everyone is served!" the lady behind me chided, cheerily brandishing what looked like a ruler. I sat back in my chair, blushing, as the other kids stared.

"Now," announced Mrs. Jones, "using your right hand, pick up the largest spoon to your right and hold it like a pencil." We obeyed. "Take up a spoonful of soup, scooping *away* from you toward the outer edge of the bowl, like this." She illustrated with a delicate swoop. "Don't fill the spoon too much, or it will spill. Bring the *side* of the spoon nearest you to your lips. And don't slurp!"

Soup successfully downed, next came the green salad on small pink plates. This time, the girl sitting across from me got thwacked. "Don't stab your food!" the server admonished. "And take just one small bite at a time. Don't put another bite into your mouth until you have swallowed the first one!"

When I tried to drink the grape juice from the nearest wine glass, I learned the hard way that the glass on my right, above the knife, and not on the left was actually mine. Because I'm left-handed, I had sipped my neighbor's juice. Bad me.

By the time the main course—chicken, mashed potatoes, and peas—began exiting the kitchen, we had all been cowed into submission. We chewed with our mouths closed. Our elbows were held correctly off the table. Sitting stiffly in my chair, I looked longingly around at the basketball hoops on the gym walls. What a colossal waste of time, I thought.

My dinner plate finally arrived. "Cut and eat one bite of chicken at a time," coached Mrs. Jones. "And when eating the peas, hold your dinner fork in your left hand, hold the main knife in your right, and use the knife to push them onto the back of the fork." This presented an obvious problem, and I struggled for a while until I figured out how to squish the peas onto the fork. It worked even better when I used the mashed potatoes as glue. Genius.

There was an answer for everything that night in the church gym: where to put your napkin, how to position your silverware when you were done, where to place your hands when you weren't using them. But I never once thought to ask why the hell a rural American kid living in the twentieth century was learning all these silly rules. It's not like eating properly was a part of our religion or even a formal part of American culture. So why bother?

ONCE UPON A time, prior to using utensils, we humans ate with our hands. For that matter, many perfectly polite people around the world still do. But sooner or later, some of us began using a knife to cut and a spoon to scoop. Though widely used among the elites of the Middle East by the tenth century, forks didn't arrive in Europe until the sixteenth century.[1] Catherine de Medici, who in 1533 journeyed from Italy to wed France's Henry II, ran the equivalent of an ad campaign for the fork. Touring France in the

1560s, she held a series of giant public festivals (free food!) that included the spectacle of her feasting with a knife, spoon, and fork. She even devised her own rules of dining etiquette, which she impressed upon rival factions by forcing them to eat at her table.

Catherine's fancy set of tined forks invited a certain scorn from French courtiers, but her publicity stunt touched off the spread of particular eating habits, as well as novel foods such as artichokes and ice cream, throughout Europe.[2] By 1633, Charles I of England proclaimed, "It is Decent to use a Fork," and the Western infatuation with eating utensils was complete; eating with hands was soon banished from upper-echelon dinner tables.[3]

Table habits have distinguished the "elect" from the "ruffians" ever since. Those who sat "above the salt" at the table received the salt first, while their less important guests, dependents, and inferiors sat "below the salt."[4] The customs of King Charles's time have gradually evolved, but what began as appropriate court behavior, or the manners of the civilized, stuck around like gum on a shoe.

Today's dining etiquette features a battery of rules that we tend to follow reflexively, assuming they have some purpose or other. But dining etiquette has nothing to do with personal hygiene, greater food control, or an increased appreciation of flavors. The real reason we have these rules, and continue to use them, is to show that we belong to an elevated social class.

As EmilyPost.com explains, "Eating a meal with others is a veritable minefield of potential blunders and gaffes, so if you're planning to dine with work colleagues, superiors or clients, it's wise for you to be fully versed in dining etiquette. Business dinners and power lunches are where so many key decisions are made and social meals are where relationships are formed."[5] In other words, you don't want to be seen as a ruffian. Much as courtly dining habits once represented membership in the aristocracy, the ability to eat "properly" remains a key component of signaling prestige and exclusivity today.[6]

But what about eating peas with a fork, specifically? British people still commonly smush peas against the backs of their forks instead of using a spoon or the fork tines as a scoop.[7] However, this decision is highly unlikely to make or break an American business dinner. These days you're more liable to face off against sushi, paella, or a burrito than loose peas. Yet there I was, young Todd Rose of Hooper, Utah, painstakingly learning to eat rogue peas as if the queen of England herself were coming to visit.

WE'RE ALL IN THIS TOGETHER

The truth that underlies the injunction to eat off the back of a fork is embedded in an old joke about life in a fishbowl. Two young fish are swimming around one day when an old fish swims by and says, "Morning, boys, how's the water?" After he moves on, one young fish turns to the other and asks, "What the hell is water?"

When we think about social influence, our minds usually gravitate toward its most egregious forms. We think about overt coercion (such as peer pressure) or crass manipulation (such as TV ads). We don't think about social norms—the unwritten rules of group consensus that determine how we should behave when we're with others—because they feel natural and predetermined, like the air we breathe. We almost never question these rules. But we really should because social norms are a primary source of collective illusions.

As we have seen, all humans share a deep, biological yearning to copy others, to belong to our groups, and to be part of the majority. These forces make us highly dependent on norms for social guidance. While the gray matter in our brains melds us from birth to our families, friends, and tribes, the much more mysterious dark matter of social norms binds us to groups of people we don't even know through an unseen yet irresistible force that gathers like storm clouds wherever people congregate.

Social norms permeate every aspect of our lives, from the way we dress to the foods we eat and how we eat them. They dictate the ways we express ourselves, the ways we communicate with each other, and even the ways we celebrate and mourn. Indeed, once you become aware of social norms, it can feel as if you've taken the red pill from *The Matrix*: it's impossible *not* to see them everywhere.

For example, we naturally say "hello" when we meet someone and often ask how they are doing, even though we really don't expect an honest answer. We say "please" and "thank you" and make direct eye contact when talking to people. We tip a server at a restaurant, say "excuse me" if we burp, and avoid picking our noses (at least in public). We try to not speak with our mouths full, to wash our hands after using the restroom, and to arrive fashionably late to a party. If we are attending a funeral, we know that we are free to wear any color we want, as long as it is black. And if you are a woman attending a wedding, don't you dare wear white unless you are the bride. Oh, and if you really want to annoy other people, stand facing them when you enter a crowded elevator. Better yet, sit next to a stranger in an empty movie theater. Or if you're a man, saddle up next to another man at a urinal.

Though their origins are misty and their purposes often murkier than the water in a dirty fishbowl, we usually treat social norms as gospel truth. But in reality, norms are almost always arbitrary, having emerged simply because long ago someone in a powerful position, like Catherine de Medici, once declared, "Make it so." And given their inherent arbitrariness, it's not surprising that norms differ dramatically across time and place. South Koreans don't use red ink because, in earlier days, people wrote the names of the deceased in the family register in red.[8] Members of the Brazilian Yanomami tribe are reassured that, when they die, their souls will be released to the spirit world through a special ceremony: fellow tribe members mix the cremated bones of the deceased with plantain to make a soup, then drink it together in a festival that celebrates and solidifies their connection to their kin and the dead.[9] And if you are in Italy and someone is making a toast, it's considered bad taste and bad luck to join in with anything but wine; toast with water, and you may be asked to leave the gathering or the restaurant.

———————

CULTURAL DIFFERENCES NOTWITHSTANDING, norms can be sorted into three general categories. "Coordination" norms exist to help us align individual behaviors in ways that benefit everyone. These generally have to do with emulating physical behavior and typically involve public safety, such as traffic rules. While I love many things about Cuba, for example, I found out that driving at night can be a matter of life and death. Over the 2018 Christmas holiday, I learned that the rules of the road in rural Cuba were more like "suggestions," and they were widely flouted. Until you've tried driving in a place where traffic laws are not really enforced, you can't appreciate the sense of calm and confidence derived from a coordination norm like driving on one side of the road.

Another category of norms has to do with belonging to one's tribe; they exclusively signal your membership in a specific group. These so-called allegiance norms can involve rules for everything from at-work dress (whether it be the robes of Buddhist monks or business attire for legions of white-collar workers), how you speak (salty slang with pals over beer, formal English at work), and how you behave while cheering on your favorite team (Go, Sox!). Allegiance norms are all about display, and they are meant to sort "us" from "them." They also explain why I had to learn to eat peas on the back of a fork; I was not to reveal myself as the farm boy I really was but rather to show that I was a well-trained member of the mannered class.

When it comes to the really meaty social norms that form collective illusions, however, my favorite category consists of what I call "I'm not an asshole" rules. These serve a dual purpose. They not only signal that one personally holds pro-social values like fairness and reciprocity; they also promote the welfare of the group by minimizing selfish individual behavior. And because they center around determining one's moral stance in a community, violations of this kind of social norm typically invite a response.

The custom of queuing in Britain and its former colonies is a good example. The first person in the line claims his or her position, and everyone else follows that person in a polite, orderly fashion. Crowding and line jumping are no-nos because they are seen as unfair. British social historians say that the norm of queuing began in the early nineteenth century, when people started moving from the countryside into cities and shopping in small stores rather than large, crowded marketplaces. It made more practical sense to stand in line when being served in a city shop than it did to crowd around and beg for attention as one did in the market. The more formal, indoor setting of the shop also encouraged calmer behavior. Later, during World War II, the queue became associated with doing one's duty and taking one's turn.[10]

Violating this particular "I'm not an asshole" norm usually provokes a passionate reaction by the people who witness it, because the violation actually imposes a burden on everybody else. I still laugh when I think about how furious my sister, Missy, became on a Black Friday in 2018 when someone cut in front of her in a line outside a Walmart before it opened. Hours before midnight on Thanksgiving, when big stores offer steep discounts on in-demand items such as toys, gaming systems, and televisions, Missy had bundled herself up in her warmest clothes, plopped herself down in a folding chair just outside the store, and nursed her thermos of coffee while reviewing her strategy, which she had planned for weeks.

Missy is a very driven person. She was in that parking lot because she meant to get her hands on a high-end seventy-five-inch flat-screen TV that normally sold for $3,000. Walmart was offering a small number of them for $1,300. She was so thoroughly invested in this fight that she had demarcated every single twelve-inch linoleum tile on that gigantic store floor in order to make the most efficient beeline to the TV section. She was going to lay her hands on that giant LED TV and not let go until it was planted on the wall of her living room, period.

"I didn't know how many of those TVs they had in there, but I was tenth in line, so I felt pretty good about my chances," she told me afterward. "But then, about an hour before the doors opened, this guy walked up to the front and simply cut into the line with his friend. Now I was eleventh in line. I was totally outraged! I ask you, what kind of person does that? It was disgusting!"

Not surprisingly, everyone else in the line went nuts over the queueing-norm violation. "We all started screaming at him, asking him what the hell he was doing," she said. "We told him to get out of line, or we would *drag* him out. It looked for a minute like things were going to get physical, but then he finally gave in and left."[11]

Now, imagine that you witness someone doing something that you think is "disgusting," as Missy described the line cutter's behavior, and consider it from a neuroscientific perspective. For example, how would you feel if you bit into a wormy apple or saw someone defecating on the sidewalk? It turns out that regardless of whether we feel physical disgust or see someone cut in line in front of us, our brains react in exactly the same way. Revulsion is a natural reflex; it's our brains telling us to protect ourselves from harm. That sense of disgust is not accidental. A dedicated part of our brains—the insula—helps track norms, and when it detects violations to them, we register the feeling as disgust. If I put you in an fMRI scanner and showed you a clip of a person cutting the line, your insula would most likely light up like Broadway. This means that if you act like an asshole, other people will perceive you in the same way they would rotten, maggoty meat.[12]

Given that social norms grease the wheels of human interactions and increase cooperation, it is not surprising that groups benefit from having them around. But we don't just care about social norms when we're in groups. It turns out that our brains absolutely *crave* them, to the point that we will literally fabricate them out of thin air.

ADDICTED TO NORMS

Let's say you're a Columbia University undergrad way back in 1927, and you've agreed to take part in a psychology study. When you arrive at the lab, a graduate student gives you a brief description of the experiment, which has to do with perception. He leads you into a pitch-black room and helps you take your seat at a table with a button on it. He tells you that you will see a light that moves, and your job is to guess how far it has gone. Then he leaves you in the dark room.

In a moment, you hear him say "ready" over an intercom, and a pinprick of light appears before you, hovering in the near distance... or is it far away? The room is so black that you can't tell. The light seems to jerk to one side for a moment. Then it's gone.

How far did the light move? It's really impossible to tell. The moon may look enormous when we see it on the horizon and small when it's up in the sky, but we know it doesn't actually change. Its relative size is just thrown into perspective on the horizon by the presence of trees or buildings. How do we make sense of what we're seeing without any such standard for judgment?

In reality, the light that appears to move in the experiment is stationary.[13] Our physiological perception of its movement has a fancy name: the autokinetic effect. We may feel like our eyes are "fixed" on that light, but our eyeballs are actually incapable of keeping completely still. When we stare at something stationary, the muscles that control the retina make tiny, involuntary movements that are then countered by other, corrective movements. It so happens that a fixed point of light surrounded by darkness highlights this little tug-of-war, which normally goes undetected.[14]

The resulting optical illusion was first recognized by astronomers in the nineteenth century, when they mistook fixed stars and planets for moving objects. In the 1940s, it confounded World War II pilots who thought they saw spots of multicolored light zipping through the darkness beside them, at the same speed as their own planes. Later these so-called foo fighters (not to be confused with the 1990s rock band from Seattle) were recognized as an example of the autokinetic effect, their stories exaggerated by rumor, speculation, and other ocular effects associated with flight and fatigue.[15]

In the 1930s, a Turkish doctoral student named Muzafer Sherif selected the autokinetic effect as the focus of his experiments at Columbia. Sherif asked, "What do we do when all external frames of reference are absent?" The answer to this question, he found, depends on whether we're alone or in a group. Over repeated exposures to the autokinetic effect, individual responses coalesced around a single range of values that became a kind of personal standard. If necessary, our brains will make sense out of nonsense by cobbling together our own relatively stable norms.

But if we are in the presence of others and everyone is speaking their answers aloud ("The light moved six inches to the left!"), we respond quite differently to the autokinetic effect. In this group setting, we tend to coalesce not around our own personal standard but around the most popular view.[16] Sherif found that this was true even when the majority response was unrealistic or didn't make rational sense and even though the people in the experimental groups had no previous relationship to each other.

Such group standards had a lasting impact: even after individuals were later separated from others and free to make their own decisions, they continued to interpret what they saw based on the shared norm of their (now nonexistent) groups.[17] Interestingly, Sherif later found that many of the individuals influenced by the majority view flatly refused to acknowledge that their opinions had changed. Sherif's study participants were actively making decisions, which means they weren't conforming automatically. But at the same time, their choices weren't entirely free, since they were so influenced by the norm.[18]

As our brains grasp for order in the chaotic, dark-room world, we seek new frames of reference. Social norms thus function like skeletons upon which we drape the muscles, skin, and clothes of our lives. But that begs a question: Why do we depend so much on them?[19]

The simple answer is that our brains are lazy.

ON A NEUROLOGICAL level, our reliance on norms is tied to the fact that our brains are energy hogs. Neuroscience has shown that 95 percent of our cognitive activities are unconscious, and these whirring hard drives in our skulls—roughly the size of your fists put together—consume about 20 percent of our physical energy. If you work on a tough cognitive task such as learning a foreign language or playing a musical instrument, you're using about one hundred more calories per hour than you would watching television (unfortunately, not enough to replace going to the gym).[20] But most of your brain's efforts go toward just keeping your body functioning normally.

Because our brains require so much fuel, norms play a critical role. Like beasts of burden, they help to carry much of our cognitive load so that we can use the executive and decision-making parts of our brains to take care of more immediate business. By providing a basic level of predictability, norms are like trusty autopilots, sparing us additional work that would otherwise cause our neurological hard drives to overheat.

Our brains crave the predictability of norms so much that we grab onto them any chance we get. As Sherif discovered, we will even sacrifice our own sense of reality for them. We prefer to rely upon a common standard, such as driving on one side of the road or standing politely in a queue, rather than devise on our own because, quite simply, it's easier to do so. When the nice church ladies tried to teach me to eat peas properly, they were saving me the trouble of having to figure out how to behave on my own. In supplying me and the rest of the kids in that church gym with the rules of the road, their norms freed our brains for other tasks—which, in my case, meant determining the best escape route to flee the etiquette dinner.

Just as seeing other people violating social norms triggers a feeling of having eaten half a worm after biting into an apple, you and I also loathe going against them ourselves. Indeed, our internal reaction to breaking some norms can feel as real and painful as an electric shock, thanks to that neurological error signal that tells us something is wrong. And the more you and I buck the group trend, the stronger that error signal, even when there is no clear right or wrong answer.

For example, the first time I went to Hong Kong (a former British colony), I unconsciously broke the queuing norm. Waiting to board a subway train with my son, I marched right up to the edge of the platform as people do in Boston or New York, positioning myself close to the doors of the oncoming train. I'd failed to notice, however, that everyone else had politely queued up farther back and to the sides to await the train. Observing the unfriendly looks around us, my son said quietly, "Dad, move over here," and guided me to my proper place in the queue. I felt deeply embarrassed at having broken this unspoken cooperative norm. It was a classic "ugly American" tourist move. When I realized my mistake, I felt the blood rush to my cheeks and my chest constrict as I fought the urge to scurry away and hide. The area of the brain that registers errors—the anterior cingulate cortex—had short-circuited my attention.[21]

But here's the interesting thing. I didn't receive that error signal ("For shame!") until my son pointed out that I was breaking a social norm. After all, I had no frame of reference for my behavior. I'd never been to Hong Kong before, and I'd spent the bulk of my time before the trip planning where my son and I would go and what we would eat rather than learning about cultural norms. The guidebook didn't mention anything about subway etiquette. So I stuck with what was familiar, and I did what Bostonians do. But the moment my son pointed out the norm, real physiological responses told me I'd made a mistake.

Another time, when I was visiting Shanghai, China, I offered to treat my tour guide to lunch at an expensive restaurant of her choice. On our way there, the guide informed me that, contrary to our custom in the United States, in Shanghai leaving a tip is considered offensive and insulting. That really surprised me. In fact, I found it hard to believe, especially since I'd once worked as a waiter myself. I half-wondered whether my guide hoped that I would give all my tipping money to her instead of dispensing it to waiters.

Throughout the meal, I kept looking for clues to verify whether what she had told me was actually true. But it was hard to tell, since the Chinese customers didn't appear to be paying for anything with cash. And since the waiter didn't speak English and I didn't speak Mandarin, and since I didn't have access to the internet on my phone, I had nobody else to trust but my tour guide. As I grappled with the tipping dilemma, I felt the buzz of error signals firing in my brain: I was stuck between a sharp discomfort, regret, and a desire to set things right. Even though I was a foreigner and might be excused for not knowing the local customs, I still felt worried that, one way or another, I could inadvertently offend the waiter.

In the end, I figured out a work-around to my tipping problem. Our table was next to a very large window, so at the end of the meal I quietly placed some cash on the windowsill rather than the table itself. I convinced myself that this was a foolproof plan: if tipping really wasn't the norm, well, since the money wasn't *on* the table, the waiter could assume that I left it there by accident; if it *was* expected, then I'd just look like the weirdo who doesn't know where to leave a tip.

In truth, the whole experience was so uncomfortable that I decided just to eat at the hotel for dinner later that night rather than feel that awful error response for a second time that day. The episode taught me that we tend to interpret our physiological response to following or breaking norms as proof that our perception reflects reality. It didn't matter what my tour guide said; not tipping *felt* wrong to me. The experience was also a powerful reminder that social norms adhere to the same Thomas theorem that governs all social influence. Though our beliefs may have nothing to do with actual reality, their consequences make them real. And so it is with social norms, even the most absurd of them.

THE CANDIDE ERROR

Imagine that you are a wealthy, lace-collared Spanish nobleman in the sixteenth century. One evening, you sit down before a roaring fire in your castle's great dining hall. On the table is a luxurious dinner of wild boar in a fragrant plum sauce, with root vegetables, freshly baked bread, and a carafe of deep-ruby wine. Your polished pewter plate also bears a strange but fragrant new fruit, a gift brought to you by the explorer Hernán Cortés, who recently conquered the Aztecs. You cut into its juicy red flesh and take a curious bite. "Mmmm! Delicioso!" you say, and happily wolf down the meal, stuffing yourself full until you have to push the plate away.

But soon you discern an odd, metallic taste in your mouth. Later that night, you are wracked by terrible cramps in your abdomen. A thundering headache overcomes you, and your fingers and toes begin to tingle. Stumbling out of bed, you vomit onto the floor. The next morning, you are found in a coma. A day later, you are dead.

The obvious culprit is the strange new fruit.

Soon after Cortés carried the first bounty of tomatoes from the land of the Aztecs to Europe, the aristocracy took note of the fruit's lethal tendencies and decided that it should never be eaten. And so, for hundreds of years, the tomato was thought to be poisonous. Yet the real culprit turned out to be the fine pewter dishware used by the nobles, which happened to contain a high proportion of lead. When the acid in the tomatoes leached out onto the plates, the food became toxic, and the diners succumbed to a mysterious disease now known as lead poisoning. Thus European aristocrats avoided eating tomatoes for centuries, but never questioned why.

And why should they have? After all, you'd be silly to test the assumption. As a result, those who believed that tomatoes were deadly simply went along with the social norm passed down to them, regardless of its basis in reality.[22] The general population ate from wooden plates; yet because they wanted to emulate the wealthy, and because there was clearly nothing wrong with the elites' pretty dishware, they too concluded that tomatoes must be poisonous. (The happy turning point came around 1800, when working-class Italians, too daring or desperate to care, began making a poor man's food called "pizza" with tomato sauce.[23])

People will go to great lengths to justify norms—particularly when those norms signal allegiance or moral values. Here, you might say, "Well, so what? If some people didn't eat tomatoes, what's the harm in that? Of course, I'm sorry those generations of people missed out on the delights of a sun-warmed tomato off the vine, drenched in olive oil with a little salt and a touch of basil. But it's not like going without was killing them." The deeper truth, however, is that people lived, for centuries, without caring whether their beliefs were actually based in reality. And they blamed tomatoes for their own ignorance.

In our unthinking complicity with norms, we tend to make a fundamental mistake, one that, if we are not careful, can easily turn social norms into collective illusions. It's what I call the "Candide Error."

As the Enlightenment dawned in mid-eighteenth-century Europe, a belief in rationality and science slowly displaced the authoritarian, cloistered worldviews of French theologians, priests, academics, and government and military leaders. *Candide, or The Optimist* is a very witty little book from this period by French gadfly and philosopher Voltaire.

In the book, a stodgy professor named Dr. Pangloss indoctrinates the naive youth Candide in the philosophy that extant reality is the "best of all possible worlds." This counsel flies in the face of all the horrible suffering Candide experiences and sees around him—earthquakes, fires, starvation, the burnings of heretics, unfairness, the pain of rejection, and so on. Yet Pangloss smooths over these awful things—and the nasty social norms that go along with them—as just a natural part of life to be shrugged off and accepted.[24] After a volcano and earthquake flatten Lisbon, Portugal, Pangloss tries to soothe Candide by saying, "This is all for the best. Because, if there's a volcano in Lisbon, it couldn't be anywhere else. Because it's impossible that things would not be as they in fact are. Because everything is for the best."[25]

As Candide begins to detach himself from Pangloss's rosy belief system, it dawns on him that "the obstinacy of maintaining that everything is best when it is worst" is sheer, blind, unadulterated, and norm-imprisoned stupidity.[26]

We tend to believe that because norms exist, they are (in Panglossian speak) good and wanted. After all, how can an old notion stick around for so long if no one really wants or even cares about it? The simple answer is that social norms are incredibly difficult to get rid of.

A story from Sweden offers a good illustration. At 5:00 a.m.

on September 3, 1967, every driver in Sweden had to switch from driving on the left-hand side of the road to the right. Dagen H (in Swedish, *Dagen* means "day," and the *H* stands for *Högertrafik*, or "right-hand traffic") forced everyone to change their habits overnight. The reason? Everybody else in Scandinavia drove on the right, resulting in too many collisions in Sweden. Still, most Swedes weren't in favor of switching. So the Swedish government deployed a massive, years-long, multi-million-dollar public relations and educational campaign. The Dagen H logo was printed on everything, including ladies' underwear and milk cartons. Each local municipality had to repaint road markings and traffic stops. The day before Dagen H, some 360,000 street signs were switched.[27]

The Dagen H conversion did seem to lower traffic accidents for a little while, but by 1969 car crashes were back up to their pre–Dagen H levels.[28] Given such results, some people in Sweden may still wonder if the whole costly effort was worthwhile. The Swedish government essentially tried to engineer a new social norm but found that this change was a lot more complex than just switching traffic signs and rewriting the law. It might as well have been asking all left-handed people to suddenly switch to using their right hands. Changing wired-in, generational habits is incredibly difficult.

Where there is far more at stake than simple coordination, norms are even harder to erase. Take, for example, the once ubiquitous practice of shaking hands. It began because someone in ancient Mesopotamia thought it was a good idea to show that he was not carrying weapons and therefore meant no ill to a stranger.[29] In other words, it was a way of displaying that one was not an asshole. That was a solid, practical idea.

The problem was that back then, nobody realized that shaking hands was also a wonderful way to spread disease. In fact, until the nineteenth century, scientists and doctors thought that diseases such as cholera or bubonic plague were caused by "miasma," or noxious air springing from decomposed matter or foul water.[30] But in 1847, a Hungarian obstetrician named Ignaz Semmelweis noticed some troubling patterns in the Viennese hospital where he worked. High numbers of women were dying of puerperal fever, which was not unusual at the time; but Semmelweis found that mortality rates varied, depending on which maternity ward a woman occupied. The ward staffed by doctors and medical students who dissected cadavers in the nearby operating theater had a mortality rate almost three times that of the ward where midwives, who were not doing dissections, worked.[31]

Suspecting that "cadaverous particles" were causing the new mothers to get sick, Semmelweis made doctors and students wash their hands with chlorinated water after their morning dissections and before examining any pregnant women. With that change of habit, the obstetric mortality rate dropped from 16 percent in 1842 to just over 2 percent in 1848.[32] Though the medical establishment at first pooh-poohed Semmelweis's theory about the spread of germs, handwashing eventually became routine among health care workers.[33] And every flu season since then, public health officials have pleaded with people to stop shaking hands or at least to wash their hands often after doing so (pretty much to no avail).

It took a global pandemic to disrupt this particularly sticky norm. With the onset of Covid-19, we all had to learn how to greet a stranger without shaking hands. To me, not shaking hands felt disrespectful, and fist and elbow bumping didn't quite satisfy my craving for the friendly, respectful old norm.

LET'S RETURN TO Elm Hollow for a moment. As you recall, one of the norms there had to do with a stricture against playing games with face cards. According to Richard Schanck, the custom originated from what he called "Puritan prejudice" against nobility.

Like a low-rent version of Instagram, face cards were seen as a way to celebrate the royal court. By prohibiting face cards, Puritans showed their allegiance to the antimonarchist cause. But in the twentieth century, Elm Hollowites were living in a country that had long freed itself from royal tyranny. The norm was no longer useful or rational, but the good citizens kept upholding it because they thought most of their neighbors agreed with it, when in fact they didn't.

This is the problem with norms. We think that since they exist and most people follow them, everyone agrees with them. Our false beliefs make it easy to become complicit in upholding unwritten rules that, underneath it all, nobody really wants. As more and more people commit the Candide Error and conform to norms that violate their personal values, we can all end up chasing the phantoms of collective illusions.

And when social norms are corrupted in this way, our conformity bias can lead us to make truly bad decisions. Indeed, entire societies can participate in destructive behaviors that people don't actually condone, such as racism, sexism, and other forms of bigotry. And because we're not aware of how this happens, corrupted norms lurk under the rocks, like rattlesnakes. We dance over them because they are mostly invisible to us, but when they attack, their poison is extremely potent. This is why the first step in divorcing ourselves from bad norms is not to ignore them but instead to be vigilant about them—all of them.

This is where some of the most important but often-overlooked people in society—our artists—play a huge role. If you stop to think about it, almost all great art scrutinizes norms and wakes the audience to new modes of perception. Millions of timeless works— including Igor Stravinsky's *The Rite of Spring*, Vincent Van Gogh's *Sunflowers*, and the plays of poets from Euripides through Václav Havel and beyond—force us to think about the norms in which we swim. Sometimes art makes us laugh at the silly things humans do to conform. Other times, it rouses us from our somnolence. Still other times, we feel offended by art that calls out our hypocrisy and destructiveness. But that's the entire point.

For instance, Shakespeare's plays are ingenious reflections on what happens when social norms are disrupted. His comedies typically hinge on the conceit of social confusion, showing what can result when we misread and misunderstand each other: men get mistaken for women and vice versa, and people from different classes change places. At its best, art allows us not only to question our norms but to appreciate how breaking the worst of them can lead to a better society.

Just as giant rhinos happily tolerate the red oxpecker birds that feed on bothersome parasites in their skin, human beings have a mutualistic relationship with social norms. The group gets greater cooperation and collaboration, and we get greater predictability and the reduction of energy demands that comes along with it. In most cases, this is truly a win-win scenario. When norms are inclusive and pro-social, and in particular when they reflect our private values, they amplify the better angels of our nature, allowing individuals and groups to flourish in ways that would not be possible without the norms.

However, because of their pervasiveness and power, and because we rarely think twice about them, we are always at risk of allowing social norms to continue past their expiration date. When social norms become corrupted—when they violate our private values and benefit the few at the expense of the many—they quickly become destructive, dragging us down into an undertow of conformity and collective illusions.

Of course, outdated norms aren't the only source of collective illusions. If they were, we wouldn't need this book, because the obvious solution would simply be to develop a healthy skepticism about norms. The second way that collective illusions form is far more pervasive and immediate. And in this case, unfortunately, we are not just the victims of collective illusions; we are the originators.

CHAPTER 6

THE REIGN OF ERROR

The most erroneous stories are those we think we know
best—and therefore never scrutinize or question.

—STEPHEN JAY GOULD

I WAS TWELVE years old when I first explored one of the dark
alleys of my own social conformity.

I lived in the tiny, Elm Hollow–like agricultural town of Hooper,
Utah, set on the briny border of the Great Salt Lake. Like most
sixth graders, I was desperate to find my place in a preferred group,
which in this case consisted of five smelly boys my age. Of course,
breaking the rules was an important rite of passage. So we naturally found ourselves gravitating toward the taboo use of tobacco.

We all thought our buddy Joe—a tall, lanky, rock-star-ish type—
was supremely cool. Martin, Joe's rebellious older brother, had
developed the nefarious habit of chewing tobacco and convinced
his younger sibling that the great nicotine rush from this illicit
drug was something very special.

So Joe rounded us up one afternoon in Mr. Ross's big irriga-
tion ditch, far removed from prying eyes and our parents' kitchen

windows. He pulled a round container from his jacket pocket and said quietly, "I'm going to show you guys something. You've got to do this! Baseball players do it. And girls love it!"

An exquisite frisson of the forbidden fluttered through us. Opening the container with care, Joe took a tiny pinch of the shredded brown stuff and pushed it inside his upper lip. "Now you try it!" he said, handing the container to me.

I stared at the tobacco, then looked around at my companions. A few had averted their eyes. I felt deeply uncomfortable, but this was a moment of truth. I took the smallest possible pinch and inserted it into the space between my upper lip and my teeth, as Joe had done. Rotten and pungent, like burning weeds, the acrid taste was accompanied by a singe of nicotine that made my eyes water.

As everyone watched, Joe told me to chew it. I did. It was awful. But I kept on chewing, like a cow with its cud. Over the next hour or so, Joe pressured all of us to cram more and more of the rancid stuff into our mouths.

Finally, the claylike gob became too much for me. Ashamed to spit it out before the others did, I gulped it down.

"Where's your chew?" Joe finally asked me, after the others had spat theirs out.

"I swallowed it," I said, instantly ashamed.

My companions all stared, aghast.

"YOU'RE NOT SUPPOSED TO SWALLOW IT!"

By then I had begun to feel really sick. I staggered home, upchucking along the way.

I headed straight for the bathroom when I got home, and my mother entered as I heaved over the toilet bowl. She was a nurse. As I sobbed out a confession, she put her hand on my pale, sweaty, rule-breaking forehead.

"Well," she said matter-of-factly, "you won't die. But I'm pretty sure you won't do that again."

Ten years later, on a visit home to see my friends and family,

I reminisced about the experience around the campfire with my old buddies one night. "Do you remember when we all did that chewing tobacco in Mr. Ross's ditch?"

"Oh, yeah," they said.

"Eew," someone laughed.

"That was so weird," said Mark.

"I have to be honest," Joe said. "I really didn't want to do that." There was a long pause.

"Are you kidding me?" I finally replied. "You pressured us all into it!"

Joe was quiet for a few moments. Then he said, "Honestly? My brother made me do it."

I WASN'T THE first or the last teenager to give in to peer pressure. I ended up getting sick. But I felt that I didn't have a choice, because standing up to the group would have been just as painful. By conforming, however, I'd also compromised my values, which brought its own kind of pain. And though I didn't realize it at the time, I'd put the rest of my friends in exactly the same awkward position, because none of them wanted to chew the cud either. Yet, one by one, we all gave in to the collective illusion that doing the same stupid, unhealthy thing we saw an older teen doing was cool and worthwhile.

Of course, all teenagers do things they come to regret as adults. And all of us conform to our peer groups when we want to feel accepted, or at least avoid embarrassment. But my youthful run-in with chewing tobacco calls into question whether our judgments of what others think and want could actually be mistaken a lot of the time. It shows the ways in which we, ourselves, can not only fall for collective illusions but actively take part in creating them out of nowhere, simply because we misread each other's intentions.

No matter where you look and no matter what the topic, you and I are likely to find ourselves mired in destructive collective illusions of our own making. To understand why this happens and how we might get the problem under control, we need look no further than the biological limitations of our own brains—namely, at the shortcuts we take in order to navigate a world that is infinitely more complex than we can possibly understand.

MIND THE GAP

As you remember from the previous chapter, your brain eats an enormous amount of energy. For example, although it's capable of capturing the equivalent of eleven megabytes of information per second from your eyes, you can only "upload" about sixty bits per second into the picture you consciously "see." This is the equivalent of facing the entire population of Paris, France, but actually seeing only eight people.[1]

To save time and mental energy, your brain does two things. First, it chooses what information to upload. It asks, "What is new here? Has anything changed? If it has, is it important? If not, I'll save my energy by relying on the norms and patterns I already know and understand." Second, it makes lightning-fast predictions, filling in missing information based on previous knowledge and experience long before any conscious thought can get involved. By making rapid inferences about what is probably there, your brain tries to make a fairly good guess about what might come next.

In other words, your brain is not like an objective computer that processes reality as it is. Indeed, the sheer effort of being 100 percent accurate about everything would be an enormous waste of cognitive power. So your brain skips over unimportant details and sticks to those you really need, so that you can make sense of what's going on in the world, anticipate changes, and react as warranted.

For example, when you're crossing a driveway and see a car

begin backing toward you, you don't wait to see what will happen next. You automatically get out of the way. But your brain also primes you for the unexpected. If the car suddenly switches into drive and pulls forward to repark, you will unconsciously compare your prediction about what would happen with what you actually experienced and, if necessary, adjust your future models. Still, since your brain relies so heavily on anticipating what *might* happen, it has a certain tendency to misinterpret reality *as it happens.*[2]

As proof, take a look at the checkerboard image below. Note the two squares, A and B. If I asked you which square is darker, what would you say? The obvious answer, it would seem, is A. Right?

Edward H. Adelson

In fact, squares A and B are *precisely the same shade of gray.* So why doesn't it look that way? Because your brain knows, from past experience, exactly what shadows do to shades of gray (spoiler alert: grays look much darker without light). So when the cylinder is placed on the checkerboard, it presents a contrast between what is actually going on (the squares are the same shade of gray) and what your brain expects to happen because of the shadow (one square is darker than the other). In the face of this difference, your expectation wins out, and your brain literally edits reality to align with your assumptions.

For additional proof, consider this version of the checkerboard with two gray lines connecting the two squares. They are the same.

Edward H. Adelson

This is how optical illusions work. As your brain fills in blanks, it often misunderstands. And if your pattern-based expectations are violated, you feel confused. So your brain tries to fix the problem by automatically slotting your perception into a pattern it already understands.

To get along in this fast-paced world, we have to constantly project our own assumptions onto what we're taking in. It's part of our self-preservation instinct. But the problem is that these expectations tint all subsequent information we receive. Especially in social situations, this makes it dangerously easy to pile on more and more guesses about what others are thinking. Though we like to believe we can discern "objective reality," that's actually impossible. Our brains function as both filters and projectors. And it turns out that we're no more correct in our inferences about individuals or groups than we are about the shades of the checkerboard squares. This inference problem is what causes us not just to fall for but also to create collective illusions.

IF YOU COULD READ MY MIND

In 2015, I went back home to Utah to say a final farewell to my beloved grandmother Ruth, who was dying in a hospital bed. I held her frail hand as she lay there with a plastic oxygen tube in her nose. In sharing our mutual memories during that last conversation, I felt free at last to get something off my chest that had bothered me for years.

"There's one thing I feel really bad about, Gramma," I confessed.

"What's that, Todd?" she asked fondly.

"All those times you and Grampa took me out to Sizzler for dinner. I know you guys didn't have much money. Going out to a restaurant was a big expense for you. I think about that a lot."

She sighed and patted my hand. "You're right, we didn't have much. But we were happy to indulge you once in a while."

"I mean," I continued, "I really just loved hanging out with you, eating the baloney sandwiches with extra pickles you made for me. I didn't really like going to Sizzler that much."

"Of course you did. You loved steak. You still love steak."

"I know, but it wasn't about the food. The food was okay. It's just that Sizzler was noisy and crowded and we couldn't hear each other. And I had to practice my table manners."

I pictured my grandparents' tiny, spotless living room with its powder-blue curtains, upright piano, and well-kept but old furniture. Their house was my after-school sanctuary for many difficult years during my childhood and youth. Gramma Ruth never ordered me to sit still and be quiet; she just accepted me as I was, which was the most loving and valuable gift she could possibly have given me.

"Go on," she said.

"Well, I was just so happy to be with you," I went on. "I really enjoyed playing Yahtzee and eating popcorn and watching Carol Burnett with you both. We didn't need to go out to eat."

She laughed and laughed, then coughed and coughed. When she recovered, she made a confession of her own. "You know what?" she said. "We didn't really like going out to Sizzler either. We even gave up our date nights so that we could afford to take you there. We just did it because we thought *you* liked it."

While outdated norms put us on the road to collective illusions, we also have terrible road signs. The reality is that it's hard to read people, even those whom you've known for a long time. And that's in part because other people distort their behavior due to social influence, just like you. But you don't realize it.

———————

WE ARE ALWAYS trying to understand what other people are thinking. The problem is that we can never really know for sure what's in their minds. We can only guess, based on what they say and do and our previous knowledge of what that means.[3]

So we give it our best effort in a process known as "mentalizing" (the cognitive work of guessing what others are thinking). By running fMRI scans of the brain in real time, neuroscientists have discovered how the same regions of the brain associated with understanding our social environments (the medial prefrontal cortex, anterior temporal lobe, temporoparietal junction, and medial parietal cortex) also kick into gear when we mentalize.[4] But these brain mechanisms have a high error rate. Regardless of whether we're trying to read the thoughts of groups or individuals, we are likely to be wrong, for the simple reason that we dramatically underestimate the impact of social influence on other people.[5]

When it comes to peer pressure, you and I know that we are affected by it, but we don't understand the degree to which others are too. Unlike anger or embarrassment, social anxiety has no obvious tells. We have no way to know for sure if other people are worried about being ridiculed or not belonging, as was the case with the chewing tobacco fiasco. I don't remember if my cheeks grew hot when I swallowed that awful stuff, but I do know that very few of us pay close attention to such subtle cues from others.

The result is a blizzard of uncertainty, false assumptions, and fear of sticking out—a combination that drives us to misread others and alter our own feelings, thoughts, and behaviors around mistaken ideas without even realizing it. Our natural proclivity to assume everything people say and do is an honest reflection of their private views only deepens the vortex because, of course, this is simply not true. If you're speeding and cut me off in traffic, I'll naturally assume you're a jerk; in reality you might be racing to get to a hospital in time to say good-bye to a dying loved one. Since we can't read minds, we simply make a guess (often in error) based on the incomplete information we have.[6]

As in the story about my grandmother, social norms can aggravate this proclivity to misread others. Consider, for example, all the little white lies we tell each other just to be nice.

Picture a Thanksgiving dinner at your friend's house, where the meal is turkey with all the trimmings. You take a bite of the meat and think, "Man, this stuff is *dry*," and push a bit of mashed potato onto your fork to help it go down.

"What do you think of the turkey?" asks your hostess.

"Delicious!" someone says, before you muster an answer. Everyone around the table nods. She beams.

"Yummy!" you add.

You would never pipe up and say, "I think this turkey tastes like firewood." Nor would anyone else there. Under the circumstances, being honest would just make you look like a jerk. You say "yummy" instead because you want to be kind to your hostess and avoid losing a friend (or friends).

It's one thing to hide your true feelings about the dry turkey. It's another to obscure the truth around big social, moral, economic, or political issues. If someone makes a racist remark while passing the gravy, and nobody objects to it, the statement might appear acceptable when it obviously isn't. And when we're dealing with crucial social issues that extend far beyond the end of a fork, this reluctance to be open and authentic can cause serious, macro-level problems.

My own organization's research, along with that of many others, shows that we shade the truth in almost every facet of our lives.[7] While refusing to speak out might work to keep the peace at Thanksgiving, on a broader level it actually fosters polarization because nobody ever hears opinions that differ from their own.[8] And if enough people fail to say what they really think, the behavior soon becomes a self-reinforcing, self-fulfilling modus operandi.

The collective illusion between my grandmother and me and the white lies about the taste of turkey are small and relatively innocuous kinds of truth shading. But what happens when misunderstandings involve far more important issues and are being spread by billions of people?

OF NOISE AND NUMBERS

When Dr. Richard Schanck visited Elm Hollow almost one hundred years ago, daily life in the small town moved along by inches. Back then, the global population numbered a little more than two billion people, and the total US population was a third of what it is today.[9] Most labor was still muscle powered by humans and animals. People pretty much got around on foot or by horse-drawn carriage, though it was possible to take a long-distance trip by train. If you needed to do laundry, you used a washboard and a big tin tub, and you boiled your sheets and whites over a fire in the backyard. Cars were still a novelty. Telephones, televisions, and electric refrigerators were marvelous new inventions too specialized and expensive for most American homes. Radio was in its cradle, so people in Elm Hollow received the majority of their information about the world from a single newspaper, its pages filled with mostly local stories. Day followed predictable day; weeks stretched into months and seasons into years in utterly expected ways, until citizens had expended their average life span of about sixty years.[10] At this slow pace, people could pretty well keep up with new information.

Today the planetary population has reached eight billion people. The expansion of democracy, technology, and globalization have brought about many social benefits, including greater access to education and reductions in poverty. At the same time, connecting with people all over the world has become exponentially easier, which means that we belong to more disembodied groups today than ever before. And while the internet has made it possible for us to follow what is happening around the globe, our brains have not had enough time to evolve the advanced mechanisms we would need to process the vast volume of information we receive from hundreds of thousands of other people.

For example, ask yourself, "How many people do I know well enough that I would feel comfortable joining them for an uninvited drink if I happened to bump into them in a bar?" The actual number, according to the British anthropologist Robin Dunbar, is 150. Back in the 1990s, Dunbar found a correlation between primate brain size and average social group size.[11] Extrapolating from his observations of primates, he proposed that the so-called Dunbar number of 150 represents how many stable relationships any one human can comfortably maintain.[12] The rest is just noise.

Today we are each encased in our own technologically driven communities, thanks to social media. Even the cybergroups that matter most to us are spread across time and space in such a way that we cannot possibly know even a fraction of their members. Still, we continue to gauge the opinions and desires of our fellow members as if we were all living in Elm Hollow, making guesses about what our groups think and want. Because our poor, clunky caveperson brains are only really able to keep track of our immediate friends, family, and most trusted social tribes, we're ill equipped to cope with an onslaught of internet-generated illusions. And yet, on a daily basis, this is exactly what we face.

For example, consider the following. On November 22, 2015, *Buzzfeed News* ran a story that opened, "Los Angeles, California— early November 22, 2015, the rapper known as Drake to his fans and Aubrey Drake Graham to his loved ones passed away in a car accident."

Buzzfeed picked up the item from a string of comments on the official YouTube video for one of Drake's most popular songs. Each comment offered condolences for the rapper's untimely death. Twenty-four hours later, the video had scored seventeen million views, and the top comments were overrun with messages of grief and mourning. Members of the online image forum 4Chan promoted the trend with a flood of likes. Soon the news swept onto Twitter and Tumblr, and Wikipedia listed Drake's date of death as November 22, 2015.

This was all news to Drake, who happened to be alive and well.

The hoax was perpetrated by users of a 4Chan discussion thread who wondered, "What if we could trick Internet users into thinking that Drake is dead?" "Operation Drake," as they called it, became a big joke.[13]

Internet hoaxes like this one happen all the time. In 2018, a site masquerading as a legitimate news source (CNN) called "Breaking -cnn.com" published a bulletin that Barbara Bush had died "peacefully in her sleep" the day before she actually died. The story garnered more than two million likes, shares, and other reactions on Facebook alone.[14] The previous year, millions of consumers devoured and spread stories like "FBI Seizes over 3000 Penises During Raid at Morgue Employee's Home," "President Trump Orders Execution of 5 Turkeys Pardoned by Obama," and "Elderly Woman Accused of Training Her 65 Cats to Steal from Neighbors"—all fake stories that went viral.[15]

Given that anonymous groups have the ability to circulate nonstop lies through social media, pinning down the majority sentiments and beliefs among our various disembodied groups has become extremely difficult. Even in person, fully knowing the minds of even a small number of other people is impossible. So how are we supposed to guess the opinions of large, nebulous, and almost entirely anonymous groups of others? At the massive scale of the internet, all we can do is guess based on our preconceived notions and information from second-hand sources.

From court gossip to Paul Revere ("The British are coming!"), we have always been eager consumers of passed-along information. We've also long recognized its limitations. Among other things, second-hand reports excel at producing caricatures—and the further they travel, the more they distort the original. There's a reason why most hearsay, or information heard from someone else who is not a witness, is not acceptable as evidence in a court of law. If you have ever played the game "telephone" (in which one person whispers something to another person, who whispers what she hears to the next person down the line, and so on), you know that the last person to receive the message and say it aloud is always hilariously off base.

———

TODAY, WE HAVE to try to make sense of second-hand information in a way that we have never had to before. Billions of people around the world are now caught up in games of telephone. How can we possibly understand what so many diverse others require or expect of us? When the groups with which we identify reach the level of thousands or millions of people, it is beyond comprehension that we should presume anything at all about our fellow members. And yet, when it comes to things like national identity or Facebook groups, we do. Thus, when online sources flood us with information that contradicts and conflicts, it becomes difficult to know whom to trust or how much weight to give any one source. It's as if three hundred Paul Reveres with radically different stories about the hostile British arrival have ridden into town, some even claiming that there is no such thing as "the British."

Sixty-something years after Elm Hollow, the birth of the internet began transforming the social experience of people around the world. From limited email connections and early government networks, computer connections expanded into Netscape and AOL in the 1990s, and from there into whole new generations of the web. Today, internet users generate about 2.5 quintillion bytes of data, or about one hundred times the total number of ants on planet Earth.[16] (With one quintillion pennies, we could cover the entire surface of the Earth 1.5 times.) A whopping 90 percent of that information was created from 2018 to 2020.[17] Today the two billion active users of Facebook, the world's largest social media platform, post an average of 510,000 comments and 293,000 status updates every minute of every day. On Instagram, users share a daily flood of ninety-five million photos and videos.[18] That's only slightly less than the number of cars that flood into Manhattan on the George Washington Bridge, the world's busiest road bridge, per year.[19]

This magnitude of information is, quite literally, mind-boggling. With the possible exception of Noah, no one in history has ever dealt with such an overwhelming flood. Those of us who spend many of our waking hours looking at screens absorb far more information than humans ever have before. Aside from work, each of us spends our leisure time consuming about thirty-four gigabytes, or one hundred thousand words, a day. In 2011, Americans consumed five times the amount of information they did in 1986, or what amounted to about 174 newspapers per day. Watching five hours of television feeds you the equivalent of twenty gigabytes of information.[20]

Of course, the internet has produced many informational wonders. You can look up anything on Google; gone are the days of searching through big card catalogs in libraries. If you suffer from a disease like cancer, you can do your own research and ask your doctor intelligent questions. Instead of spending all day on the phone waiting for a call center to pick up, you can find the answer to your question on a company's website. But given the slow speed at which our human brains are able to process visual information, it's laughable to pretend that we can possibly digest all the data floating around out there today.[21] As a result we have now become a world where most of the information directed at us has been tailored, personalized by us or by algorithms. In other words, we now only see the information that we want to see.

You might think that all this knowledge would lead to greater wisdom, but that doesn't appear to be the case. The speed at which we are fed information and our natural impulse to download as much of it as we can far outpace our ability to process it. Facing the digital age with our antiquated mental machinery is a bit like trying to upload photos to Facebook using one of those old IBM PCs from the 1980s, with their pixelated text and blinking green cursors. The scramble to keep up is hopeless. So our brains spin ceaselessly like overheated hard drives, trying to figure out which bits of information to select and absorb.[22]

Seeking relief, we rely on unconscious cognitive shortcuts. We narrow our sources of information to our tribes. We draw comfort from belonging to groups whose members we believe agree with us, regardless of whether our inferences about them are correct or not. While such shortcuts can momentarily calm us, they generate their own set of problems.

Deliberate misinformation and fake news are one thing. But our focus on these issues obscures the far greater damage being wrought by an information deluge. Unfortunately, the combination of our brains and the internet has produced not just greater connection but also an unprecedented explosion of misunderstanding that threatens to envelop us all.

LIFE IN THE HALL OF MIRRORS

As the checkerboard example shows, it's difficult to trust your own eyes. We can even be wrong about those whom we think we know intimately, as my grandmother and I were about each other. Online communication has aggravated this effect. And given that our inferences about others are often so wrong to begin with, it's important to understand exactly how social media in particular magnifies our collective illusions.

The web is structured to collect, curate, dispense, track, and magnify any and all information that users consume. Relatively few people generate most of its content. This all but ensures that you will never be able to read the majority stance of your Facebook community or Twitterverse correctly, even if you're discussing something as comparatively benign as your favorite Drake video.

Instead of one gigantic, all-you-can-eat buffet where you can choose what to see or read based on what's truly available, the internet is more like a prix fixe menu: what you consume is curated *for you* based on the algorithms generated by your previous online behaviors. In other words, your digital environments are hyper-personalized to feed you what the algorithms think you want. So if you search for information about violent protests or Antifa, guess what shows up in your news feed? More stories about violent protests and Antifa.

This problem is intensified by a weird cranial quirk called the "repetition bias." Simply put, the more you hear a story, the more likely you are to think that it's both true and commonly understood as true, even if you know that one person is actually just repeating it over and over. The repetition acts like a rainstorm that gradually wears little rivulets into a muddy path. Repetition works for corporate ads and government propagandists because they say the same thing so often that familiarity trumps rationality and the repeated lie starts to feel like truth. Quite simply, the more often we see something, the faster our brains tend to process and accept it as truth (the only exception being the most extreme and obviously false pieces of information, such as "humans are cold-blooded animals").

Consider, for example, the current phenomenon of fake news. In 2018, a team of Yale researchers found that simply exposing someone on Facebook to the same piece of false information repeatedly, regardless of its credibility, increased its perceived accuracy. And all it took was a sliver of potential truth to set the wheels in motion, such as the headline "Trump on Revamping the Military: We're Bringing Back the Draft." Between their first and second exposure to this plausible but clearly false headline, the number of subjects who said it was accurate *doubled*. The authors concluded that social media inflates repetition bias by acting as a dangerous incubator and a kind of hamster wheel for false information. Indeed, study subjects believed a familiar piece of information to be true even when fact checkers had already exposed it as false or when it contradicted the subject's political views.[23]

Unfortunately, in real-world situations in which our brains are processing information in a lightning-fast, often distracting environment, the involuntary familiarity of a statement often wins out over our more objective assessments of sources or existing knowledge. Indeed, research has shown how our ability to access objective memory gets impaired when our attention is split among several different things, intensifying our repetition bias. In this context, familiarity with a piece of information becomes more important than whether it is actually true.[24]

The philosopher Ludwig Wittgenstein rightly compared our belief in oft-repeated information to buying a second copy of the same newspaper just to see if the first one was right.[25] Like a glitch in our biological software, repetition has no logical connection to truth. Yet it has somehow become a trap door to our beliefs. Sadly, governments, bullies, and leaders have used this trap for generations. To take just one example, Hitler's *Mein Kampf* identifies a number of core principles for successful propaganda—among them, "to employ constant repetition of just a few ideas, using stereotyped phrases and avoiding objectivity."[26]

Social media throws gasoline on the bonfire by amplifying the loudest voices, regardless of their knowledge or expertise. On Twitter, for example, the largest volume of tweets in the United States comes from a small minority of users: in 2018, only 10 percent of tweeters accounted for a whopping 80 percent of all tweets.[27] Freed from the limitations of time and space, vocal minorities thus create the false impression that they are speaking for the majority. And this strategy works. Since most of us tend to mistake repetition, confidence, and volume for generally accepted truth, loud minority statements become accepted reflections of reality, regardless of their veracity.

Russian trolls deployed the enormous power of this strategy when they successfully interfered in US politics during the 2010s. In one instance, a few Americans shared their disgust, in 2017, over Maine Republican senator Susan Collins's support for the Affordable Care Act. Within days, the Russian bots had created a full-blown Twitter storm. Flooding the platform with rage, they accused Collins of being a "traitorous sellout." Their repetitive barrage of insults amplified emotions and quickly built the impression that this was the majority view. Suddenly thousands of Maine residents from both parties were pulled into the cyclone, whether they cared deeply about the Affordable Care Act or not.[28]

In swaying this and countless other issues, Russian trolls enjoyed a roaring success. On Election Day 2016, a single group of false Twitter accounts fired off a steady stream of repetitive messages, posting the hashtag #WarAgainstDemocrats more than seventeen hundred times. In the weeks and months after Bernie Sanders ended his campaign and endorsed Hillary Clinton, Facebook pages supporting Sanders were flooded by suspicious new users posting the hashtag #NeverHillary and calling for "The Revolution" to continue.[29] By posing as Americans and deploying targeted ads, false news articles, and social media posts and tools, Russian trolls were able to reach and mislead tens of millions of American social media users.[30] And because the bots were active on both sides of the political divide, Americans began to see their own parties as more fringe than they actually were. Republicans and Democrats alike started to look hyperextreme.

Using some three million tweets collected between 2009 and 2018, Clemson University researchers Patrick Warren and Darren Linvill have pinpointed exactly how the bots manipulated public opinion. The Russian social media posts were generated en masse by an industrial-style system created by Russia's Internet Research Agency. Employing a simple user template that could be repeated and tweaked according to specialized types of information, these so-called troll factories manufactured lies in much the same way a bottle factory churns out plastic soda bottles. And it worked. The bot posts looked just human enough to be believed, and the angrier and more extreme they were, the more enraged other users became.[31]

One of their most insidious skills was to pile support behind a few human outliers. This way the extreme sentiment comes from a real American, while the bots are agreeable but just polarizing enough to tip the scales. As Linvill has observed, "People are persuaded by things they're already inclined to believe, not by someone yelling at you. The trolls were trying to be your friends, not your enemies."[32]

Worst of all, the bots' stealthy emotional impact tends to linger long after they are discovered and kicked off social media. This, Warren argues, is where the true danger lies, because their influence is "like an infection. It spreads into the social media ecosystem. And even when you take away that vector, you've done lasting damage to the body."[33] This body is not just the Twitterverse but American society and democracy itself. As the US Senate's Select Committee on Intelligence notes, the Russian trolls intend to "stoke anger, provoke outrage and protest, push Americans further away from one another, and foment distrust in government institutions."[34]

THERE'S ANOTHER REASON why fringe ideas become so powerful on social media that they mess with our perception of popular opinion and reality itself. It relates to what scientists call the "friendship paradox." The paradox goes like this: on average, your friends have more friends than you do. At first blush this seems counterintuitive, but it's actually fairly straightforward. Basically, in all social networks some people are *really* social. When I was a kid in Hooper, I had about twenty friends. One of those friends was Joe, the cool kid who looked like a rock star. Because Joe was far more popular than me or most of my friends, he had about one hundred friends. This meant that, on average and taken as a group, my friends had more friends than I did, because Joe threw off the average.[35] And because he had more friends, he also had an outsized influence on my thinking. Ergo the tobacco disaster.

Social media takes the friendship paradox to the extreme. Let's say you have one hundred followers on Twitter, including some who have, say, one thousand followers. These people see more diverse information and post more than you do. As a result, a few highly connected people on your Twitter network give the impression of being very popular and expressing a majority view. In fact, as we've seen, it just takes a few people to tweet something that ricochets around like a sonic-speed ping-pong ball until their opinion appears to be everywhere. Despite the fact that these few folks are decidedly not representative of most people, you end up thinking that they hold the majority view, when they don't.

None of this would matter much if the loud 10 percent were more or less like the rest of us in their attitudes and preferences. But the loudest voices on the internet are decidedly *not* like the rest of us; they are more like the Mrs. Salts of modern society or the online heckler who went after the young adult fantasy author Laurie Forest. They often hold fringe opinions, they don't mind expressing them, and they have a massive megaphone for reaching the rest of us in ways you and I cannot deflect.

Together, our various built-in biases, the internet's amplifying effect, and the friendship paradox turn the web into a carnival room full of distorting mirrors. The result is that everything becomes bloated and misshapen, and it's almost impossible to sort truth from falsehood, perception from reality.

If we don't do something to get out of this hall of mirrors, we become willing participants in creating and feeding still more distorted illusions.

GENERATIONAL CONSEQUENCES

If you recall from the introduction the Populace study that examined collective illusions around success, you remember that there is a yawning gap between what people think others believe and what they actually strive for in their personal lives. Of study respondents, 97 percent defined personal success as following "their own interests and talents to become the best they can be at what they care about most." Yet almost the same number, 92 percent, said that society views success as the achievement of fame and fortune.[36]

In other words, our private understanding of success is entirely different from how we think everyone else sees it. The "good life," as measured by education, relationships, and character, matters most to nearly all of us, while status is the least important.[37] Generally speaking, we all want the same things: to be loved and cared for, to have enough resources to be comfortable, to be good parents, to be happy at work, to be healthy, and to be contributors to our communities.

But our kids aren't getting the message. Take fame, for example. In the absence of anyone speaking up about how little fame means to them, which message do you think our kids are absorbing?

A study conducted by psychologists from the University of California, Los Angeles (UCLA), pertaining to the values transmitted by television shows reveals an answer. Back in 1967, sitcoms like *The Lucy Show* and *The Andy Griffith Show* focused on family and community. In the 1970s, *Laverne & Shirley* and *Happy Days* focused on community values too. Until 1997, the number one value transmitted by television shows was community feeling; benevolence (being kind and helping others) was also big, right up until 2007. Then something changed.[38]

The change was the advent of the internet. By 2007, the Web had reached 1.1 billion users and more than 17 percent of the world's population.[39] And the first fully digital generation was soaking up a new set of values: fame, followed by achievement, popularity, image, and financial success. These were reflected in shows like *American Idol* (a reality show about people who compete in a singing contest) and *Hannah Montana* (about a high schooler who works as a rock star at night).

During this decade, YouTube, Facebook, and Twitter exploded in popularity, encouraging greater focus on the self, including selfies, and a whole new susceptibility to narcissism. Today, the number one goal among kids is to be a YouTube star. According to a 2018 study conducted by Pew Research, 37 percent of teens felt social media put them under pressure to look good to others and to garner "likes."[40] "My friends and I are making a YouTube Channel," one eleven-year-old boy told an author of the UCLA study. "Our goal is to try and get a million subscribers." The kid wasn't interested in showcasing a talent—his only interest seemed to be in garnering numbers. "Given that these digital media invite you to broadcast yourself, share your life, and then hope for attention that is counted by number of views, likes, or comments," the author asked, "can you blame him?"[41]

Despite this wisdom, most American kids think success is all about chasing the fame phantom and looking good in an illusory world. Advertisers make a point of selling this fantasy because they are caught up in illusions too. They think we all want fame because we all think we all want it, and so they give us what we think we want. Thus, the education of our children and the very future of our society have become tangled up in collective illusions.

Our submission to these illusions isn't just about us; it has an effect on others. The same inference problems we encounter with our closest family members and friends also come into play in our groups, leading to misunderstandings of majority opinion. Chasing the success phantom leads us into the kind of cut-throat, zero-sum trap we see on competitive reality TV, where our win means someone else must lose.

But the greatest tragedy lies in the fact that, as I said at the outset, most other people hold the same unspoken views we do; we just don't realize it. The giant storm of information, magnified minority voices, and our own cognitive shortcuts prevents us from seeing and celebrating everything we share. It blinds us to the common reality we don't discuss for fear of upsetting the Mrs. Salts of the world or not garnering "likes."

This horrifying trend is dangerous for all of us. As successive generations shape their own behavior based on the cultural practices and social norms of their elders, they use imitation to figure out who they are and what it means to belong. One generation's collective illusion becomes the next generation's private opinion.

Social media is now a fact of life, and we can't solve this problem by asking more of technology or media. The solution lies with us. We can start by realizing that most of what we think about our groups is just wrong. We can control whether or not those illusions affect our behavior and, more importantly, whether we allow them to influence how we see the people in our real-life communities. It is entirely possible to do this, and each one of us can. We have to recognize that we can't trust our brains to give us an accurate read on social reality anymore. When you combine the fact that we are so bad at reading other people with the fact that technology has made us so dependent on second-hand information, you see how easy it is to be wrong about each other. And in being so wrong, we end up hurting ourselves and one another.

The good news about collective illusions is that, as powerful as they are, they are also fragile. They only exist because we allow them to. We can get to a society free of illusions—one that is better for each one of us. But to do that, each one of us has to take responsibility for our part in creating and sustaining illusions.

Part III

RECLAIMING OUR POWER

The most common way people give up their power is by thinking they don't have any.

—ALICE WALKER

CHAPTER 7

THE VIRTUE OF CONGRUENCE

The privilege of a lifetime is to become who you truly are.

—CARL GUSTAV JUNG

BOB DELANEY IS a seventy-year-old, broad-shouldered, round-faced fellow with short-cropped silver hair, denim-blue eyes, and a thick "Joisey" accent. He is one of the smartest, kindest, most ethical and compassionate human beings you could ever hope to meet and a bona fide hero to thousands. He can also tell you, better than just about anyone else, exactly what happens when illusion takes over your life.

Bob grew up in the close-knit Irish-Italian neighborhood of Paterson, New Jersey. The upstanding son of a state trooper, he was cherished by his family, friends, and neighbors. He thrived in a life highly structured by the strict norms of his Catholic school and the strict routines of sports, and he even thought he might one day become a priest. Graced with a sharp eye and a keen mind, he never got into trouble. ("Growing up Irish Catholic means you wake up guilty in the morning," he quips.) In high school, he loved the energy and jittery anticipation of stepping onto the basketball court for a big game. He was an honest, hard-working kid with every intention of becoming an exemplary adult.

Thus, when he was twenty-one, Bob naturally followed his father into duty as a state trooper, and he fell in love with the job. Like his dad, he took great pride in putting on his crisp uniform, badge, and spit-shined shoes. He gleaned so much satisfaction from police work that he lived in the troopers' barracks even on his days off. In his daily "miles and smiles" beat on the state highways, he was delighted to help out the smaller communities that lacked their own police forces. He had a mission.[1] "I was a Dudley Do-Right kind of kid," he remembers. "I just wanted to catch the bad guys."[2]

One day in 1975, Bob got a mysterious request from division headquarters. A lieutenant had taken notice of the eager young trooper and wanted to know if Bob would like to be drafted into a six-month assignment investigating organized crime. At that time, the Jersey waterfront was infested with mob members who extorted millions from the owners of small businesses, forcing them to make payoffs they couldn't afford for "protection" from other mobsters. These were the same vulnerable, law-abiding citizens Bob had sworn to protect and defend as a state trooper. He immediately jumped at the opportunity.

The state police and the Federal Bureau of Investigation (FBI) were working together on this special project, whose goal was to infiltrate the infamous Genovese, Bruno, Gambino, and DeCavalcante families in order to gather evidence of their crimes. Enthusiastic, naive young Bob agreed to what he thought was a "cool" half-year assignment, believing the experience would help him pursue his dream of becoming a detective. "Project Alpha," as it was called, consisted of two state troopers (Bob and his partner) and three FBI investigators. They were told to set up a local trucking business that would attract the mobsters' attention, ultimately allowing them to befriend the wise guys.

Accepting the job meant that Bob had to make a near-total break with his former life. He abruptly resigned from his trooper job, without any explanation. His friends, including his state trooper partner, worried that he had somehow landed in serious trouble. But he deflected their questions, bound to silence by the inherent threats of his secret assignment. He couldn't even tell his family about what he was doing. "Just like that, I was gone from the face of the earth, about to enter the dark side," he noted.

Working undercover, Bob became someone else. He donned a completely new identity as "Bobby Covert" (oddly enough, Covert is a common Irish surname whose actual meaning did not raise suspicions in the early 1970s), and an alternate version of himself began to emerge. Gone was the trim young cop. In his place was an "armpit with eyes," as Bob described himself, disguised as a slovenly man four years older and thirty pounds heavier, who sported a droopy Fu Manchu mustache and curly hair (courtesy of the rollers he applied a few times a week).

The mob was soon siphoning 25 percent of the profits from Bob's new trucking business. Pat Kelly, a former mobster turned FBI informant, was brought in as Bob's business partner and became a kind of mentor. Eager to stay out of prison, Pat taught Bob everything he needed to know about mafiosos and how they operate. He also used his connections, helping Bob to gain the mobsters' trust. Mob members began hanging out on the upper floor of the trucking operation, watching TV, sipping wine, and planning their next scam. Meanwhile, Bob and Pat worked up to fifteen hours a day running the trucking company. The trucks moved what the mobsters called "swag"—stolen bicycles, clothing, electronics, and so forth—and Bob, Pat, and the building itself were wired top to bottom. The FBI overheard everything: every movement, conversation, and casual curse was recorded.

In order to survive in this "world that revolved around deceit and danger," Bob became a better liar. Consciously at first, and then unconsciously, he adopted the swagger and callousness of his new companions. He became foulmouthed and aggressive. And the more high-rolling, upper-echelon mobsters he befriended, the more he was absorbed, like an amoeba, into the wise guy culture. His former identity began to erode. "Without realizing it, I had started to change," he recalls. "I was thinking like a real mob guy."[3]

The Feds were pleased with Bob's work and eager to collect more evidence. They extended his contract and underwrote the expansion of the trucking firm, with Bob as its new president. As the months rolled into years, Bob took to wearing the same kind of shiny, three-piece suits the crime bosses wore and even driving the same kind of car: a Lincoln Mark V. He shared inside jokes with professional criminals and treated them to expensive dinners. He also spent time with some of their families. He began to feel at home in Bobby Covert's shoes.

But his new life wasn't entirely comfortable either. He found it almost impossible to relax, and he couldn't shake a lingering sense of disgust at who he'd become. "It was like living in the toilet," he says. "Stay in the toilet long enough, and you start to stink."[4]

By his third year in Project Alpha, Bob was certain he'd be whacked if the mobsters ever found out the truth about what he was doing. He knew too much. The intense anxiety and stress of constantly living under the threat of discovery was taking its toll: he had heart palpitations and woke up in sweat-drenched sheets. His levels of the stress hormone cortisol were so high that his adrenal glands—which regulate the metabolism, immune system, and stress response—stopped functioning. He suffered from chronic diarrhea, and there were times when he had to pull his car over to the side of the road to vomit. At one point he thought he was having a heart attack. Though he tried to ignore these signs of ailing health, Bob knew they weren't normal for a guy in his twenties.

He hit his moral nadir one evening while riding in a car with a couple of mobsters. Pat was beside him in the backseat, and Larry and Tino, two of the worst wise guys, were up front when Bob clicked open the latch of his briefcase. Everyone in the car stiffened; the sound was like a gun being cocked. As they all gradually relaxed once again, Bob, whose tension was almost at the breaking point, entertained a terrible thought: "What if next time I actually had a gun in my briefcase? I could end this whole freaking mess. I could snap open the briefcase and this time Tino wouldn't notice. I would pull out a pistol and fire into the back of his head. Before Larry could act, I would shoot him too. And to make sure there were no witnesses, I would have to turn the gun on Pat—hard as it might be—and squeeze the trigger."[5]

In moments of despair, a person can rationalize anything.

A DIVIDED LIFE

Bob never went totally *Goodfellas* because his character, upbringing, and values wouldn't let him. But his double life exacted an enormous price, generating a sustained cognitive dissonance that wreaked havoc on his psyche. As a state trooper, he thought of himself as highly moral, a person who believed in God, the rule of law, truth, and justice. Yet there was no way to reconcile this self with Bobby Covert, the immoral trucking company executive who paid shameless fealty to thieves and murderers. The longer crooked Bobby Covert palled around with wise guys pretending to be their friend, and the more he snitched on those fake friends to the New Jersey State Police and the FBI, the more estranged he grew from Bob Delaney. Bob was splitting away from himself in multiple directions, shredding an identity he'd spent his life building and cherishing.

When he at last fingered the bad guys, Bob was given 24/7 protection for several weeks. After that, he was on his own. He kept a gun at his bedside and took it everywhere he went. Sneaking around his own apartment at 2 a.m., he would yank aside the shower curtains, terrified of finding an attacker. His family, friends, and everyone he knew saw him as a hero, but he didn't feel heroic at all. Little things triggered him. Once, when he went out to fetch the paper in his driveway, he saw a helicopter flying low over his house and immediately thought he'd been put under mob surveillance. Terrified, he raced back inside and slammed the door. It turned out that the helicopter was spraying for mosquitos.

Then there was the battery of distinctly unsavory habits he'd picked up while he was undercover. He cursed like a criminal and recklessly threw money around, trying to feel like he belonged. He had violent impulses and repeatedly punched holes in the walls of his apartment, which he then had to cover up with cheap framed posters from Kmart.[6] ("Visitors wondered why I had so much art on the walls," he laughs.[7])

Bob was profoundly damaged by living what Carl Rogers would have called an "incongruent" life.[8] A humanistic psychologist and pioneer of psychotherapy, Rogers defined "congruent" as being in agreement or harmony; to be incongruent, then, is to be in conflict with oneself. Incongruent people, Rogers argued, are untrue to themselves and must therefore work hard to maintain their dishonest self-concept.[9] At a deeply personal level, Bob learned how destructive this incongruence can be.

Bob's case may have been extreme, but he is hardly alone. In fact, today's America incentivizes incongruence. Dishonesty and cynicism are the status quo. We don't expect truth from people we don't know, much less from our leaders. We often view being genuine as silly and naive, and even if we'd like to be more honest with one another, we're frequently afraid of exposing ourselves to criticism. So instead of being clear about what we truly believe, we focus on how we appear to others. "Impression management" is a special gift of social media: just think of how users of Instagram, who know it isn't real life, keep pretending that it is. Like it or not, our lives are shot through with a thousand little lies, pretenses, and hypocrisies.

Because we're so accustomed to living these artificial lives, we don't really notice the damage that incongruence does to us, both personally and collectively. Living incongruously sends an invisible message through our social networks that it's okay to lie, begetting more lies, destructive norms, and bad behavior.[10] In this loamy soil, collective illusions germinate and set down deep roots. Spreading their canopies wide, they bear fruitful lies that destroy our shared reality and stunt the vital saplings of societal progress. At their worst, they warp our ability to understand ourselves and others, prompting still more collective stumbles and driving us into what Henry David Thoreau called "lives of quiet desperation."[11]

How did we arrive at such a pass? Once again, the answer lies in the biology of our brains and the deeply social foundations of our individual thoughts and actions. While we tend to view our beliefs as a fairly stable bedrock that anchors our identities, they are actually molded by a host of unseen social and cognitive processes operating outside conscious thought. Deep in the recesses of our unconscious brains, the discomfort of cognitive dissonance works to guide how we justify our behavior and ultimately how we behave.

Indeed, cognitive dissonance can push us into lying to ourselves in order to feel less conflicted. As what we objectively know to be true clashes with what we feel or want to be true, an internal battle ensues between our beliefs and our behaviors. And more often than not, if we have already done something that conflicts with our values, then we instinctively adjust where we can. We resolve the discomfort by nudging our beliefs in one direction or another in order to feel more aligned.[12]

The problem is, this mental balancing of self-image with self-interest changes our behavior too. Bit by bit, what we normally consider as objective reasoning shifts and contorts, reshaping rationality to fit incongruent thoughts and actions.[13] Next come the excuses, which we use to justify our small deceptions. Soon we begin releasing ourselves entirely from responsibility, blaming others for things that we did. We rationalize our behavior by subtly retooling exactly what we did and why. Far too easily, this turns into a habit and then a norm, and soon we find ourselves using logical justifications for more and more serious offenses.

THE SLIPPERY SLOPE

The reporter Jayson Blair, who resigned from the *New York Times* in 2003 after being called out for plagiarizing and fabricating his stories, described his own experience as "a slippery slope" effectively greased by cognitive dissonance. As he told CBS News in 2012, "Once you realize that you can get away with something, once you cross over that line, you somehow have to rationalize how 'I'm a good person and I did this. So somehow this has to be okay. I've got to make this okay.' So then it becomes a lot easier to do it."[14] Small initial infractions thus tend to snowball, giving rise to greater moral detachment and the justification of our misdeeds. Indeed, research has found that the gradual exposure of subjects to increasingly serious unethical behaviors (or "slippery-slope conditions") more than doubled the rate of such behavior.[15] In short, as long as we can justify our behavior and maintain our vision of ourselves as decent people, we go right on doing the wrong thing until we're caught.

Remember the experiment in Chapter 2 where people were paid either $1 or $20 to lie about how interesting the test was? The people who were paid just $1 viewed the objectively mind-numbing experience more positively than those who received $20. The experimenter, Leon Festinger, concluded that the $1 subjects reinterpreted reality to justify their fib. "Just as hunger impels a person to eat, so does dissonance impel a person to change his opinions or his behavior," Festinger wrote.[16] And when we act incongruently for small personal gains—as we do when we tell little white lies we consider harmless—we're more likely to internalize the beliefs behind those behaviors. Almost without our noticing, they become habit.

One way or the other, your brain will always work to drag you into alignment. But as Bob learned, prolonged deceit is exhausting. Every single day, he put enormous brainpower into being both an undercover agent and a friend to mobsters. Unbeknownst to him, each time he was untrue to the stand-up guy he thought he was, alarm bells went off, sending an error signal pinging through his neural networks. As his brain worked overtime to constantly dissimulate in two directions, he lost the ability to relax. He became hypervigilant.[17] This effort to deceive requires a seamless web of cognitive responses and interactions, known to psychologists as one of the highest-order mental activities a human brain can handle.[18] While lying involves simply creating a fictional answer, deceiving requires both concealing the truth and creating a fiction to actively mislead others, a process that keeps our brains firing on all cylinders.[19]

Beneath the surface, Bob's incongruence drew upon his long-term memory and cognitive control, even as other mental processes worked to integrate and balance the lies he was creating with his true feelings. Thus, in the high-anxiety state that was Bob's status quo, his brain struggled to conceal his deception through both regulating the emotional part of his brain and exerting greater, more conscious control over his decisions and actions.[20] The maintenance of this false identity placed much greater, more complex demands on his brain than simply following orders or telling the truth.[21]

A meeting between Joy Hirsch, a neuroscientist at Columbia University, and Steve Silberman, a writer for *Wired*, revealed the true magnitude of how incongruence impacts our brains. In 2006, Silberman agreed to take a lie detector test—not the standard one with a polygraph, which yields iffy results and is easily duped by expert liars, but a different version that relies upon fMRI.

In the first phase of the procedure, Silberman launched into an internal monologue relating to his personal life, silently forming the words in his mind "as if to a telepathic inquisitor." Then, after a signal, he began to silently lie. He thought, "I've never been married. I had a girlfriend named Linda in high school back in Texas. I remember standing at the door of her parents' house the night she broke up with me." Silberman actually grew up in New Jersey, didn't have his first relationship until he went to college, and had been happily married since 2003.[22]

The experiment showed a distinct difference in Silberman's brain function when he was honest versus when he was lying about himself. When he was truthful, all the parts of the brain associated with emotion, conflict, and cognitive control were quiet (these same neural centers are also responsible for the fight-or-flight response). When he was lying, however, these areas glowed with activity.[23]

The research also demonstrated that, regardless of what you believe, your brain knows better. And it's keeping score. In other words, you can lie to yourself all you want, but you'll never escape your own internal judgment.[24]

At a subconscious level, Bob knew what lying was doing to him. "I was not proud of who I was as I lived a lie and of becoming friends with people while knowing they were criminals," he says.[25] Having lost much of his connection to his former life, he was plagued by self-doubt and even questioned his own self-worth. By the time the mobsters—some of whom had become real friends—were finally arrested, his three years of incongruence had worn him down.

WANTED: SELF-WORTH

The central symbol of my life back in 1996 was an old, broken-down, rust-colored Chevy Chevette that served as my family car.

That thing had a hole in the floor of the backseat so big you could see the road flying by below. We had to tell passengers to keep their legs on the seats to avoid stepping through the floor as we drove.

I'd had a rough time as a kid. Though my family was stable and loving, I performed terribly at school. As a high school junior, I had grades so poor that the administrators wouldn't let me play sports, the only thing I really loved to do. I didn't even graduate.

Try as I might, everything I touched seemed to fall apart, just like that old car. At the age of twenty-one, I had a wife and two young kids I couldn't support. Aside from the pitiful minimum wage I earned working at a bagel shop in Ogden, Utah, we lived on welfare and food stamps. I was so down, as the saying goes, that everything looked like up to me.

Like a self-fulfilling prophecy, my feelings of inadequacy, self-loathing, and incongruence led others to reject and ostracize me. I had very few friends.[26] Still, I was a decent chameleon, and I found belonging by adapting endlessly to my surroundings. I pretended to be religious with Mormon people, a jock around jocks, or a tough guy with the tough guys. I constantly made excuses, and I blamed others for every mistake I made. And I played it cool, pretending not to care that I was a failure. Barely past the legal drinking age, I had such an eviscerated sense of self-worth that I'd given up all hope of reform, believing any effort to improve myself and earn people's respect would inevitably bomb.

"But you're so smart!" people would tell me, their eyes snapping with judgment. "You could be successful if you really tried!" Their disappointment only made me feel worse. I felt like the setup to a bad joke: What's worse than being a loser? *Being a smart loser.* My best defense was just to say, "Screw it," and decide to own that neon "Smart Loser" sign on my forehead. I embraced the identity of a guy who had blown his potential, someone who would never be anything more than a smart loser.[27] I knew my life wasn't working, but I had no idea how to fix it. I'd given up hope.

Then one day, on a lunch break from the bagel store, I wandered into the self-help section of a Barnes & Noble. The book I happened to pull off the shelf was *The Six Pillars of Self-Esteem* by psychologist Nathaniel Branden. It looked interesting, but I couldn't afford to buy it, so I sat down and read it right there in the store.[28] Branden explained that to have self-esteem is "to trust one's mind and to know that one is worthy of happiness."

A few particular passages from the book struck me. "Self-esteem is an intimate experience; it resides in the core of one's being. It is what I think and feel about myself, not what someone else thinks or feels about me," Branden wrote. "The ultimate source of self-esteem is and can only be internal—in what we do, not what others do. When we seek it in externals, in the action and responses of others, we invite tragedy."[29]

I'd always thought that my self-worth came from my adherence to the views of others, but here was a psychologist saying the opposite. If bad things happened to me, he explained, I had no one to blame but myself. I was the cause of my own misery because I was betraying my own integrity. Something clicked when I realized what this guy was telling me: My life was a mess not because I was born to be a failure but because my underlying beliefs didn't match my outward behavior. The idea seemed so novel that it made my skin tingle. What if being a wretchedly poor, albeit smart, loser wasn't who I really was? I needed to take a serious look at my belief system.

I had learned the hard way how failing to meet one's own personal standard can erode self-esteem and expose a person to greater risk.[30] Realizing that I had never thought through my beliefs, I began keeping a journal, a practice that was surprisingly therapeutic.[31] In my writing, I questioned my conformities. I acknowledged what I was good at, where I fell down, and how and in what instances I lied to myself. I began to see that when I received negative feedback, I had a hard time dismissing it. I finally understood why I'd felt so conflicted and anxious to be accepted by people I didn't actually care about.[32]

Slowly, I began to accept the fact that it's okay to ask for help. I began to question. Before I knew it, I was shedding my old, incongruous, smart-loser, conformant life like a snake loses its skin, and underneath was a shiny new me. I gained self-trust. I felt real hope. Eventually I told myself, "I can make good choices now." For the first time in my adult life, I experienced the kind of quiet calm that comes with self-understanding.

Ultimately, I learned that feelings of self-worth and congruence are the same thing.

A congruent person, Carl Rogers argues, is someone who is open, sincere, accepting, empathetic, and genuine. Such a person can achieve what Abraham Maslow called "self-actualization": the complete realization of one's potential in the world (and also the highest level on Abraham Maslow's hierarchy of needs).[33] In simpler terms, when you are living congruently and according to your personal values, you experience more satisfaction with your life. You become happier.

Living with greater congruence, I earned my GED. I went to college and became a psychology major. I graduated with highest honors. Five-plus years after entering that bookstore, I started graduate school at Harvard. One day in 2007, eleven years after my life hit rock bottom in the bagel store, I donned a crimson robe with three black velvet stripes on its sleeve and received my doctorate. If you'd told the "smart loser" that story, he would have taken it as a big fat joke.

But enough about me; let's take a look at the data.

_____

MY ORGANIZATION'S RESEARCH has shown that the only way to really succeed in life is by being true to yourself. Indeed, "success" has nothing to do with conforming to what other people think. Instead it is a deeply personal thing. Out of the more than five thousand people in our study, no two gave the same answer about the meaning of personal success.[34] In reality, the things that make you feel as if you have lived a "successful" life are as unique as your own thumbprint. This means that the only real way to achieve fulfillment is to advance the things that matter most to you personally, regardless of what anybody else thinks. In other words, it's about being congruent.

In addition to putting us on a more reliable path to a successful life, becoming more congruent with ourselves also actively facilitates happiness by boosting our ability to be trustworthy, have better relationships, and achieve greater life satisfaction.[35] Populace's research has shown that when we spend 20 percent more time accomplishing things we find personally rewarding—gardening, playing with our pets, making music, spending quality time with our kids and grandkids, enjoying chocolate ice cream instead of someone else's preferred vanilla, you name it—*the improvement in life satisfaction is the same as if we have been given a 50 percent pay raise.*

Just stop and think about that for a minute.

We also found that those who achieve and succeed at things they think *other* people want them to do—earn a lot of money, buy a big house, get famous on YouTube, and so on—accrue no such dividend in their quality of life.[36]

Of course, striking off down your own path is easier said than done. Part of the problem relates to how we learn new things. These days, even if you don't know how to do something like replace the runners on a kitchen drawer, you can simply look it up online and learn all you need to know. But what if you were in a workshop where several other people were already repairing their own sets of kitchen drawers? What would you do in that case?

Naturally, you'd copy the others. The less you know about how to do something, the less confidence you have in your own knowledge and abilities and the more you will rely on imitation. When individuals or even whole communities feel they are lacking in knowledge or skills, they are much more likely to follow the actions of prominent individuals, and this is true regardless of whether the copied behaviors are good or bad.[37] And it only gets scarier from there because, as we know, the copycat trap leads straight into collective illusions.

Economists have shown that for every incremental increase you feel in self-confidence, you give three times less weight to the actions of others.[38] By the same token, the more your skills improve, the less likely you are to copy. You become less sensitive to social feedback, and your self-esteem grows, along with your overall health and happiness.[39] This boost to your psychological immune system makes you both more resilient in the face of adversity and less vulnerable to developing depression, anxiety, or eating disorders.[40]

Initiating this kind of self-development is much easier than it may appear. In fact, you can improve your congruence by actively learning and practicing it, just as you might gain skill and confidence in repairing a kitchen drawer. Our own brains, it turns out, are custom-built for a life of congruence.

WIRED FOR TRUTH

The "Homo economicus" view of humanity suggests that people are economic agents who make choices chiefly to benefit themselves. But if this were true, then what would happen if people could lie without any threat of punishment? Would you and I deceive others simply to enrich ourselves, knowing we can get away with it?

To answer this question, a team of researchers conducted an experiment in which they called German people at home and asked them to flip a coin. Subjects who got tails received a gift certificate;

heads won them nothing. From a purely economic perspective, all the participants should have chosen to maximize their payoff by lying, since tails would clearly win them money at no apparent cost to themselves. There was no way they could ever be called out for lying, since the experimenters on the other end of the line couldn't see the coin themselves. Participants were entirely immune to external judgment. So why shouldn't they all lie? Because, as it turns out, they were judging themselves.

Instead of 100 percent tails, the experiment yielded a roughly 50 percent split between heads and tails, with more "heads" reported. Thus, despite the lack of any tangible downside to lying, most or all of the participants appeared to have answered honestly. The researchers concluded that, in contrast to the generally cynical assumption that moral fortitude will crumble in the face of monetary incentives, many people actually have an "intrinsic aversion to misreporting their private information."[41] Indeed, being aligned in this way gives us a nice hit of dopamine, which makes us not only happier but more social and fairer toward others.[42] Like a kind of truth serum, the invisible and inevitable psychological costs of lying, combined with the benefits of honesty, motivate us to tell the truth.

While deceiving others triggers a destructive "Beware!" signal in our brains, telling the truth does the opposite. We have a natural craving for congruence, trust, and sharing rooted in our need to survive. As we have seen, the hormone oxytocin increases social attachment. From the time of nomads and cave dwellers, the survival of our infants, families, and tribes depended on the sharing of resources and food. The breaking of bread together isn't just a popular holiday ritual; it has promoted group bonding through the ages.[43] Even very young babies are alert to fairness and can discern the difference between good and bad behavior. At just three months of age, infants are drawn more to puppet characters that are "nice" than those that are "mean." At one year, they begin to understand that everyone should get an equal portion of cookies.[44]

Our adult brains retain this preference for perpetuating good, fair behavior. Simply perceiving ourselves as people who do good deeds and behaving accordingly motivates us to do greater good in the future. In one paid study of one hundred college students, subjects who wrote down a list of past good deeds and were then asked to donate money to a charity gave, on average, over half the earnings they'd made from the study—almost twice as much as those who had been instructed to recall previous bad deeds or neutral conversations. In addition, subjects who'd taken pains to describe not only how they'd been nice to others but how people responded were likely to donate significantly less than those who focused purely on the actions themselves. In other words, people who seemed concerned about appearances (e.g., the impact of their good deed, as much as the deed itself) were less generous than those who cared more about doing good for its own sake.[45]

Consciously reflecting on how you have helped others also improves your perception of yourself as a moral being, which makes you more likely to continue helping others. The opposite is also true, however: if you view yourself as insincere to begin with, then you are more likely to be artificial or dishonest.[46]

The first step in fighting our conformity bias is to understand that personal congruence is a sacred virtue. The personal virtues that we deeply believe in—honesty, integrity, generosity, compassion, and others—transcend social norms. They define who we really are unconditionally. We hold them close not because other people hold them but because we believe in them no matter what. They allow us to look in the mirror, as Bob did, and say, "I'm a decent human being."

In the end we are not purely economic, utilitarian beings, because even when it's not in our own self-interest, we opt for congruence. We tend to tell the truth. The community-based chemistry of our brains drives us to prefer sincerity in our own behavior and that of others. Quite simply, being honest makes us feel better than lying does.

SINCERITY AND AUTHENTICITY

Of course, the struggle for congruence is nothing new. In fact, human society has been wrestling with the tension between personal sincerity and collective illusions for centuries.

In Shakespeare's *Hamlet*, the creaky royal counselor Polonius advises his son, Laertes, "This above all: to thine own self be true / And it must follow, as the night the day / Thou can'st not then be false to any man." In Polonius's case these words carry a touch of irony, since he himself is a doddering old fool who routinely lies and spies from behind arrases, a fault that ultimately costs him his life. But the tip is not a bad one, as fatherly advice goes.

Still, what exactly does it mean to be congruent, or true "to thine own self"? In English, this quality can be parsed under two subheadings: "sincerity" and "authenticity."

In Western culture, being sincere—defined as "being free from pretense, deceit, or hypocrisy"—has been understood, at least since the time of Aristotle, as absolutely central to an ethical life.[47] Derived from the Latin *sincerus*, meaning "clean, sound, or pure," sincerity means having and cultivating congruence between what one avows to others and what one actually feels privately. In ancient times, it was applied to material things that weren't broken, falsified, patched up, or adulterated (thus, a group of Spartans who popped open an amphora of "corked" wine might have said it was not "sincere"). In the early sixteenth century, Protestant (and later Puritan) reformers were the first to begin using the word in moral terms. Thus, one who lived a sincere life—focused inward rather than outward—was cultivating an admirable existence, free from the lies and dissimulation that were then strongly associated with the Catholic Church. A sincere person's words and deeds were therefore congruous with his or her beliefs.[48]

This virtue of sincerity was further captured by the French Renaissance writer Michel de Montaigne, who was greatly inspired by Seneca (and who also influenced Shakespeare). For Montaigne, sincerity was about self-awareness. "When I religiously confess myself to myself," he wrote, "I find that the best virtue I have has in it some tincture of vice."[49] To be sincere, then, requires not only honesty but an open acknowledgment of both personal and societal imperfections. Montaigne's essays feature a man who is trying to be true to himself, striving to present the same self in public as he believes himself to be in private.

Western civilization has had a curious relationship with sincerity ever since, vacillating between valuing it as a virtue (perhaps even as *the* civic virtue) and dismissing it as irrelevant, foolish, or naive compared to deception. Thus, for contrarian Renaissance philosophers like Niccolò Machiavelli, being genuine was for dunderheads—though fake sincerity, as a form of manipulation, could get you somewhere. At the French courts of Louis VIII and his namesake son, Le Roi-Soleil, dissimulation and artifice evolved into high art. Sincerity gave way to enormous powdered wigs, thick makeup, and heels, while its banishment was enforced by absurd, ornate, and tyrannical norms that assured deference to authority in everything from personal hygiene to knocking on the king's door (which one did by scratching on the door frame with an overly long pinky nail, grown uniquely for that purpose).[50] In the early Enlightenment, Voltaire poked fun at Candide's naive sincerity and, by the end of the book, had hardened his protagonist into more of a realist.[51]

The Genevan philosopher and writer Jean-Jacques Rousseau had much loftier plans for sincerity, however, and ultimately raised this virtue to a whole new level. He and his fellow Romantics believed that preserving the integrity and congruity of the self—that is, one's heart and soul—was of utmost importance. In their world, sincerity's ancient interpretation as cleanliness, soundness, or purity became a moral value and a deeply held personal responsibility. Across the pond in America, Benjamin Franklin followed their lead and helped infuse the foundations of our democracy with reverence for personal integrity and congruence.

This idealization of sincerity soon waned, however, in favor of much more exciting flavors, such as snark, falsehood, and irony. Long "before Hallmark strip-mined it down to muck," as *New York Times* writer Laura Kipnis put it, sincerity was past its prime and put out to pasture.[52]

We now speak, instead, of being "authentic," a less moralistic term that refers to being real as opposed to false. Authenticity *sounds* good, but it isn't necessarily a call to ethical action. An authentic leader—a creature much praised in business literature— is meant to be genuine, self-disciplined, self-aware, and values driven.[53] Yet authenticity has nothing to do with virtue; one can be authentic and have good or bad values, just as one can be authentically good or bad. Until his conversion following the visitation of the three spirits, Scrooge was true to his own vision of himself as a "tight-fisted hand at the grindstone . . . hard and sharp as flint." As Charles Dickens made clear, this total and utterly unapologetic allegiance to money was authentic, because it reflected his reality.[54] But it didn't make him a good person.

So if sincerity's off among the daisies and authenticity comes up short, where does that leave us?

THE QUALITY OF *CHENG*

Centuries before our classic Western philosophers wrestled with the notion of sincerity, there was *cheng*. The Chinese philosopher Confucius (born 167 years before Aristotle, in 551 BC) developed this more complex notion, which combines personal congruence— or being in harmony with oneself—with our obligations to others.

Yanming An, a professor of Chinese and philosophy at Clemson University, says *cheng* is about one's relationship not just to oneself and others but to the universe as a whole. While the Romantics lauded sincerity as fidelity to oneself—one's heart or soul—*cheng* demands a less individualistic vision of the self as one who shares in essential attributes common to all human beings. In fact, *cheng* makes no distinction between the personal and the social: it's a call to be true simultaneously to oneself *and* to others.

Cheng is about trust, truthfulness (or the acceptance of a shared reality), and congruence between what we privately feel and how we behave in the world. Because it encompasses trust, *cheng* assures positive consequences for both ourselves and society at large. Essentially unselfish and highly responsible, *cheng* is "beneficial to all people, anytime and anywhere." It's worth quoting An in full here:

> The emphasis is put on the side of universality, a feeling of "respect" between two parties, who differ in their understanding of social issues... The reasoning would be that, no matter what you believe in, correct or incorrect in my view, you still have my respect and admiration so long as your attitude toward your belief itself is honest, and you have truly sacrificed for your belief. Here the point is not that I accept the content of the truth in which you believe, but that I respect your attitude toward the truth. The content differentiates you from me, while the attitude underscores the commonality of us.[55]

Cheng, he adds, is an "independent value from the very beginning, the root or substance of all the other virtues, and the sole path to the solution of the contradiction between knowledge and action. In principle, it precludes any probability of 'doing bad sincerely' *(as one can do when one is 'authentic')* and therefore, in theory, will never lead to negative social consequences."[56]

This is why *cheng* is a civic virtue. Indeed, it comes close to what Benjamin Franklin was trying to nail down during the founding of the United States. Although not familiar with *cheng*, Franklin believed sincerity to be absolutely essential in republican forms of government because it is the polar opposite of Machiavellianism. In his view, the best society would be one in which people openly communicated with one another about their motives. Writing about sincerity in his "Thirteen Virtues" (1730), Franklin advised readers to "use no hurtful deceit; think innocently and justly, and, if you speak, speak accordingly."[57]

Unfortunately for our democracy, Franklin's words, much like his dress style, have long since faded out of fashion. But just imagine getting a reputation for tactful but complete truthfulness in today's world. The embodiment of *cheng*, you are trustworthy and sincere. You have the kind of integrity others know they can count on. For all the people who truly care more about truthfulness than protecting their egos or sheltering illusions, you would become an enormous resource. Your *cheng* would not only build respect and lasting relationships for you but also benefit the group by helping to break down illusions and restore a shared reality. And the more you and others affirmed this common ground, the stronger your relationships and self-esteem would become. In acting upon who you really are and approaching your greatest potential, you would put yourself on a path toward Maslow's self-actualization.

Cheng becomes a kind of flywheel, bringing everyone and society at large enormous benefits. Today, as I write this, I believe we are at an inflection point. Call me idealistic, but if history is any guide, we may be transitioning from a long period of falsity into a reckoning and, ultimately, the blossoming of something new and more congruent.

THE UPSIDE OF CONGRUENCE

It took Bob Delaney a while to metamorphose back into the man he had been before his prolonged foray into the Jersey shore's dark and dirty underbelly.

A fellow detective with a psychology degree noticed some red flags following the Project Alpha assignment and invited Bob to talk about his experience. Bob also shared his struggles with one of his former psychology professors, who helped him put a name on what he was going through: posttraumatic stress disorder (PTSD). The more Bob talked about what it was like to live in the shadows, the better he began to feel.

Slowly, over the course of a few years, he adapted to a new, more congruent, *cheng*-like life. Changing his habits was difficult at first, but his self-investigation was rigorous and unrelenting. He read just about every self-help book he could lay his hands on, and in each one he found parts of himself. He literally held conversations with himself in the mirror. He told himself repeatedly that what he'd been through was abnormal and that, deep down, he was a good guy. He found these reflective conversations between Bobby Covert and Bob Delaney freeing. He could almost feel himself shedding his mob-infected skin.[58] "It was like learning to drive in snow," he says. "Turning the wheel in the direction of the spin is completely counterintuitive, but with practice it became easier."[59]

In his gut, Bob knew that this process of self-affirmation could help build his self-esteem.[60] He also took a lot of notes, which ended up becoming fodder for the books he would one day write. In a memoir about his underground experience (*Covert: My Years Infiltrating the Mob*), Bob explains, "I found myself still searching for balance and meaning in a world that had been turned upside down for a very long time. I discovered that what I was looking for was ... on the hardwood floors of my youth."[61]

Bob had always been athletic. He played all-state basketball in college, and the thrill of stepping onto the court had never left him. As he found himself returning to basketball, it became his therapy. "There are rules and boundaries in basketball, and this placated my hypervigilance and playing released endorphins," he recalls. "My passion for the game led to a completely different profession."

Bob dropped the thirty pounds he'd gained as Covert and began volunteering as a referee. He became a member of the International Association of Approved Basketball Officials Board 194, officiating high school games in New Jersey. He found himself having fun again and finally felt some measure of relief from his undercover work. One night, the commissioner of the Jersey Shore Summer Pro League approached him and suggested that he sign up as a referee. Eventually, Bob caught the eye of Darrell Garretson, the supervisor of officials for the National Basketball Association (NBA). By the mid-1980s, he says, "I'd gone from jumping through hoops in the mob shadows to officiating hoops in the sports spotlight."[62]

Bob found a way to transform himself. He took early retirement from his police job and became an NBA referee. He earned a master's degree in leadership. He began teaching PTSD survivors how to come to terms with their own horrific experiences. He married happily. He authored two books. Eventually he rose to become NBA vice president and director of officials. He earned numerous awards, including the National Collegiate Athletic Association's highest honor, the Theodore Roosevelt Award, in 2020.

Today, Bob is a good friend of mine who is living his best life, and he's come a long way to get there. A vibrant seventy-year-old, he is an example of how our lives can change when we move from deceit and hypocrisy to congruence and *cheng*.

With the perfect storm of political polarization, social strife, and rapidly evolving digital technology upon us, we each have a moral responsibility to follow Bob's example. No matter where we are in our lives, it is never too late to start aligning our private and public selves. When you commit to congruence, you not only tap into what can become an immeasurably better life but also become a person who doesn't contribute to illusions and, through integrity, can help to dismantle them where they exist. In other words, adopting the virtue of congruence is truly a win-win decision. Indeed, it is the most important thing we can do for ourselves and each other.

CHAPTER 8

TRUSTING STRANGERS

It is mutual trust, even more than mutual interest, that holds human associations together.

—H. L. MENCKEN

DURING THE SAME awful year or so that I drove that old Chevy Chevette with the hole in the floor, one of my jobs involved giving enemas to people who were ill and homebound. Awful as it was, I considered it better than the bagel shop, because it paid an exorbitant $7 per hour (compared to the then minimum wage of $4.25). My wife added to our income by selling her blood plasma. We also shared a newspaper route, waking up early to whirl morning papers out onto driveways on alternating days. My parents helped out with my night school fees, but they were still supporting my younger siblings. I knew my folks couldn't do much more for us.

I had never been so broke or desperate in my life, but I was also proud. I loathed the idea of accepting any kind of handout. Eventually, however, my father offered me a perspective that made it easier to take the government assistance we needed. "Todd," he told me, "welfare exists to help people like you and your family. It's not an entitlement. You have to think of it as an investment. Look around at your neighbors. They're taxpayers who are investing some of their hard-earned money in people like you so that you can improve your life. And when you accept their help for a little while, you have an obligation to pay back more than you took, later on."[1]

With that smart counsel in mind, I felt a little better about accepting our monthly allotment of food stamps. But it didn't make shopping for groceries any easier. My wife and I made a special effort to go to the store late at night in order to avoid the judgmental looks of strangers. I dreaded every visit to the register, when we had to sort out the items we were allowed to buy with taxpayer money (including baby food, formula, milk, cheese, cereal, fruits, vegetables, eggs, and peanut butter, but only specific brands) from the things we had to purchase on our own dollar.[2]

I will never forget the time I was buying a jar of chunky peanut butter for my toddler Nathan, who absolutely craved the stuff. The store was packed that night, full of long checkout lines and tired, impatient customers. As the cashier began scanning our food stamp items, she picked up the jar and glared at it, then at me. "You're not allowed to buy chunky peanut butter on food stamps!" she bellowed. She might as well have broadcast it over the PA system.

I wanted to crawl into a hole. It was as if she'd poured lye on my already smarting conscience. Burning under countless pairs of eyes, I felt judged by the cashier and everyone else. I was an irredeemable "taker."[3]

After that episode, we began seeking out a particular cashier at a different grocery store, one we knew was kind. As she scanned each of the government-approved items, she nodded at us sympathetically. "I know how you feel," she confided to me, sotto voce. "I'm on food stamps too." From then on we shopped there, taking care to go during her shift.

Among other things, my experience with the federal food stamp program taught me that the bureaucrats running it didn't trust me to buy the "correct" foods for my own kids.[4] As angry as I was (and still am) about this situation, I have since come to understand this level of distrust as a broader characteristic of our government, one that reaches far beyond any efforts to control poor Americans. It's a symptom of a much larger, more profound problem: the sense that people, in general, cannot be trusted. Our entire society has become so entrenched in this view of distrust that it is baked into our norms and institutions. And the lies it reinforces are terrible for all of us, both as individuals and as Americans.

We are not born suspicious; we become that way through negative experiences and the distrustful systems we inherit from our forebears. But by internalizing these pernicious doubts, we become the architects of our own misery. Quite simply, congruence can only emerge through trust. If we don't deal with the broader problem of distrust, then there is no way we can build a culture in which we can all live congruently and begin to dismantle harmful collective illusions. So how do we learn to practice greater trust? We can begin by understanding why we are so suspicious of others in the first place.

THE COST OF PATERNALISM

I believe that the root cause of our distrust is paternalism. Derived from the Latin for "father," paternalism is defined as "actions or practices that infringe on the personal freedom and autonomy of a person (or class of persons) with a beneficent or protective intent."[5] Simply put, paternalism involves treating others as if they are children who need to be controlled for their own sake. Today, when we refer to something as "paternalistic," we mean that it's not just authoritative and coercive but condescending.

Paternalism has, of course, been around forever. Philosophers from Plato to Kant accepted and even promoted it as part of the natural hierarchy of things; those in charge of maintaining and promoting social order were essentially seen as benevolent dictators. Kings, religious leaders, the nobility, and heads of state all represented a ruling, unquestioned, and largely male authority that "knew better" and therefore determined the laws and virtues most valued by their societies.[6]

Paternalism has been woven into American history since the day the Puritans landed at Plymouth Rock. Though we typically think of it in the context of sexism and religious repression, it's also been used to justify slavery, control immigrants, and persecute Native Americans.[7]

In 1911, American paternalism reached new heights with the help of Frederick Winslow Taylor's *Principles of Scientific Management*. Named "the most influential book on management ever published" by the Academy of Management in 2001, the book established Taylor as the father of white-collar management practices. In a single stroke, it also industrialized paternalism and systematized distrust.[8]

Taylor believed that businesses should be run on the basis of science and knowledge rather than tradition, an innovation he called "scientific management." In more humane hands, such a shift might have been positive. But Taylor promoted scientific management for all the wrong reasons. An elitist to his core, he used his powerful position to shape popular perceptions of industry and reframe workers, whom he loathed, as the weakest link.

In his youth, Taylor was set to attend Harvard when declining eyesight derailed his plans. Unable to continue his studies after graduating from the prestigious Phillips Exeter Academy, he turned his attention to learning a trade. Signing on as an apprentice at a steel company whose owners were friends of his wealthy Philadelphia parents, he quickly climbed the ranks to become chief engineer at a different company.[9] His knack for innovation drove a series of key changes, and by the time he left, he had doubled the company's productivity.[10]

Taylor leveraged what he learned to further his ambitions and solidify his sense of superiority over the people he had come to know at the factory. He based his new theory of management on a hard line between "educated" owners (who sought to squeeze "maximum productivity and maximum profit" from their businesses) and "stupid" factory workers. Thus the essential issue, he argued, was that "what the worker wants and what the employer wants are fundamentally at odds."[11] Taylor's own words drip with scorn in his assessment of workers: "One of the very first requirements for a man who is fit to handle pig iron as a regular occupation is that he shall be so stupid and so phlegmatic that he more nearly resembles in his mental make-up the ox than any other type... [H]e is so stupid that the word 'percentage' has no meaning to him, and he must consequently be trained by a man more intelligent than himself into the habit of working in accordance with the laws of this science before he can be successful."[12]

Believing that animalistic factory workers were intrinsically worthless unless they could be tightly controlled, Taylor devised a system that made them as machinelike as possible, limiting their every movement based on "scientific" calculations. Conveyor belts moved at a speed set by factory managers and strategized for maximum production, rather than what worked best or was most sustainable for the laborers. Everything was measured and meticulously timed.

In his 1936 movie *Modern Times*, Charlie Chaplin satirized this new system of production. In one scene, the Little Tramp finds himself working in a factory assembly line, where he is reprimanded by his boss for not going fast enough. But he struggles to keep pace with the rapidly moving conveyor belt. When a bee buzzes in his face, the manager helpfully swats at it with a meaty hand, smacking Charlie's forehead instead. Unable to keep up, Charlie hops aboard the conveyor belt and disappears into the machine itself, where he is rolled and pressed among the cogs. He becomes an actual part of the machine. He emerges a crazed man who runs around tweaking the noses of coworkers and managers with his two wrenches. Immune to social norms, he harasses ladies and violates personal space in his blind pursuit of more nuts to tighten. His transformation to an automaton is complete, but the result is disastrous.[13]

Since Taylor's book came out more than a century ago, institutions around the world have embraced, internalized, and incorporated his paternalistic approach to managing people. Taylor's method filled not just his pockets but those of business owners and the scientifically trained managers who occupied the upper reaches of organizational charts. Thus the organization man (and later woman) was born, along with droves of management consultants, business schools, and the *Harvard Business Review* (whose founding mission is to "improve the practice of management").[14]

Thanks to its assimilation by the business world, Taylorism has also seeped into the workings of modern society as a whole. Today, just about every manager-run American organization and institution—schools, law courts, prisons, businesses, government programs, you name it—operates on the assumption that the managed cannot be trusted to make good decisions for themselves.

Top-down Taylorism is so pervasive that we don't even notice it; it's the water we're all swimming in. And as we know, what we believe defines what we perceive as reality. Thus, in little more than a hundred years, Mr. Taylor's "scientific" approach toward our work, our lives, and our attitudes toward others has become as self-evident and unquestionable as the law of gravity.

Alex Tabarrok, an economist at George Mason University, has studied the fallout caused by Taylorism, including economic damage and massive social distrust. Paternalists, he argues, are more likely to be corrupt. Among other things, they are inclined to false zero-sum thinking (i.e., "There is only so much pie. The more I get, the less there is for you"). This makes them greedy, selfish, and prone to investments that are hard for other groups to share in.

They are also more likely to redistribute wealth in their favor, which lowers trust among the general population and harms the overall economy.[15] Harvard researchers studying this problem found that what Tabarrok calls the "distrust trap" is self-reinforcing, as civil servants and business owners alike become more likely to treat people badly.[16]

Thus, because our Taylor-inspired institutional overlords tell us we are untrustworthy, we tend to incorporate that belief into our own self-images. And our subscription to this paternalist lie spawns a distrust bias that snowballs: since we feel like we shouldn't be trusted, we assume other people can't be trusted either. We become suspicious of them and resist trusting because we think they don't care about being trustworthy; but this, in turn, means they'll distrust us too. Thus our mutual wariness, cycled and recycled like a poison through all our interactions with others, becomes a destructive, self-fulfilling prophecy.

At an individual scale, the distrust bias also accelerates the splintering of the self. Our suspicion of others makes us more likely to fall into the traps of copying, belonging, and silence. We become more susceptible to peer pressure and conspiracy thinking, and congruence becomes extremely difficult. Distrust hurts our relationships and intensifies anxiety and stress. It also makes it harder for us to think clearly, driving us to become more cautious, inflexible, and angry.[17] Compounded across an entire society, these characteristics become truly damaging.

EVERYONE IS SUSPECT

Trust comes in many flavors. At a fundamental level, it's about having confidence in other people. It's the basic assumption that others will uphold their expected roles and fulfill their responsibilities to us. It also represents an implicit, unspoken contract of shared reality. It is why, if you're crossing the street just about anywhere in the United States, you can generally assume that I won't run over you with my car, even if you're jaywalking. Driving among other cars on the road, we trust those around us to follow the same rules we're following, and that helps keep us safe. When you go to a restaurant, you trust other diners not to steal your food. If I fix the electrical wiring in your house, I assume you will pay me for my services once I've completed the job. And if you are my employer, I count on you to pay me a decent wage in exchange for my work. Billions of such trust-based, mutually assuring handshakes enable our individual and collective security.

Like the experience of merging onto the highway for the first time, trust is about exposing yourself to risk. Once you're cruising along at sixty-five miles per hour, there's always a chance the person in front of you could slam on their brakes. But you're willing to take that risk in order to enjoy the benefits and convenience of the highway. You trust the other drivers to be sober and alert. And each time our mutual trust is validated, on the road or elsewhere, it confirms our shared reality and our connection to one another. The trust we have in each other and in our institutions is a measure of social health around the world.[18]

The dark stain of Taylorism on the social fabric of America helps explain why every single American generation since 1940 has been more distrustful than the preceding one.[19] A 2020 study by the Pew Research Center revealed that 64 percent of Americans in 1997 felt a good deal of trust in their fellow citizens; by 2020, however, that percentage had dropped by nearly half. Most of the 2020 respondents also said they didn't trust other Americans when first meeting them.[20]

This trend points to some serious structural issues in our society. Trust in America is on life support. In late 2020, *New York Times* columnist David Brooks noted the consequences of this massive problem in *The Atlantic*: "Falling trust in institutions is bad enough; it's when people lose faith in each other that societies really begin to fall apart." In a bleak analysis, Brooks outlined the extent of the fallout: in 2020, rates of clinical depression and suicide rose to an all-time high.[21] A June 2020 Gallup poll found that American national pride was lower than at any time since 2001, the first time it was measured.[22] Another poll by NBC News and the *Wall Street Journal* showed that 71 percent of Americans were angry about the state of the country, and 80 percent thought America was "out of control."[23] "By late June [2020]," Brooks wrote, "it was clear that America was enduring a full-bore crisis of legitimacy, an epidemic of alienation, and a loss of faith in the existing order... The distrust doom loop was now at hand."[24]

The epidemic of distrust has become so dire that it is endangering our democracy.[25] Fearing imaginary threats, increasing numbers of Americans are being drawn to the illusory security of political extremism and paternalistic authoritarianism. Both right- and left-wing authoritarians (and their bots) happily espouse the Taylorist approach of flattening identities and voices, feeding the flames of polarization and bias.

Clearly, if we want a healthier, safer, and more equitable society, we need to restore our trust in one another. But we can't do that until we dispel the ultimate collective illusion afflicting us all.

THE DISTRUST ILLUSION

In May 2014, Joe Cornell was living in a Salvation Army rehab center in Fresno, California, trying hard to kick a meth habit. He didn't have a job, and he and his wife were behind on rent and car payments. One day, a Brinks truck driver accidentally left a bank bag containing $125,000 on the sidewalk, and Cornell happened to find it. Whereas others might have been tempted to make off with the cash, Cornell returned the money to the bank.

Afterward Cornell told a local news station that his first concern was for the people who might lose their jobs if he took the money.

"Deposits from businesses and stuff...could have trickled down to a lot of people's jobs, who knows what? So I just figured it was the right thing to do," he explained. "What type of man do I want my grandkids to think I am? I want them to think I'm a just man that...did the right thing."

Brinks rewarded him with a $5,000 debit card, and his family was very proud. The media loved the story.[26] But beyond his belief in personal integrity, Joe Cornell was motivated by the importance of social trust. He thought about how being dishonest might negatively affect others.

You're probably thinking Joe must be a rare jewel; but think again. Joe's story is far from exceptional. In fact, people everywhere do the right thing millions of times a day. And especially once you look closer to home, the distrust illusion begins to crumble. Why? Because, like Joe, we all have to look ourselves in the mirror every day.

Let's say you find a wallet on the street and turn it in to someone working at the local post office, police station, or museum. What do you think the odds are that the cash stays intact or that the wallet makes it back to its rightful owner?

In a 2019 study published in *Science*, researchers sought to answer this very question. Experimenters turned in wallets they pretended to have found on the street to the folks working at front desks in 350 cities around the world. Each wallet contained a clear ID, an email address, and a grocery list. Some contained no cash; others held about $13; still others contained $100. The researchers wanted to see whether the recipients of the lost wallets would actually try to contact the fictitious owners.

And what did they find? In almost every country, people tried to return the wallets. When the wallets contained the greatest amount of money, they tried even harder to reach the owner. And when the wallets contained a key—something that mattered only to the owner—they tried hardest of all.

The researchers then conducted surveys asking people in the United States, the United Kingdom, and Poland to estimate the rate of returned wallets based on whether they contained no money, $13, or $100. Both laypeople and professional economists thought the return rate would be highest when there was no money in the wallet and lowest when it contained $100. In reality, the opposite was true.[27]

Clearly, a collective illusion was at play here. "In this naturalistic test, with real money on the line and nobody observing their behavior, people have moral concerns that come into play that outweigh the material benefits you'd get from keeping the wallet," said David Tannenbaum, one of the study's coauthors. "Doing a big cross-country study like this and getting a consistent result suggests that you might be tapping into something that's really deep about the human condition." The researchers concluded that a large majority of us like to think of ourselves as honest, moral, and altruistic, even though we may not think the same thing of others. In short, we're actually a lot like Joe.[28]

Our own certainty that we can be trusted, even when others cannot, ties into our feelings of self-worth. When Populace researchers looked into the American public's private beliefs about the qualities of a successful life, we found that out of seventy-six possible attributes, being considered trustworthy ranked number three (although, not surprisingly given the collective illusion around trust, they thought most people would rank it at number thirty). Moreover, 93 percent of respondents perceived themselves as pretty reliable, agreeing with the statement "I personally can be trusted to make good decisions." In fact, 47 percent of those who agreed did so *strongly*, hinting at the personal importance of this quality.[29]

Together, these findings point to an enormous and terribly destructive collective illusion. Having bought into Taylorism and all its false assumptions about human nature, we end up thinking that most *other* people don't value being trustworthy and cannot be trusted to make good decisions; yet the overwhelming majority of us believe that we ourselves have both of these qualities. Obviously, these two things cannot simultaneously be true. Thus, either the people Populace surveyed were lying to us and to themselves, or they had misread the majority. Since the methodology for Populace's Success Index is nearly impossible to game, the answer is clear: people, as a whole, *are* trustworthy; we just operate under the collective illusion that they aren't.

So we know what's wrong, and it boils down to a distrust rooted in illusion. But what can we do about it?

OUR SHARED VALUES

If the media are to be believed, Americans today are at each other's throats. And certainly, at a superficial level, it looks like liberals and conservatives share no common values at all. An October 2019 poll by Pew found that people in both the Republican and Democratic parties thought those on the opposite side were "closed-minded," "unintelligent," "lazy," and "unpatriotic" (although Republicans tended to be more negative toward Democrats). In comparison to their responses in 2016, members of both parties were also substantially more likely to say that those in the other party were less moral than other Americans.[30]

People on opposite sides of the political fence are actually much more alike than we think, however. Here's why.

At the moral root of all trust lies a set of common beliefs. These so-called salient shared values are the kinds of basic ethical tenets—such as trustworthiness, honesty, and integrity—that matter most to each of us, especially when it comes to our fundamental identities, our goals, and the methods we use to reach them.

Shocking as it may seem, and despite our raw political hostilities, we privately share a majority of salient values. In 2021, a study conducted by Populace revealed that, by nearly every measure, *most of us share the same hopes and priorities for our own lives and the country as a whole.* Americans across the political spectrum privately agree that individual rights, high-quality health care, leadership accountability, neighborhood safety, an unbiased criminal justice system, and equality are all important for themselves personally and for the future of America. We also share the same conception of fairness and want the same things from our institutions, from work and education to health care and criminal justice. Indeed, out of the top twenty ranked aspirational values, we privately agree on fifteen—including respect for one another, creating a thriving middle class, developing a modern infrastructure, and ensuring equal opportunity for all.[31]

Of course, keeping things more polarized suits both politicians and the media, and so they emphasize our differences and cloud reality, making it difficult for us to recognize how much we actually agree. Take the issue of climate change, for example. Our research shows that Americans of all political stripes agree on the need to address climate change, privately ranking the issue's priority at number three, right behind individual rights and health care. Yet when we asked respondents where they thought *other* Americans would rate its importance, it came in at number thirty-three.[32] This glaring difference between our public and private views illustrates, again, the dangerous way false assumptions can warp our beliefs.

Understanding and accepting that we agree more often than not is crucial because our shared values are the moral foundation for trust. Since we long ago lost the habit of relying on people whom we don't know personally, our default has become to distrust them until they prove themselves trustworthy. Guilty until proven innocent. Yet the resulting inferences we make about one another are primarily off base. And anyway, how can strangers ever prove their trustworthiness if we never give them the opportunity to do so? It's the old chicken-or-the-egg problem.

TRUST BEGETS TRUST

Imagine you're fifteen years old, standing in the tiled hallway of your high school and making the call on whether to skip English class to, ahem, practice your tobacco-consumption skills with some friends. Of course, you know that cutting class is wrong, but you decide to skip anyway. So then the question becomes what lie to tell your parents if they find out.

And what if you can't actually lie about it, because your dad is one of the world's foremost experts on lie detection?

For Eve Ekman, this wasn't hypothetical. Her father, Paul Ekman, named one of the most influential psychologists of the twentieth century, revolutionized the use of science to decode how nonverbal cues convey specific emotions and reveal deception. His strategies for detecting and catching lies have been used in classrooms and police stations and by the US Department of Homeland Security.

In her tumultuous teen years, Eve had to face Dr. Ekman each time she went out on a weeknight or snuck home after curfew. Sound like a personal nightmare? Surprisingly, it wasn't.

When she was twenty-eight, Eve asked her father, "Do you ever remember catching me for anything when I broke your trust, or a time when you caught me dead in a lie?"

Ekman's answer: "Nope."

The trick, he explained, was in actively trying *not* to catch his daughter in a lie and instead inviting her to disclose the truth when he knew she'd done something wrong. His own greatest challenge growing up, he said, was learning how to outwit his parents, and this led him to cultivate "an entirely secret life," which he grew to regret.

Ekman argues that by making themselves vulnerable and trusting their children, parents can invite trust in return. For any kid, he says, "the most important thing is to feel they can trust that their parents, whether they approve or disapprove, will always be available for help and support." One of the best ways to cultivate this relationship and raise trustworthy children is to start out on the right foot. Quite simply, give them your trust.[33]

But how does trust work exactly? And is it possible to teach ourselves to trust more?

The neuroeconomist Paul J. Zak (also the pioneer of a new field called neuroeconomics) has devoted years to answering this question. Zak began by studying hormones. Experiments on rats had shown that the bonding hormone oxytocin surges when one rat decides another is safe to approach.[34] Zak wondered whether it might have a similar effect on humans. Could a single hormone make us more trusting or trustworthy?

He decided to use a common social science experiment known as the "trust test." Participants were given some money and told that they could transfer any amount of it to a stranger online. They were also informed that each time they sent cash, it would triple in value, but there was no guarantee whether the unknown recipient would then reciprocate by sharing some of their winnings with the sender. Under these circumstances, the more trusting sender would send more money, counting on the fact that the recipient would at least return the original amount that had been shared. Of course, this would also expose them to the risk of having their trust betrayed. The more trusting sender was therefore more vulnerable as well.

Zak measured the amount of oxytocin being released before and after the senders made their decision about whether to trust a stranger with their cash (since senders could choose exactly how much money to send, a greater amount of cash indicated a higher level of trust). He also tracked the recipients' oxytocin levels to see how they changed when people were trusted and when they chose to share their winnings.

The findings were striking. Participants were, of course, happier the more money they received (higher quantities of money prompted an increase in oxytocin production). But this elevated level of oxytocin also correlated with the decision to share winnings. In a subsequent study to test this connection, senders were given a nasal spray to boost their oxytocin before sending the money. Participants who had received oxytocin sent more than double the cash those with a placebo chose to share.[35]

Oxytocin, it turns out, isn't just the bonding hormone. It also encourages us to be more trusting and trustworthy. (On the flip side, other studies have illustrated how anxiety suppresses the production of oxytocin, helping to explain why we are often grumpy or antisocial when stressed. This also lends support to the link between oxytocin and trust.)[36]

The story of Ekman and his daughter points to something much bigger than the relationship between parent and child. It tells us that the single best predictor of whether someone will behave in a trustworthy way is if they, themselves, are being treated as trustworthy. As circular as it sounds, trust behaves like a widening spiral, expanding its reach each time we choose to be vulnerable. Just as the spiral of silence isolates and shuts people down, trust connects and opens them up.

OPENING THE DOOR

Variations on the trust game have shown that when receivers believe senders are trusting them with all of their money, they are more likely to follow their example by sharing their own money with another player. In other words, you're more likely to trust strangers if you've been trusted by a stranger.[37] The research also shows that people who trust are seen as more trustworthy than those who do not. This means that just one act of vulnerability, by any one of us, has the power to create a group norm that guides all of our subsequent interactions. If I am willing to trust you, anonymous reader, with my wallet, then that single decision can trigger an exponential growth of both trust and trustworthiness throughout our groups and our society as a whole.

Imagine that you, all by yourself, can double the amount of social trust in the world just by being willing to believe in and rely upon others a bit more. David Brooks calls this "the outrageous gesture of extending vulnerability in a world that is mean, by proffering faith in other people when that faith may not be returned." And taking this leap has, in fact, been shown to open the door to change. Sometimes, Brooks adds, "trust blooms when somebody holds you against all logic, when you expected to be dropped. It ripples across society as multiplying moments of beauty in a storm."[38]

We can begin this process with the simple step of extending more trust and respect to our family and friends. From there, we can work to expand social trust by changing how we *think* about one another. Most of us see ourselves as honest and generally tend to behave honestly, as Joe Cornell did.[39] Actually facing this truth, however, requires recognizing that our assumptions about the beliefs and values of others are plain wrong most of the time. It forces us to confront all the ways these false ideas cultivate distrust. Above all, taking personal responsibility for our own assumptions is important because, as we've seen, our tendency to emulate one another makes each of us a behavioral model for others.

Trusting someone can begin with something as elementary as our choice of words. In an extended version of the trust game, participants were given multiple chances to either trust or distrust the other player. To test whether preconceptions of "friend" or "foe" might influence this interaction, psychologists also primed subjects by referring to the other player as either a "partner" or an "opponent." The results revealed that both sides had the same initial expectations of trust, but the reciprocation of trust (or trustworthiness) among "partners" was more than double what was observed among "opponents." In other words, people were over twice as likely to reciprocate trust if they'd been led to believe a stranger was a collaborator rather than a competitor.[40]

Now I can almost hear you thinking, "Hold on a second, Todd. This all sounds pretty naive. My neighbors down the street aren't exactly the kinds of people I feel like trusting. Are you asking me to just take a leap and bring them a spare key to my house? And if we just suddenly start trusting everyone, aren't we setting ourselves up to be duped?"

Of course I'm not saying that everyone is trustworthy. There are plenty of people around who don't deserve your trust. I *am* saying that, thanks to our distrust bias, it's easy to feel like those exceptions are the rule. It's perfectly okay to distrust some people if they've given you a real reason for doing so. But I think it's important to ask yourself, "Is this person truly untrustworthy, or am I just looking for confirmation of my distrust bias?" Because for everyone you suspect of having less than honest motives, there are thousands of Joe Cornells.

And by the way, if you think that people who are more trusting are more likely to become victims of mischief, the opposite is true. One Canadian study found that "high-trusters" are actually better lie detectors than "low-trusters." While low-trusters are generally suspicious of everybody, high-trusters are more discerning in their judgment of others, thanks to the wisdom they've gleaned from their past mistakes.[41]

Still, you're probably wondering, "What about situations where a possible betrayal of trust could cause real harm to you or others?" In such cases, of course, you should withhold your trust unless you're sure of the other person. It's also worth remembering that in most of our daily interactions with other people, the stakes are not high. And if you ask yourself, "Could I live with the cost of a betrayal of my trust?" in each everyday interaction and the answer is yes, then go ahead and let go. Because, at that point, you are dealing with a massive mechanical advantage. Like someone lifting a load of bricks with the help of a pulley, you can generate enormous benefit to others (and yourself) by taking on extremely little risk to yourself. The trade-off and the risk are similar to driving your car on a busy highway each day in order to keep the job you love or feed your family. If we can just look at things objectively, it's clearly well worth it.

And if that isn't convincing enough, then trust others for the sake of your own health. Studies have shown that trust makes us healthier, more tolerant and productive, and generally happier.[42] Simply put, when you feel you can trust others, the world just feels like a better place.

THE OPPOSITE OF TAYLORISM

Eight-year-old Mauricio Lim Miller arrived in the United States from Mexico back in the 1950s, along with his mother and sister. He remembers watching his sharp, resourceful mom repeatedly try, and fail, to climb America's socioeconomic ladder. "She was a Latina with a third-grade education, and nobody would trust her," he told the *East Bay Times*. "She was talented, but the system was not set up to recognize that."[43]

Miller went on to spend much of his career working at nonprofits, trying to boost people out of poverty by helping them to find housing and jobs. But after more than twenty years of doing this, he began seeing the adult children of program participants sign up for the same services themselves. For years he'd been working under the belief that the assistance his organization provided would launch these kids and their families into the middle class.[44] What were they doing wrong?

Miller's own family managed to escape poverty through the support of other immigrants who pooled their knowledge, money, and resources.[45] Inspired by this experience, Miller left his old job and launched UpTogether (originally called the Family Independence

Initiative), a community-based nonprofit that gives disadvantaged families the network of trust and support they need to innovate and direct their own lives. Indeed, over twenty years' worth of poverty data show how enabling self-determination, fostering supportive communities, and focusing access to resources around people's strengths can increase the economic and social mobility of disadvantaged Americans.[46] UpTogether acts upon this knowledge, shifting the poverty narrative from that of the helpless "charity case" to that of the creative, courageous warrior fighting to improve his or her life. The goal is to both trust and invest in families.[47]

UpTogether's online platform delivers monthly, unrestricted cash payments to families who are independently working to improve their lives.[48] It also provides members with social networks, or online "groups" of other families and individuals who can share their own experiences, collaborate, and help participants to achieve their goals. Miller has described this as a "pure model where no one is telling the families what to do."[49] It's about cutting out management and empowering people to find their own way forward, free from the oppression of paternalism. As one Austin, Texas, UpTogether member, Ivanna Neri, commented, "People don't really want a hand out. They want a hand up."[50]

One of those people was Tanya Jones. After joining UpTogether in 2019, Tanya was able to improve her credit score, put additional funding into her business, and finally pay off the bills she had been meaning to pay for months. In March 2020, on the brink of a global pandemic and economic crisis, Tanya was able to use her UpTogether funds to make a down payment on a home. Getting approved for her mortgage felt "so surreal," she said. Her family was able to move into their new house in May 2020.[51]

In 2020, UpTogether rapidly distributed some $130 million to more than two hundred thousand individuals and families suffering from the financial impacts of the Covid-19 pandemic.[52] In the communities where it has programs, UpTogether has driven an average decrease of 36 percent in welfare subsidies and increased monthly income by 23 percent. Its members have also seen a 77 percent increase in their monthly business income, doubled their retirement savings, and improved their children's school grades.[53] Among the participating families in Boston, 41 percent of those that start below the poverty line climb above it in three years. Member families also report improvements in health, more savings, and less debt.[54] In the words of one UpTogether member named Arial, "We all are in tight situations and trying to fight to better ourselves... and we as a small group realized that together we are stronger!"[55]

The success of UpTogether is one reason why I prefer cash transfers as a way to both support and empower people facing poverty. Growing evidence around the world suggests that increasing people's dignity and independence really does make a positive difference. Giving poor people cash without conditions attached improves their lives and increases their future earning potential. And when you start doing that across all the families in a community, the level of cooperation and social trust rises.

For example, one study in California showed that when people were given $500 per month for two years without being told how to spend it, 26 percent of them paid off their debt, landed full-time jobs, and showed measurable improvements in their emotional health.[56] Another experiment in rural Mexico looked at whether giving people cash or food assistance was more effective. They found that transfers of money led to positive health outcomes, in part because it allowed recipients to spend their cash on necessities such as medicine and transportation. As it turns out, the cash programs also cost 20 percent less to administer.[57] Yet another study conducted in Canada involved giving fifty homeless people a lump sum of $5,700, then following their lives over a period of a year and a half. Those who'd received the money were able to find food and housing faster than those enrolled in social assistance programs, and they also spent 39 percent less on alcohol, cigarettes, and drugs.[58]

This and other research has exposed Taylorism for the zero-sum power game it has always been. Yet these paternalistic roots remain deeply embedded in our institutions. If we really want to stamp out the distrust bias, we must therefore deconstruct the institutional foundations supporting it. This is already starting to happen in the very place Taylorism was born: business.

BASED IN THE agricultural heart of California, the Morning Star Company is the United States' largest processor of tomato products. It's also the polar opposite of a traditional hierarchical organization. Rather than ensuring employee productivity via managers and overseers, Morning Star relies upon "self-management," where employees shape their own positions and goals within the company. Anyone can dip into the Morning Star coffers to buy what they need, without having to get approval from a higher-up. "Colleagues" have a voice and a choice about the work they do and how they do it. Employees are in charge of initiating the hiring process, and they are expected to freely voice concerns and suggestions about any and all aspects of the company. Encouraged to innovate, "colleagues" set their own annual "personal commercial missions" based on their evolving skills and interests.[59]

This topsy-turvy system works extremely well. For the past twenty years, Morning Star has kept up an unbroken streak of double-digit growth, and the company's 550 full-time employees generate over $800 million a year.[60] Even by Tayloristic standards, these results are remarkable.

So what's the secret? How does this company take a recipe for anarchy and turn it into a thriving, smooth-running business?

In a word, the answer is trust. And it begins with the opposite of

Taylor's prescription: namely, the company's decision to cede control to the workers. Liberated from the bureaucratic and financial weight of bosses and managers, colleagues are empowered to work freely and collaboratively, in a way that maximizes their skills. Suspended in a web of some three thousand letters of agreement among colleagues, the company operates through a network of commitment and responsibility that does all the work a team of managers might, at no charge.[61]

One could argue that Morning Star has placed itself in a vulnerable position by relying so heavily on its employees' ability to make good decisions. Yet, by exposing its soft underbelly, it has proven that trust can be highly profitable. Morning Star is also a very attractive place to work. All else being equal, most people would choose to work at a place like Morning Star rather than at an organization committed to Taylorism.

Morning Star is what business academics call a "high-trust" company, and the rest of the business world is gradually waking up to what such companies have known for a long time: trust matters. Research from Paul Zak and others has found that people working at companies with the highest levels of overall trust are happier, more productive, and more engaged. Those in high-trust workplaces also feel more aligned with the goals of their employers. They are more loyal and closer to their colleagues, and they earn more money. Moreover, high-trust companies are more productive, innovative, and, ultimately, profitable.[62]

A GLIMPSE OF THE FUTURE

So what would high trust look like if we could scale it up to a national level?

Norway has one of the highest levels of neighbor-to-neighbor trust on the planet. To throw this into perspective, Scandinavians in general have been shown to trust other people twice as much as Americans. Through the social support and structure of their communities and government programs, these countries cultivate security and trust. As a result, they are less burdened by legal and administrative procedures that do more to compound costs and complexity than ensure integrity.[63]

If you really want to see the kind of future that high levels of social trust could unlock, look no further than the Norwegian prison system. In Norway, the goal is not so much to punish inmates as to rehabilitate them so that they can return to the community as contributing citizens. Norwegian penal policy basically says, "You've lost your freedom to participate in the outside world, but now you have the opportunity to rehabilitate, so use this time inside to reflect and learn from your mistakes."

For example, Halden is a Norwegian maximum-security prison that houses some 250 men convicted of crimes such as drug trafficking, assault, rape, and murder.[64] In America, this would mean a walled fortress reminiscent of the prison in *The Shawshank Redemption*. In Norway, the seventy-five-acre Halden site instead resembles a small village or an open college campus. Cells look like dorm rooms, complete with flat-screen televisions and private bathrooms. Modern kitchens and comfortable chairs adorn the common rooms. Works of art decorate the walls. Large windows admit plenty of daylight, and landscaped green space abounds, both in the central courtyard and around the perimeter. There's a recording studio, a gym, and athletic fields.[65] Prisoners live and work together, as well as with the staff, and they serve as contributing members of a community, learning valuable skills such as auto repair and computer programming.[66] "All aspects of the prison are designed to reduce psychological distress and interpersonal conflicts, and promote rehabilitation," says one of Halden's senior architects, Gudrun Molden.[67] The numbers tell the story: compared to the average US recidivism rate of nearly 70 percent within two years of release, Halden has a rate of just 20 percent.[68]

The contrast with America's penal system could not be starker. Traditionally designed to punish rather than rehabilitate, American prisons force people to lose their independence, their identity, and, too often, their dignity. While criminals are purportedly placed behind bars to protect society, the American prison system demonstrates a certain lust for vengeance and scapegoating. And this lust costs a lot: America locks up an astonishing seven hundred people per one hundred thousand residents, at a cost of $180 billion in taxpayer money each year.[69]

Of course, every country has its own strategies for how to handle criminals. But the example offered by Norway opens the door to what has previously seemed unimaginable in America. By exposing the American prison system as the product of a collective illusion rooted in Taylorism and committed to discipline and punishment, it shows us how we might reform a whole variety of paternalist institutions.

This isn't to say that we can fix our social trust problems overnight. Far from it. But what we can do, to begin, is recognize the role of paternalism in perpetuating these issues and breaking down our ability to rely on each other.

We can start to communicate better, on the basis of our many common values, and stop simply accepting what the media would have us believe about our differences. As individuals, each of us can strive for greater honesty and personal congruence in our own lives, a practice that promises exponential dividends. Changing our institutions feels more like a Herculean task, but if we take our lead from UpTogether, Morning Star, and Halden Prison, other public institutions in education, criminal justice, health care, and government can follow.

None of this is possible without trust, however. Trust is what we owe each other because, without it, the social fabric of our society and our ability to live congruent lives dissolve. With trust, we enable tolerance. We welcome diverse views. We empower people with choice. This combination of tolerance and self-determination ensures that people can integrate their inner and outer selves. When we trust one another, we allow social norms to work in our favor—making it unacceptable for anyone to silence others or use control to strip them of their dignity.

If we can all be just a little more vulnerable and let trust blossom even a tiny bit, America will come out of its cultural tailspin. We would begin to have more faith in our institutions, and they in turn would grow and improve through placing their trust in us. With these small steps, we could set a positive cycle into motion.

CHAPTER 9

LIVING IN TRUTH

The world changes according to the way people see it, and
if you can alter, even by a millimeter, the way people look
at reality, then you can change the world.

—JAMES BALDWIN

BACK IN THE 1970s, there was a man who sold fruit and vegetables from a store in what was then Communist Czechoslovakia.
Each day when he opened his shop, he'd put a sign in the window
that read "Workers of the World, Unite!"

Nobody paid attention to the sign because every other store
and office in the city displayed the very same one. Under the
Communist regime, the sign was just a bit of cliché propaganda.
It demonstrated that the greengrocer not only belonged to but was
also a cooperating participant in a repressive system.

Putting the sign in the window wasn't the greengrocer's idea
because he wasn't acting of his own volition. The sign was a life-
saving requirement. He knew that if he failed to conform to the
Czech government's authoritarian norms, there would be hell to
pay. His shop might be forced to close. His suppliers might suddenly

stop working with him. His children might not be allowed to go to college. He would be bullied and ostracized for not going along with the status quo. And so, fearful for his own and his family's safety, he dutifully put the sign up in the window even though he didn't believe in what it said or what it stood for. In so doing, he helped perpetuate a system he secretly despised.

The greengrocer's story is the centerpiece of a celebrated 1978 essay titled "The Power of the Powerless," written by the poet, playwright, dissident, statesman, and, later, president of the former Czechoslovakia, Václav Havel.[1] At the time of the essay's publication, Havel's country lay in the grip of a spy-ridden Communist bureaucracy that carefully proscribed what one could say and do, under threat of arrest or worse. In other words, as Havel observed, the system didn't actually care whether or not the grocer believed in his sign or not. It was enough that he and everyone else feigned support for their own safety, which made them all complicit in the lie and ultimately kept the system in place.

Then one day, Havel notes, the greengrocer decided he'd had enough of living a lie, and he refused to put the sign in his window. He stopped voting in farcical elections. He started speaking up at town meetings. And surprisingly, with amazing speed, he began to gain support for the simple reason that everyone else in the city felt exactly the same way he did. Tired of living under oppression, the tailor and the baker and the office worker followed his lead. The moment the greengrocer stopped cooperating, he sent a signal to everyone else that they could do likewise.

Havel explains, "Because the emperor is in fact naked, something extremely dangerous has happened: by his action, the greengrocer has addressed the world. He has enabled everyone to peer behind the curtain. He has shown everyone that it is possible to live within the truth." As when a magician's tricks are suddenly unveiled, the impact of this step is enormously powerful. "By breaking the rules of the game, [the grocer] has disrupted the game as such. He has exposed it as a mere game...he has demonstrated that living a lie is living a lie."[2]

Following the publication of his seminal essay, Havel—already a celebrity—was thrown in prison for four years by the Czech authorities. But while the writer suffered behind bars, the quiet spark he had struck slowly grew into a flame among the everyday people of his country, who privately revered him.

Ten years after "The Power of the Powerless" appeared, everything in Czechoslovakia changed abruptly, almost overnight. On November 17, 1989, riot police suppressed a student demonstration in Prague. Within a week, nearly a million people formed a massive protest against the government. A few days later, the citizens of Czechoslovakia joined in a general strike. And twenty-four hours after that, the Communist government surrendered its power without a single shot fired. The following month, Havel was elected president by a unanimous vote of the Federal Assembly. Havel subsequently negotiated the removal of all Soviet troops, and in June 1990, the country held its first democratic elections in forty-four years.[3]

This "Velvet Revolution"—so named because it was "soft" and nonviolent—is a true historical anomaly. Most revolutions are bloody fights that last many years and claim hundreds of thousands or even millions of casualties, but this one was the opposite. The size and speed of the Velvet Revolution has long puzzled experts, who are still trying to understand why and how the country's government fell apart in the way it did. Nobody—not even Havel himself—saw it coming. A student protest did not seem likely to intimidate an authoritarian state capable of suppressing any sort of demonstration. Even foreign governments thought little of the strikes and protests.

From my perspective, the most important factor in the Velvet Revolution is also the most overlooked. I believe Communist Czechoslovakia collapsed because it was based on a collective illusion that was as fragile as glass, and Havel knew it. This lie had nothing to do with the workers of the world uniting and everything to do with the Communist bureaucrats' hold on power. Communism and the Soviet occupation of Czechoslovakia ended because the people took Havel at his word. He set the country on a path of resistance to their collective illusion, and it worked.

Havel had already begun opening the public's eyes many years before. In 1963, he penned an extremely popular play titled *The Garden Party*, a Kafkaesque comedy that caricatures the stultified government. The play features a middle-class boy named Hugo, whose parents want him to meet an influential man named Mr. Kalabis. Expecting to meet the great man at a garden party held by the government's "Liquidation Office," Hugo instead finds himself wandering through a string of encounters with bureaucrats whose absurdly ideological language was horribly familiar to the Czech public. Eager to impress, Hugo apes them and learns to speak in the same nonsensical clichés. Thus he ascends to become the proud head of the "Central Inauguration and Liquidation Committee" and subsequently loses his identity so completely that even his own parents fail to recognize him.[4]

The play was a cultural phenomenon, the *Hamilton* of its day, with ridiculous lines such as "Not even a hag carries hemp seed to the attic alone" and "He who fusses over a mosquito net can never hope to dance with a goat."[5] Quotes from it became part of that generation's vernacular, akin to familiar lines Britons and Americans cite from Monty Python skits. Most importantly, the satire went after the Communist system in a way that wasn't easy for the authorities to suppress.[6]

The play made Havel famous, cementing his role as one of the country's smartest dissidents. His art was so cleverly funny that he was able to expose the repressive regime for what it was without drawing its heavy club down upon his head. And people who understood the play and later absorbed his 1978 essay clearly got the underlying message. Complicity was silly because the regime's bureaucracy was silly too.

The story of the Velvet Revolution has more to tell us about our contemporary situation than we realize. It shows us how ordinary people can solve the problem of collective illusions.

DESCENT INTO POWERLESSNESS

In "The Power of the Powerless," Havel laid bare how blind conformity to norms is exactly the same thing as surrendering to them. Suddenly it was clear that by submitting to the norms of a repressive system, the Czech people were upholding the very thing that oppressed them and thus causing their own suffering. For decades, they had been crushed beneath the wheels of the Soviet system, whose rules were often imposed upon them at gunpoint. They thought they were powerless. But then they woke up to the absurdity of communism. As the Velvet Revolution showed, they weren't powerless at all.[7]

In America today, we face a similar situation. Churned beneath the gears of Taylorism and systemic paternalism, we tend to think we're powerless too. In reality, we actively surrender our power when we participate in a system that rewards compliance and punishes dissidence. We have come to accept that blind obedience is the price we pay for belonging to our tribes. Whether we realize it or not, this makes us collaborators in a web of awful collective illusions that hurt us all. And unlike the prerevolutionary Czechs, we have done this to ourselves—no need for bombs or bayonets.

WHEN WE ARE incongruent—whether because we are copying others, falling victim to cascades, or silencing ourselves and others—we do lasting damage to our own self-worth, diminish our well-being, and make it more difficult to realize our full potential.

Paradoxically, our conformity also hurts our groups, because when we fall into silence, we deny our in-group the very things it needs to improve and grow. When truth, trust, honesty, and new perspectives are ignored, repressed, punished, or flatly denied, progress stops. The resulting collective illusions prevent the group from uplifting its members. In succumbing to these illusions, the group members begin to work against their interests. At that point, they become more like zombie-esque ritualists, merely belonging for belonging's sake. The apparent alternative of social rejection and isolation terrifies them, so they justify the personal and collective costs of their decisions.

This is why blind conformity is arguably the most selfish thing that any of us can indulge in.

As you now know, collective illusions have led us to see division, even when the reality is unity. They mask our shared values. They fuel our fear of each other, they impair our ability to cooperate, and they block social progress. So we find ourselves in a crisis of confidence, plagued by a dark and dangerous feeling of power-lessness. But the truth is that we aren't powerless at all. Collective illusions are just made-up fantasies that can be dissolved by, if not a snap of the fingers, something pretty close to it.

You and I are like Dorothy with her ruby slippers. We may not be aware of our own power yet, but it's already there, hiding in plain sight. In Havel's own words, "The real question is whether the brighter future is really always so distant. What if, on the con-trary, it has been here for a long time already, and only our own blindness and weakness has prevented us from seeing it around us and within us, and kept us from developing it?"[8]

HOW TO CURE OURSELVES

In 1990, the government of Vietnam turned to the US arm of Save the Children, an international nongovernmental organization

(NGO), for help in confronting a terrible plague of childhood malnutrition. At the time, 63 percent of Vietnam's children—even those from relatively well-off families—were malnourished. Save the Children sent its program director, Jerry Sternin, accompanied by his French wife and working partner, Monique, to Hanoi to see what could be done to help.

The Sternins not only shared a lifelong romantic connection but were also bonded by what you might call a "mission-driven" marriage. When they arrived in Vietnam, however, they realized that this particular mission was close to impossible.

In addition to the language barrier, the American-French couple were eyed suspiciously, due in part to their respective countries' colonial histories and decades-long war in Vietnam. (At the time, the United States was also enforcing a trade embargo against Vietnam.) The Sternins also faced two perennial problems traced to the traditional, paternalistic model of international "assistance." This "we came, we fed, we left" model is a Band-Aid solution that creates unsustainable dependency. Jerry called this model "True but Useless," or TBU: "While you are there, things improve" under this strategy, he observed, "but as soon as you leave, things revert back to the baseline."[9]

The Vietnamese government gave the Sternins a narrow six-month time frame to show that malnourished kids could be rehabilitated and that a more sustainable model could be developed. If no substantial changes had occurred in childhood malnutrition by then, the couple would be booted out. Given that the average time to roll out a brand-new, countrywide pilot program was one year, there wasn't a lot of room for maneuvering. The Sternins had no staff, no office, no supplies, no command of the Vietnamese language, and no expertise in nutrition. But they did bring with them a novel approach to local behavioral change that Jerry had discovered while working with Save the Children in Bangladesh.

Rather than coming into poor villages as patriarchal experts from on high, armed with ready-made solutions, they cultivated two core notions, neither of which had been wholly codified. The first was the belief that, in every community, there are people who hold the keys to solving local problems. The second was that once the solution is found, the locals—not the experts—must be the ones to share it and act upon it.

Rather than seeing themselves as problem solvers, the Sternins acted as humble questioners and catalysts. They approached the task wondering what the local people knew that they didn't. They started out by working with the Vietnamese Women's Union to weigh village children and rank families based on how poor they were. Then they asked their local volunteers to use the resulting data to answer a simple question: "Is it possible for a very poor child here to be well nourished?"

The resounding answer, based on the tally they had collected, was yes!

So the next question, of course, was "Who are these well-nourished children?"

With the help of the Women's Union, the Sternins located these unusual children and found that their families had no more resources than those of the malnourished kids. However, the mothers of these kids did things somewhat differently from the norm. For example, they supplemented their children's meals with tiny bits of shrimp and crabs from the rice paddies where they worked, along with sweet potato greens (considered a low-class food). They also fed their kids three or four times a day, though most parents fed their children just twice.

The nutritious foods these mothers added to meals were widely available to everyone. But the vast majority of people didn't even think to use them, because it simply wasn't the way things were done. Conformity to this bad norm prevented the malnourished children from getting the calories they needed. The majority of (malnourished) Vietnamese children were fed haphazardly, their parents too busy with work to pay attention to their kids' diets. The rice harvests were often scanty, and families would get more substantial meals only when external food relief was provided. One or two daily meals of mostly rice, with little else, was normal. Shrimp was also thought to be bad for children, and so in most households it wasn't offered to them (not unlike those "poisonous" sixteenth-century tomatoes). Meanwhile, the mothers who fed their children more nutritious meals hadn't shared their practices publicly for fear of going against these norms.

In short, everyone was suffering from the collective illusion that because they were poor, their children would only get enough to eat through greater access to the powdered milk, oil, protein biscuits, and other processed foods they'd been given as a form of foreign aid. Most villagers didn't realize that some among them had already found a way around the problem. But the Sternins pulled back the curtain on this collective illusion. They called the poorest families who had well-nourished children "the bright spots."[10]

Having discovered the illusion, the next step was key: making public the crucial private information they had found. Recognizing that the messenger was as important as the message, they knew that the usual, sterile government propaganda (typically trumpeted by loudspeaker) and blanket guidance wasn't going to solve the problem. So to spread the word about the minority best practices, the Sternins asked villagers (a collection of locals you might call "people like us") how best to share their newfound knowledge. After a series of community meetings, they settled on a plan to have these locals invite the mothers of the healthy kids (other "people like us") to share their hands-on wisdom.

Each woman from these networks would invite eight to ten mothers with malnourished children into her home for a kind of potluck and ask them to bring contributions of shrimp, crabs, and sweet-potato greens. Together, the women and the mothers then cooked a meal for the entire group. Within a few weeks, the mothers of the malnourished kids overcame their fears and followed the best practices of the healthy kids' moms. Before long, they saw how the new foods were making their own children healthier too, which drove further spread of the new norm.

The Sternins applied two favorite sayings to this form of hands-on practice: "Seeing trumps hearing, but doing trumps seeing" and "It's easier to act your way into a new way of thinking than to think your way into a new way of acting."[11]

Within six months, the Sternins were able to demonstrate to the Vietnamese government how the children whose families broke the norm gained weight. "You should have seen the faces of the parents who explained how they rehabilitated their children," Monique later noted.[12] The couple was allowed to stay on in the country, and within two years as much as 80 percent of the formerly malnourished kids in the program were getting all the nutrients their bodies needed.[13] The Vietnamese government became a huge fan. A "living university" where people could touch, sniff, watch, listen, and copy was created to promulgate the new nutrition practices. "Graduates" of this university then went on to spread the strategy further afield. By the end of the 1990s, more than five million families had returned their sick children to health, and many of their younger siblings enjoyed the benefits of better nourishment too.[14]

POSITIVE DEVIANCE

The formal term for the Sternins' humble and unique, inquiry-driven approach is "positive deviance," or deviation from a negative norm in a positive direction.[15] (The Sternins have noted how they often think of it in the same terms they've heard people around the world use. In Bangladesh, for example, it's called "Why Not?" To the members of the Mocua tribe in Mozambique, it's "The far away stick cannot kill the nearby snake."[16] Still others refer to it as "David and Goliath."[17]) Positive deviance principles are grounded in respect for the local context, an emphasis on empowering communities that already hold the secrets to solving their own problems, and a belief that human ingenuity is the most powerful asset of any group.

The Sternins' approach has made gains everywhere it's been applied. It has boosted health education among Rwandan youth, helped stem the spread of drug-resistant staph infections in US hospitals, prevented AIDS among transvestite sex workers in Indonesia, and even improved the performance of Fortune 500 companies.[18]

Positive deviance has proved particularly useful in resolving problems anywhere collective illusions have taken root. One particularly tough example is the practice of female genital mutilation (FGM), a brutal, dangerous, centuries-old, and very powerful norm. Practiced mainly in northern Africa, the operation involves the removal with a razor of some part, or sometimes all, of a female child's or pubescent girl's clitoris, prepuce, and labia. At its most extreme, it can also include the surgical narrowing or sewing up of the vaginal opening.[19] Believed to keep women virtuous, marriageable, and uninterested in sex, the practice is used as a strategy to guarantee "purity," and those who aren't cut are seen as unattractive and immoral. Enduring the procedure is part of assuming one's full status and womanhood in society. The dishonor of remaining "uncircumcised" is seen as a threat to not only a girl's future but that of her family.[20]

In addition to the physical torture and riskiness of FGM, there is the added posttraumatic stress of having been betrayed by mothers and other norm-enforcing relatives who trick young girls into being cut, bribing them with cookies or other enticements.[21] Women have reported that such betrayal destroyed their familial trust, and those subjected to FGM suffer greater risk of mental illness, anxiety, and low self-esteem.[22] Many women who have been mutilated do not actually support the practice. Research in Egypt has shown how parents who privately disagree with FGM still worry that their grown-up, marriageable daughters will be publicly shunned if they are not cut. So they make a devil's bargain:

they sacrifice their daughters' trust and risk their health or even their lives in order to save their futures.[23] Yet almost no one dares to talk about this terrible situation for fear of social stigma and ostracism.

In 2002, Monique Sternin was hired as a task force consultant to work on this issue. Her mission was to apply the positive deviance model to FGM in Egypt, where cultural pressure to follow the norm was intense. Armed with the lessons she and Jerry had learned in Vietnam, Monique began humbly, by gently asking people questions about FGM. She also looked for positive deviants within the existing population: families that might not have cut their daughters.

"What about the women who aren't circumcised?" she wondered. "Was it in fact possible to be a virtuous woman without undergoing the procedure?"

Finding these women and their families was somewhat trickier than locating well-nourished children, because Monique was looking for what people were *not* doing. But by asking her questions in small community sessions, she was able to encourage a shift from fatalism to curiosity:

One director fixed me directly with his eyes as if to administer a lie detector test: "Aren't you circumcised?" he asked.

"No. In France, no women are circumcised," I responded.

He was dumbstruck and, after an awkward silence, excused himself.

Remaining behind, his female assistant, present throughout and listening intently, timidly asked: "If you are not circumcised, don't you want sex all the time?"

"No, sometimes I have a headache," I retorted.

This was received with much laughter, proof that some feminine strategies are universal.[24]

In the spirit of learning about each other, Monique was able to slowly foster rapport with community volunteers. She found a few women and men willing to talk about the harm caused by FGM—at first not in person but instead on videotape. One was a grandmother; another, a doctor. Still another was the father of four girls, all of whom had excellent reputations in their community. His two eldest had been circumcised, but after the second daughter almost bled to death, he had decided not to circumcise their younger sisters. In a group interview session, he spoke up and said, "Look at me! I have four daughters. All, as you well know, are good and virtuous girls. Two are circumcised and two are not. The only difference between them is two I badly hurt and the other two I saved."[25]

Emboldened by the community sessions and the knowledge that they weren't alone, these positive deviants began to have real conversations about this sensitive subject with their families and neighbors. Slowly, the norm started to shift within their spheres of influence and then spread, forming a new, positive kind of cascade. The rusty lock of FGM began to open.

Five years after Monique set foot in Egypt, the government launched an FGM abandonment program based in part on positive deviance. By 2007, the program had touched 1,693 families in forty communities. The more people saw evidence of how others "just like them" had abandoned the practice, the more things began turning around.[26] Greater education among women appears to be helping this shift: according to one study, FGM has been steadily declining across all segments of Egyptian society for decades.[27]

Looking at all the massive, intractable problems in the world, it's easy to believe that the solutions will have to be equally complicated. The Sternins' work shows otherwise. Positive deviance is the single most powerful method I know for addressing complex social problems. Its greatest lesson is that change always lies hidden in the hands of everyday individuals. You and I have a role to play in dismantling collective illusions. As Mahatma Gandhi supposedly said, we are responsible for being the change we want to see in the world.

RECLAIMING OUR POWER

The call to reclaim our power is more than an empty slogan. It is real, it is practical, and it starts within our own hearts. It requires making a daily commitment to personal congruence, being vulnerable, and trying to open up cracks in our collective illusions, so that the light can come in.

Havel called for taking "authentic responsibility" for our own congruence in "the hidden sphere" of our private lives. Because we're so out of practice, however, we have to consciously start flexing our congruency muscles. Having endured decades of oppression and silencing, Havel's fellow citizens had likewise lost the habit of being congruent. They had long ago surrendered to the bureaucrats. And though he was seen as naive for his emphasis on authentic self-expression, Havel knew something that his critics did not: a system based on a lie cannot survive the light of truth.[28]

But simply knowing the truth is not enough. Personal congruence requires working, as Bob Delaney did, to live according to the truth and follow the guidance of one's soul and conscience rather than the external dictates of whatever collective illusions are blinding us.

Nor is it enough to privately agree with what you have learned in this book; indeed, staying silent can be dangerous, as we have learned. Thus, taking authentic responsibility also requires a willingness to set an example for everyone else. You and I may not be visionaries like Václav Havel or Jerry and Monique Sternin. But we are the mother in the Vietnamese village. We are the greengrocer in Czechoslovakia. We are the father and mother who refuse to hurt their daughters. If the mother of a healthy Vietnamese child had felt a responsibility to share her knowledge, rather than shame at her difference, the government would have had no need of the Sternins' help. If the parents of Egypt's uncircumcised girls had publicly contested the need to cut a girl to prove her marital value, Monique would not have had to encourage that conversation. Like them, you and I have an obligation to hold open, honest discussions about our own norms, especially those we feel are darkening our mutual doors. It's never too early, and never too late, to start these conversations—as long as we find the courage to have them.

Taking a public stand doesn't mean blabbing to online, disembodied hordes on social media who will twist your thinking (and may not even be real to begin with). Nor does it mean recklessly exposing yourself to ridicule or danger. Instead, being congruent is about uniting your beliefs and your behaviors among the flesh-and-blood people of your communities. It's about aligning yourself with the truth on the outside, as well as the inside.

This may seem like a tall order. But think back to how simple it was for the Sternins to solve that massive malnutrition problem. All it takes is a powerful truth, mounted on the wheels of social connection, and you've got yourself a race car. You can start by deploying the skills you've picked up from this book. Refuse to be silent when conscience calls. Ask "Why?" or "Why not?" to open up sensitive but important discussions. Embrace the differences in yourself and others. Be wary of your assumptions, and don't be afraid to face them. Trust a stranger when there's no obvious reason not to.

If we can manage to make that first crack in a collective illusion, you and I can contribute more to our families, friends, neighbors, and communities than we can possibly imagine. When the pastor of that church in Elm Hollow decided to play cards with the locals, the entire social character of the place changed. And make no mistake, we know that it only takes one courageous person, like the little boy in the Hans Christian Andersen tale, to speak the truth out loud and shift public opinion. Havel's greengrocer destabilized the Communist regime when he began speaking up at town meetings. Surprisingly, and with amazing speed, he gained support because everyone else in the city felt exactly as he did.

"A better system will not automatically ensure a better life," Havel wrote. "In fact, the opposite is true: only by creating a better life can a better system be developed."[29] The smallest choices you and I make, every single day, can change the world for better or worse. The simple act of refusing to live a lie has the power to transform who we are and what we are capable of, both as individuals and as a society. In other words, trying our best to live a congruent life is one of the most important things we can do for ourselves and each other.

The truth is, there isn't anything we can't solve together. We already have the answers to our social problems hiding in plain sight. We're not as divided as we're told. We share common values. We are trustworthy, and we want the best for each other. When we recognize our own private power, commit to congruence, and stand up publicly for what we believe, we can dispel the fog of collective illusions and live up to the promise of a better society.

In everyone there is some longing for humanity's rightful dignity, for moral integrity, for free expression of being and a sense of transcendence over the world of existence. Yet, at the same time, each person is capable, to a greater or lesser degree, of coming to terms with living within the lie. Each person somehow succumbs to a profane trivialization of his inherent humanity, and to utilitarianism. In everyone there is some willingness to merge with the anonymous crowd and to flow comfortably along with it down the river of pseudo-life.

—VÁCLAV HAVEL

ACKNOWLEDGMENTS

I AM DELIGHTED to say that writing *Collective Illusions* was a truly collaborative endeavor. My partner in the work was my dear friend, colleague, and story architect, Bronwyn Fryer. She helped me with everything from getting the ideas into book form to contributing storytelling, research, wordsmithing, and editing. This book would not be what it is without her passion, dedication, and contributions. It was an absolute joy to collaborate with such a talented and kind human being.

I am also grateful for my editor at Hachette, Lauren Marino, who understood the potential of this book from the beginning and helped ensure that the insights could reach the widest possible audience. I would also like to thank Fred Francis, Jennifer Kelland, and Mollie Weisenfeld for their work on behalf of the book.

I want to extend a special thanks to my incredibly talented agent and friend, Keith Urbahn. He helped turn my rough idea into a commercial project and contributed in so many ways to the final product. Thanks, as well, to the phenomenal team at Javelin, including Frank Schembari, Robin Sproul, Matt Latimer, and Matt Carlini.

This book benefited immensely from the insights and efforts of my colleagues at Populace: Walter Haas, Debbie Newhouse, Dewey Rosetti, Parisa Rouhani, Bill Rosetti, Mimi Gurbst, Kelly Royal,

ACKNOWLEDGMENTS

Brian Daly, Teresa Kalinowsky, and Tanya Gonzalez. I am grateful to be part of such an incredible team.

Special thanks to Emily Donaldson, who contributed in so many ways to the book, including research, writing, copyediting, and fact checking; the brilliant data scientists at Gradient—Tom Vladeck, Kyle Block, Brendon Ellis, and Stefan Musch—for helping us advance the methods to discover collective illusions; Bob Delaney, for being a wonderful friend; and to Joann McPike, who inspires more than she realizes.

In addition, many scholars have influenced my thinking about collective illusions, most notably: Yanming An, Abhijit Banerjee, Regina Bateson, Gregory Berns, Cristina Bicchieri, Sushil Bikhchandani, Roy Baumeister, Marilynn Brewer, Daniel Campbell-Meiklejohn, Tanya Chartrand, Nicholas Christakis, John Darley, Robin Dunbar, Thomas Gilovich, Marco Iacoboni, Vasily Klucharev, Timur Kuran, Bibb Latane, Cathy McFarland, Andy Meltzoff, Dale Miller, Elisabeth Noelle-Neumann, Erik Nook, Deborah Prentice, Sonia Roccas, Monique Sternin, Cass Sunstein, Alex Tabarrok, Kipling Williams, and Paul Zak.

Kaylin, Austin, and Nathan—thank you for your patience with me and your contributions to the book. Your support means the world to me. I thank my parents, Larry and Lyda Rose, who are wonderful role models, and to whom I owe more than even I realize. And to my Godchildren, Audrey, Emily, and Natalie, for bringing joy and happiness to all our lives.

NOTES

INTRODUCTION
The Secret of Elm Hollow

1. These quotes are paraphrased.

2. Richard Louis Schanck, "A Study of a Community and Its Groups and Institutions Conceived of as Behaviors of Individuals," *Psychological Monograph* 43, no. 2 (1932).

3. Schanck, "A Study," 73.

4. Schanck, "A Study," 74.

5. Hans Christian Andersen, *Fairy Tales Told for Children, First Collection* (Copenhagen: C. A. Reitzel, 1837).

6. Populace and Gallup, "The Success Index," Populace.org, 2019, https://static1.squarespace.com/static/59153bc0e6f2e109b2a85cbc/t/5d939cc86670c5214abe4b50/1569955251457/Populace+Success+Index.pdf.

7. E.g., Douglas J. Ahler and Gaurav Sood, "The Parties in Our Heads: Misperceptions About Party Composition and Their Consequences," *Journal of Politics* 80, no. 3 (2018): 964–981; Christine M. Baugh et al., "Pluralistic Ignorance as a Contributing Factor to Concussion Underreporting," *Health Education & Behavior* (2021), https://doi.org/10.1177/1090198121995732; M. Ronald Buckley, Michael G. Harvey, and Danielle S. Beu, "The Role of Pluralistic Ignorance in the Perception of Unethical Behavior," *Journal of Business Ethics* 23, no. 4 (2000): 353–364; Leonardo Bursztyn, Alessandra L. González, and David Yanagizawa-Drott, "Misperceived Social Norms: Female Labor Force Participation in Saudi Arabia" (Working Paper 24736, National

Bureau of Economic Research, 2018); Lucy De Souza and Toni Schmader, "The Misjudgment of Men: Does Pluralistic Ignorance Inhibit Allyship?," *Journal of Personality and Social Psychology* (2021), https://doi.org/10.1037/pspi0000362; James J. Do et al., "Gender Bias and Pluralistic Ignorance in Perceptions of Fitness Assessments," *Military Psychology* 25, no. 1 (2013): 23–35; William P. Eveland Jr., Douglas M. McLeod, and Nancy Signorielli, "Actual and Perceived US Public Opinion: The Spiral of Silence During the Persian Gulf War," *International Journal of Public Opinion Research* 7, no. 2 (1995): 91–109; Daniel E. Flave-Novak and Jill M. Coleman, "Pluralistic Ignorance of Physical Attractiveness in the Gay Male Community," *Journal of Homosexuality* 66, no. 14 (2019): 2002–2020; Nathaniel Geiger and Janet K. Swim, "Climate of Silence: Pluralistic Ignorance as a Barrier to Climate Change Discussion," *Journal of Environmental Psychology* 47 (2016): 79–90; Julian Givi, Jeff Galak, and Christopher Y. Olivola, "The Thought That Counts Is the One We Ignore: How Givers Overestimate the Importance of Relative Gift Value," *Journal of Business Research* 123 (2021): 502–515; J. Roger Jacobs, "Pluralistic Ignorance and Social Action on Climate Change," *EMBO Reports* 20, no. 3 (2019): e47426; Kerry M. Karaffa and Julie M. Koch, "Stigma, Pluralistic Ignorance, and Attitudes Toward Seeking Mental Health Services Among Police Officers," *Criminal Justice and Behavior* 43, no. 6 (2016): 759–777; Esther Michelsen Kjeldahl and Vincent F. Hendricks, "The Sense of Social Influence: Pluralistic Ignorance in Climate Change," *EMBO Reports* 19, no. 11 (2018): e47185; Matthew S. Levendusky, "Our Common Bonds: Using What Americans Share to Help Bridge the Partisan Divide" (unpublished manuscript, University of Pennsylvania, 2020); Tagart Cain Sobotka, "Not Your Average Joe: Pluralistic Ignorance, Status, and Modern Sexism," *Men and Masculinities* (2020), https://doi.org/10.1177/1097184X20901578.

8. Ashley Mandeville, Jonathon Halbesleben, and Marilyn Whitman, "Misalignment and Misperception in Preferences to Utilize Family-Friendly Benefits: Implications for Benefit Utilization and Work-Family Conflict," *Personnel Psychology* 69, no. 4 (2016): 895–929.

9. Kengo Nawata, LiHua Huang, and Hiroyuki Yamaguchi, "Anti-Japanese Public Attitudes as Conformity to Social Norms in China: The Role of the Estimated Attitude of Others and Pluralistic Ignorance," *Japanese Journal of Applied Psychology* 42 (2016): 16–24.

10. Takeru Miyajima and Hiroyuki Yamaguchi, "I Want to but I Won't: Pluralistic Ignorance Inhibits Intentions to Take Paternity Leave in Japan," *Frontiers in Psychology* 20, no. 8 (2017): 1508.

11. Douglas J. Ahler, "Self-Fulfilling Misperceptions of Public Polarization," *Journal of Politics* 76, no. 3 (2014): 607–620.

12. Joshua Levine, Sara Etchison, and Daniel M. Oppenheimer, "Pluralistic Ignorance Among Student-Athlete Populations: A Factor in Academic Underperformance," *Higher Education* 68 (2014): 525–540.

13. Unpublished survey data from Populace, "Project Delta 2.0 Results," 2020, 7.

14. A study of the 2018 US elections by the Reflective Democracy Campaign (a project of the Women Donors Network dedicated to examining demographics in American politics) looked at some thirty-four thousand candidates at the federal, state, and county levels and found that women and people of color won elections at the same rate as white men. "The Electability Myth: The Shifting Demographics of Political Power in America," Reflective Democracy Campaign, June 2019, https:// wholeads.us/research/the-electability-myth.

15. Regina Bateson, "Strategic Discrimination," *Perspectives on Politics* 18, no. 4 (2020): 1068–1087.

16. "Beliefs About Gender in America Drive Perceived Electability," Avalanche Insights, accessed May 17, 2021, https://www.avalanchein sights.com/beliefs-about-gender-in-america-drive-perceived-electability.

17. Indeed, the same problems faced by women also confront people of color. Bateson notes that shortly after Egyptian American Dr. Abdul El-Sayed began running in the 2018 Democratic primary for governor of Michigan, " 'very powerful people who call a lot of the shots in the party' sat him down for a little chat. According to El-Sayed, these party insiders told him, 'We think you're great. You just, you know, it's not that we're racist. It's just that we think that people outside of Southeast Michigan are racist, and so you can't win.' " Bateson, "Strategic Discrimination."

18. Kristin Munger and Shelby J. Harris, "Effects of an Observer on Handwashing in a Public Restroom," *Perceptual and Motor Skills* 69 (1989): 733–734.

19. Erik C. Nook and Jamil Zaki, "Social Norms Shift Behavioral and Neural Responses to Foods," *Journal of Cognitive Neuroscience* 27, no. 7 (2015): 1412–1426.

20. A similar crisis occurred back in 1973, when *The Tonight Show*'s Johnny Carson casually mentioned a fictional toilet paper shortage, sending consumers into a TP tizzy that lasted four months. Kay Lim, "Remembering the Great Toilet Paper Shortage of 1973," CBS News, April 5, 2020, https://www.cbsnews.com/news/remembering-the-great-toilet-paper-shortage-of-1973.

21. William I. Thomas and Dorothy Swaine Thomas, *The Child in America: Behavior Problems and Programs* (New York: Alfred A. Knopf, 1928).

22. Kari Paul, "Zuckerberg Defends Facebook as Bastion of 'Free Expression' in Speech," *The Guardian*, October 17, 2019, https://www.theguardian.com/technology/2019/oct/17/mark-zuckerberg-facebook-free-expression-speech.

23. Shadi Bartsch and Alessandro Schiesaro, eds., *The Cambridge Companion to Seneca* (Cambridge: Cambridge University Press, 2015).

24. Lucius Annaeus Seneca, *Moral Essays*, trans. John W. Basore (Cambridge, MA: Harvard University Press, 1928).

25. One of the things Seneca loathed most was blind conformity. By allowing ourselves to be unconsciously swept along with the group, he said, we surrender our autonomy and harm both ourselves and those around us. Recognizing that his society was both immoral and fickle, he liked to quote from one of Aesop's fables: "We do not consider whether the way itself is good or bad, we just count the crowd of footsteps, but none of the steps are coming back." G. D. Williams, *Seneca: De otio; De brevitate vitae*. Cambridge Greek and Latin Classics (Cambridge: Cambridge University Press, 2003).

CHAPTER 1

Naked Emperors

1. Michael V. Cusenza, "You Could Be a Hero: Hamilton Beach Man Needs Another Kidney Transplant," *The Forum*, November 14, 2014, http://theforumnewsgroup.com/2014/11/14/you-could-be-a-hero-hamilton-beach-man-needs-another-kidney-transplant.

2. Steven McCann, Yuanchen Liu, and Faith Bernstein, dirs., *Waiting List* (Washington, DC: *The Atlantic*; New York: ShearWater Films, 2016).

3. "Statistics," The Kidney Project, University of California San Francisco, accessed March 5, 2021, https://pharm.ucsf.edu/kidney/need/statistics.

4. Robin Fields, "God Help You. You're on Dialysis," *The Atlantic*, December 2010, https://www.theatlantic.com/magazine/archive/2010/12/-god-help-you-youre-on-dialysis/308308.

5. "Organ Donation Statistics," United States Health Resources and Services Administration, accessed March 5, 2021, https://www.organdonor.gov/statistics-stories/statistics.html.

6. Olivier Aubert et al., "Disparities in Acceptance of Deceased Donor Kidneys Between the United States and France and Estimated Effects of Increased US Acceptance," *Journal of the American Medical Association Internal Medicine* 179, no. 10 (2019): 1365–1374.

7. Juanjuan Zhang, "The Sound of Silence: Observational Learning in the U.S. Kidney Market," *Marketing Science* 29 (2009): 315–335. Hospitals and transplant centers also play a role since they filter which kidneys are offered to patients based on the urgency and specific circumstances of each patient's situation. As noted by the National Kidney Foundation, "Many factors contribute to whether or not an organ will be offered to you [by your transplant center], including, but not limited to: blood type, how long you have had kidney failure, medical urgency, where you live (an organ must be safely transported the distance to the transplant hospital), and in some instances your weight and size compared to that of the donor." Extra priority is also given to patients who are extraordinarily hard to match due to, for example, high levels of antibodies from prior transplants, previous blood transfusions, or pregnancies. See "The Kidney Transplant Waitlist—What You Need to Know," National Kidney Foundation, accessed March 24, 2021, https://www.kidney.org/atoz/content/transplant-waitlist.

8. Zhang, "The Sound of Silence."

9. See Fiona Grant and Michael A. Hogg, "Self-Uncertainty, Social Identity Prominence and Group Identification," *Journal of Experimental Social Psychology* 48 (2012): 538–542.

10. Bibb Latané and John M. Darley, "Group Inhibition of Bystander Intervention in Emergencies," *Journal of Personality and Social Psychology* 10, no. 3 (1968): 215–221.

11. Kipling D. Williams, "Ostracism: Consequences and Coping," *Current Directions in Psychological Science* 20, no. 2 (2011): 71–75.

12. Jaime Posada et al., "Death and Injury from Motor Vehicle Crashes in Colombia," *Revista panamericana de salud pública* 7, no. 2 (2000): 88–91.

13. Deysi Yasmin Rodríguez, Francisco José Fernández, and Hugo Acero Velásquez, "Road Traffic Injuries in Colombia," *Injury Control and Safety Promotion* 10, no. 1–2 (2003): 29–35.

14. Mara Cristina Caballero, "Academic Turns City into a Social Experiment," *Harvard Gazette*, March 11, 2004, https://news.harvard.edu /gazette/story/2004/03/academic-turns-city-into-a-social-experiment.

15. "Mimes Make Silent Mockery of Those Who Flout Traffic Laws," video uploaded to YouTube by AP Archive, October 16, 2011, https:// www.youtube.com/watch?v=6YcK05z--n8.

16. Antanas Mockus, "The Art of Changing a City," *New York Times*, July 16, 2015, https://www.nytimes.com/2015/07/17/opinion/the-art -of-changing-a-city.html.

17. Caballero, "Academic Turns City."

18. Caballero, "Academic Turns City."

19. "Crocodile Blamed for Congo Air Crash," MSNBC, October 21, 2010, https://www.nbcnews.com/id/wbna39781214.

20. James Surowiecki, *The Wisdom of Crowds* (New York: Doubleday, 2004).

21. Abhijit V. Banerjee, "A Simple Model of Herd Behavior," *Quarterly Journal of Economics* 107, no. 3 (1992): 797–817.

22. Charles Mackay, *Memoirs of Extraordinary Popular Delusions and the Madness of Crowds* (London: Office of the National Illustrated Library, 1852), viii.

23. Mackay, *Memoirs of Extraordinary Popular Delusions*, 87.

24. Gregory A. Petsko, "The Wisdom, and Madness, of Crowds," *Genome Biology* 9 (2008): 112.

25. Mackay, *Memoirs of Extraordinary Popular Delusions*, 91. Despite its recent exposure as an occasionally exaggerated and not entirely factual account, Mackay's colorful telling of this story has elevated it to popular fame among economists and bankers.

26. Andrew Odlyzko, "Charles Mackay's Own Extraordinary Popular Delusions and the Railway Mania" (working paper, SSRN eLibrary, 2011), https://papers.ssrn.com/sol3/papers.cfm?abstract_id=1927396.

27. Odlyzko, "Charles Mackay's Own."

28. John H. Cushman Jr., "U.S. Urges Users of New Well Pumps to Drink Bottled Water," *New York Times*, April 19, 1994, https://www.nytimes .com/1994/04/19/us/us-urges-users-of-new-well-pumps-to-drink-bottled -water.html.

29. Jan Conway, "Per Capita Consumption of Bottled Water in the United States from 1999 to 2019," Statista, November 26, 2020, https:// www.statista.com/statistics/183377/per-capita-consumption-of-bottled -water-in-the-us-since-1999; "Global Bottled Water Market Share Expected to Grow USD 400 Billion by 2026: Facts & Factors," Intrado GlobeNewswire, February 10, 2021, https://www.globenewswire.com /news-release/2021/02/10/2172833/0/en/Global-Bottled-Water-Market -Share-Expected-to-Grow-USD-400-Billion-by-2026-Facts-Factors.html.

30. Jan Conway, "U.S. Bottled Water Market—Statistics & Facts," Statista, February 12, 2021, https://www.statista.com/topics/1302 /bottled-water-market.

31. To add insult to injury, these companies often fail to pay their own water bills on time. Dasani and Aquafina have both accumulated tens of thousands of dollars in past-due water balances for bills that weren't paid off for months afterward. Their water has never been shut off, despite Detroit's otherwise strict policy to shut off water to its private citizens who fall behind by $150 on their water bills. Ryan Felton, "How Coke and Pepsi Make Millions from Bottling Tap Water, as Residents Face Shut-offs," *Consumer Reports*, July 10, 2020, https://www.consumerreports.org /bottled-water/how-coke-and-pepsi-make-millions-from-bottling-tap -water-as-residents-face-shutoffs; Julia Conley, "Report: 64% of Bottled Water Is Tap Water, Costs 2000x More," *Ecowatch*, February 21, 2018, https://www.ecowatch.com/bottled-water-sources-tap-2537510642.html; Conway, "Per Capita Consumption."

32. Conway, "Per Capita Consumption."

33. Conley, "Report."

34. Maria McCutchen, "Here Are the 10 Most Expensive Bottled Water Brands in the World," *Money Inc*, accessed March 24, 2021, https://money inc.com/10-expensive-bottled-waters-world.

35. Laura Parker, "How the Plastic Bottle Went from Miracle Container to Hated Garbage," *National Geographic*, August 23, 2019, https://www .nationalgeographic.com/environment/article/plastic-bottles.

36. "The Great Pacific Garbage Patch," The Ocean Cleanup, accessed March 24, 2021, https://theoceancleanup.com/great-pacific-garbage -patch.

37. Nicholas Christakis, "The Hidden Influence of Social Networks," TED, February 2010, https://www.ted.com/talks/nicholas _christakis_the_hidden_influence_of_social_networks.

38. It turns out that human beings are not unlike bees when it comes to emotional contagion. When an intruder enters a nest, bees diffuse hormonal chemicals, called pheromones, that tell the other bees to attack. And the more pheromones enter their atmosphere, the more other bees are socially influenced to attack too. Like bees, we emit pheromones that help us communicate sub rosa, without even realizing it. See Henry Farrell, "This Is How Donald Trump Engineers Applause," *Washington Post*, January 23, 2017, https://www.washingtonpost.com/news/monkey-cage /wp/2017/01/23/this-is-how-donald-trump-engineers-applause.

39. Mary Francis Gyles, "Nero: Qualis Artifex?," *Classical Journal* 57, no. 5 (1962): 193–200; Karen Rile, "Bring Your Own Applause: What Donald Trump and Roman Emperor Nero Have in Common," *JSTOR Daily*, February 9, 2017, https://daily.jstor.org/bring-your-own-applause -what-donald-trump-and-roman-emperor-nero-have-in-common.

40. Farrell, "This Is How Donald Trump."

41. Zhang, "The Sound of Silence."

42. Based on a true story.

43. Kat Odell, "Ask a Somm: How Do I Know if a Wine Is Corked?," *Eater*, June 1, 2016, https://www.eater.com/2016/6/1/11824138/wine -corked-smell-flaw-tca-sommelier.

44. Ángel V. Jiménez and Alex Mesoudi, "Prestige-Biased Social Learning: Current Evidence and Outstanding Questions," *Palgrave Communications* 5, no. 1 (2019): 1–11.

45. Joseph Henrich, *The Secret of Our Success: How Culture Is Driving Human Evolution, Domesticating Our Species, and Making Us Smarter* (Princeton, NJ: Princeton University Press, 2015).

46. Jiménez and Mesoudi, "Prestige-Biased Social Learning."

47. Brad J. Bushman, "Perceived Symbols of Authority and Their Influence on Compliance," *Journal of Applied Social Psychology* 14, no. 6 (1984): 501–508.

48. Charles K. Hofling et al., "An Experimental Study in Nurse-Physician Relationships," *Journal of Nervous and Mental Disease* 143, no. 2 (1966): 171–180.

49. Daniel Campbell-Meiklejohn et al., "Independent Neural Computation of Value from Other People's Confidence," *Journal of Neuroscience* 37, no. 3 (2017): 673–684.

50. Jean Braucher and Barak Orbach, "Scamming: The Misunderstood Confidence Man," *Yale Journal of Law & the Humanities* 27, no. 2 (2015): 249–290; Karen Halttunen, *Confidence Men and Painted Women: A Study of Middle-Class Culture in America, 1830–1870* (New Haven, CT: Yale University Press, 1982).

51. Alan D. Sokal, "Transgressing the Boundaries: Towards a Transformative Hermeneutics of Quantum Gravity," *Social Text* 46/47 (1996): 217–252.

52. Janny Scott, "Postmodern Gravity Deconstructed, Slyly," *New York Times*, May 18, 1996, https://www.nytimes.com/1996/05/18/nyregion/postmodern-gravity-deconstructed-slyly.html.

53. Scott, "Postmodern Gravity."

54. Alan Sokal, "A Physicist Experiments with Cultural Studies," *Lingua Franca* (May/June 1996).

55. Cass R. Sunstein, "Academic Fads and Fashions (with Special Reference to Law)" (working paper, SSRN eLibrary, 2001), https://papers.ssrn.com/sol3/papers.cfm?abstract_id=262331.

56. Reputational cascades are so damaging that institutions can be driven to great lengths to stop them. For example, when someone is being tried in a US Navy court-martial, the judges now vote in reverse order of rank, which does away with the problem of deference to authority. Sushil Bikhchandani, David Hirshleifer, and Ivo Welch, "A Theory of Fads, Fashion, Custom, and Cultural Change as Informational Cascades," *Journal of Political Economy* 100, no. 5 (1992): 992–1026.

57. Zhang, "The Sound of Silence."

58. Diana I. Tamir and Jason P. Mitchell, "Disclosing Information About the Self Is Intrinsically Rewarding," *PNAS* 109, no. 21 (2012): 8038–8043.

59. Tamir and Mitchell, "Disclosing Information."

60. Tamir and Mitchell, "Disclosing Information."

61. Einav Hart, Eric VanEpps, and Maurice E. Schweitzer, "I Didn't Want to Offend You: The Cost of Avoiding Sensitive Questions" (working paper, SSRN eLibrary, 2019), https://papers.ssrn.com/sol3/papers.cfm?abstract_id=3437468.

CHAPTER 2

Lying to Belong

1. Rebecca Moore, "The Demographics of Jonestown," Alternative Considerations of Jonestown & Peoples Temple, San Diego State University, July 25, 2013, https://jonestown.sdsu.edu/?page_id=35666.

2. Chris Higgins, "Stop Saying 'Drink the Kool-Aid,'" *The Atlantic*, November 8, 2012, https://www.theatlantic.com/health/archive/2012/11/stop-saying-drink-the-kool-aid/264957; "Losses Linger 25 Years After Jonestown," *ABC News*, January 6, 2006, https://abcnews.go.com/GMA/story?id=128197&page=1.

3. Federal Bureau of Investigation (FBI), "Q042 Transcript, FBI Transcription," File RYMUR 89-4286-2303, Alternative Considerations of Jonestown & Peoples Temple, San Diego State University, accessed March 9, 2021, https://jonestown.sdsu.edu/?page_id=29081.

4. "Nightmare in Jonestown," *Time*, December 4, 1978, https://time.com/vault/issue/1978-12-04/page/34; Higgins, "Stop Saying."

5. Timothy Lisagor, "Jim Jones and Christine Miller: An Analysis of Jonestown's Final Struggle," Alternative Considerations of Jonestown & Peoples Temple, San Diego State University, July 25, 2013, https://jonestown.sdsu.edu/?page_id=30294.

6. Higgins, "Stop Saying."

7. FBI, "Q042 Transcript, FBI Transcription."

8. Michael Bellefountaine, "Christine Miller: A Voice of Independence," Alternative Considerations of Jonestown & Peoples Temple, San Diego State University, July 25, 2013, https://jonestown.sdsu.edu/?page_id=32381; Higgins, "Stop Saying."

9. Bellefountaine, "Christine Miller."

10. Eunice U. Choi and Michael A. Hogg, "Self-Uncertainty and Group Identification: A Meta-analysis," *Group Processes & Intergroup Relations* 23, no. 4 (2020): 483–501.

11. Nathaniel M. Lambert et al., "To Belong Is to Matter: Sense of Belonging Enhances Meaning in Life," *Personality and Social Psychology Bulletin* 20, no. 10 (2013): 1–10.

12. Roy F. Baumeister and Mark R. Leary, "The Need to Belong: Desire for Interpersonal Attachments as a Fundamental Human Motivation," *Psychological Bulletin* 117, no. 3 (1995): 497–529.

13. K. W. De Dreu Carsten and Mariska E. Kret, "Oxytocin Conditions Intergroup Relations Through Upregulated In-Group Empathy, Cooperation, Conformity, and Defense," *Biological Psychiatry* 79, no. 3 (2015): 165–173.

14. John Hughes, dir., *The Breakfast Club* (Universal City, CA: Universal Pictures, 1985).

15. Paul E. Smaldino, "Social Identity and Cooperation in Cultural Evolution," *Behavioural Processes* 161 (2019): 108–116.

16. Adam Smith, *The Theory of Moral Sentiments* (London: George Bell & Sons, 1892), 497.

17. Smaldino, "Social Identity."

18. Kirsten G. Volz, Thomas Kessler, and D. Yves von Cramon, "In-Group as Part of the Self: In-Group Favoritism Is Mediated by Medial Prefrontal Cortex Activation," *Social Neuroscience* 4, no. 3 (2009): 244–260; Samantha Morrison, Jean Decety, and Pascal Molenberghs, "The Neuroscience of Group Membership," *Neuropsychologia* 50, no. 8 (2012): 2114–2120.

19. Russell Golman et al., "The Preference for Belief Consonance," *Journal of Economic Perspectives* 30, no. 3 (2016): 165–188.

20. De Dreu Carsten and Kret, "Oxytocin Conditions Intergroup Relations."

21. Mina Cikara, Matthew M. Botvinick, and Susan T. Fiske, "Us Versus Them: Social Identity Shapes Neural Responses to Intergroup Competition and Harm," *Psychological Science* 22, no. 3 (2011): 306–313.

22. "And Stay Out: In Ancient Athens, Ostracism Did the Job of Impeachment," *The Economist*, January 4, 2020, https://www.economist .com/books-and-arts/2020/01/02/in-ancient-athens-ostracism-did-the -job-of-impeachment; James P. Sickinger, "New Ostraka from the Athenian Agora," *Hesperia: The Journal of the American School of Classical Studies at Athens* 86, no. 3 (2017): 443–508. Apologies to *The Economist* for borrowing their brilliant article title for this section.

23. Naomi I. Eisenberger, Matthew D. Lieberman, and Kipling D. Williams, "Does Rejection Hurt? An fMRI Study of Social Exclusion," *Science* 302 (2003): 290–292.

24. Geoff MacDonald and Mark R. Leary, "Why Does Social Exclusion Hurt? The Relationship Between Social and Physical Pain," *Psychological Bulletin* 131, no. 2 (2005): 202–223.

25. Eisenberger, Lieberman, and Williams, "Does Rejection Hurt?"

26. Mark R. Leary et al., "Teasing, Rejection, and Violence: Case Studies of the School Shootings," *Aggressive Behavior* 29 (2003): 202–214.

27. John B. Nezlek, Eric D. Wesselmann, and Kipling D. Williams, "Ostracism in Everyday Life," *Group Dynamics: Theory, Research, and Practice* 16, no. 2 (2012): 91–104.

28. Frank M. Schneider et al., "Social Media Ostracism: The Effects of Being Excluded Online," *Computers in Human Behavior* 73 (2017): 385–393.

29. Our fear of exclusion is a survival instinct, with roots stretching back to our common ancestors. Early humans excluded from social groups had less access to food and resources and a reduced pool of potential mating partners; some died as a result. See Karen Gonsalkorale and Kipling D. Williams, "The KKK Won't Let Me Play: Ostracism Even by a Despised Outgroup Hurts," *European Journal of Social Psychology* 37 (2006): 1176–1186; Eisenberger, Lieberman, and Williams, "Does Rejection Hurt?"

30. Kipling D. Williams, "Ostracism," *Annual Review of Psychology* 58 (2007): 425–452.

31. Kipling D. Williams, "Ostracism: Consequences and Coping," *Current Directions in Psychological Science* 20, no. 2 (2011): 71–75.

32. Gonsalkorale and Williams, "The KKK."

33. Eric D. Wesselmann, Danielle Bagg, and Kipling D. Williams, "'I Feel Your Pain': The Effects of Observing Ostracism on the Ostracism Detection System," *Journal of Experimental Social Psychology* 45 (2009): 1308–1311.

34. Gonsalkorale and Williams, "The KKK."

35. Jean Evans, "Case Reports: Johnny Rocco," *Journal of Abnormal & Social Psychology* 43 (1948): 357–383.

36. National Academy of Sciences, *Stanley Schachter*, Biographical Memoirs 78 (Washington, DC: National Academies of Science Press,

2000), 224; Stanley Schachter, "Deviation, Rejection, and Communication," *Journal of Abnormal & Social Psychology* 46, no. 2 (1951): 190–207.

37. Schachter, "Deviation, Rejection, and Communication."

38. T. M. Mills, "A Sleeper Variable in Small Groups Research: The Experimenter," *Pacific Sociological Review* 5 (1962): 21–28.

39. Eric D. Wesselmann et al., "Revisiting Schachter's Research on Rejection, Deviance and Communication (1951)," *Social Psychology* 45, no. 3 (2014): 164–169.

40. For a comprehensive understanding of preference falsification and its consequences, see Timur Kuran's excellent *Private Truths, Public Lies: The Social Consequences of Preference Falsification* (Cambridge, MA: Harvard University Press, 1997).

41. Leon Festinger, "Cognitive Dissonance," *Scientific American* 207, no. 4 (1962): 93–106.

42. Thomas Gilovich, Kenneth Savitsky, and Victoria Husted Medvec, "The Illusion of Transparency: Biased Assessments of Others' Ability to Read One's Emotional States," *Journal of Personality and Social Psychology* 75, no. 2 (1998): 332–346.

43. Gilovich, Savitsky, and Medvec, "The Illusion of Transparency."

44. Gilovich, Savitsky, and Medvec, "The Illusion of Transparency."

45. Thomas Gilovich and Kenneth Savitsky, "The Spotlight Effect and the Illusion of Transparency: Egocentric Assessments of How We Are Seen by Others," *Current Directions in Psychological Science* 8, no. 6 (1999): 165–168.

46. Jeff Sharlet, "Inside America's Most Powerful Megachurch," *Harper's Magazine*, May 2005, https://harpers.org/archive/2005/05/inside-americas-most-powerful-megachurch.

47. Bill Gallo, "A New Life Big as Church," *Rocky Mountain News*, August 11, 2007, https://web.archive.org/web/20090520195128/http:/www.rockymountainnews.com/drmn/local/article/0,1299,DRMN_15_5668662,00.html; "Amid Allegations, Haggard Steps Aside," *Rocky Mountain News*, November 2, 2006, https://web.archive.org/web/20061107224943/http://www.rockymountainnews.com/drmn/local/article/0,1299,DRMN_15_5112770,00.html.

48. Rachel Grady and Heidi Ewing, dirs., *Jesus Camp* (New York: A&E IndieFilms; Brooklyn, NY: Loki Films, 2006).

49. "Evangelical Leader Admits Buying Meth, Denies Gay Sex Claims," *CBC News*, November 3, 2006, https://www.cbc.ca/news/world/evangelical-leader-admits-buying-meth-denies-gay-sex-claims-1.620653.

50. Dan Harris, "Haggard Admits Buying Meth," *ABC News*, November 12, 2008, https://abcnews.go.com/GMA/story?id=2626067&page=1.

51. Kevin P. Donovan, "Focus on the Family VP Joins Haggard Restoration Team," *Christian Post*, November 15, 2006, https://www.christianpost.com/article/20061115/focus-on-the-family-vp-joins-haggard-restoration-team.

52. More specifically, research suggests that lying may trigger the release of stress hormones and increase heart rate and blood pressure. See Leanne ten Brinke, Jooa Julia Lee, and Dana R. Carney, "The Physiology of (Dis)honesty: Does It Impact Health?," *Current Opinion in Psychology* 6 (2015): 177–182.

53. Hubert J. O'Gorman, "White and Black Perceptions of Racial Values," *Public Opinion Quarterly* 43, no. 1 (1979): 48–59.

54. Hubert O'Gorman, "Pluralistic Ignorance and White Estimates of White Support for Racial Segregation," *Public Opinion Quarterly* 39, no. 3 (1975): 313–330.

55. Hubert O'Gorman and Stephen L. Garry, "Pluralistic Ignorance—a Replication and Extension," *Public Opinion Quarterly* 40, no. 4 (1976): 449–458.

56. O'Gorman and Garry, "Pluralistic Ignorance—a Replication."

57. History.com Editors, "Jonestown," *History*, October 18, 2010, https://www.history.com/topics/crime/jonestown.

58. Sonia Roccas and Marilynn B. Brewer, "Social Identity Complexity," *Personality and Social Psychology Review* 6, no. 2 (2002): 88–106; Richard J. Crisp and Miles Hewstone, "Multiple Social Categorization," *Advances in Experimental Social Psychology* 39 (2007): 163–254.

59. Marilynn B. Brewer and Kathleen P. Pierce, "Social Identity Complexity and Outgroup Tolerance," *Personality and Social Psychology Bulletin* 31, no. 3 (2005): 428–437.

60. Brewer and Pierce, "Social Identity Complexity and Outgroup Tolerance."

61. Thomas Mussweiler, Shira Gabriel, and Galen V. Bodenhausen, "Shifting Social Identities as a Strategy for Deflecting Threatening Social Comparisons," *Journal of Personality and Social Psychology* 79, no. 3

(2000): 398–409. Under the right conditions, this impulse to protect our own egos can turn ugly. When we feel threatened, we tend to shift the identities of others and characterize them based on more negative identities or harmful stereotypes in order to make ourselves feel superior. For example, in one study where subjects were praised by a black doctor, they identified him first as a doctor. But when they were criticized by the same doctor, they jumped to emphasize the fact that he was black and incompetent and failed to mention his elite professional status. Lisa Sinclair and Ziva Kunda, "Reactions to a Black Professional: Motivated Inhibition and Activation of Conflicting Stereotypes," *Journal of Personality and Social Psychology* 77, no. 5 (1999): 885–904.

62. De Dreu Carsten and Kret, "Oxytocin Conditions Intergroup Relations."

63. Roccas and Brewer, "Social Identity Complexity."

64. In one study, researchers asked 222 Ohio residents about their most important group memberships and their views on people who fell outside those preferred in-groups. The more complex a person believed their in-groups to be, the more likely they were to support affirmative action, multiculturalism, and the equal treatment of outgroup members such as Muslims or LGBTQ individuals. Brewer and Pierce, "Social Identity Complexity and Outgroup Tolerance."

CHAPTER 3

The Sound of Silence

1. Vasily Klucharev et al., "Reinforcement Learning Signal Predicts Social Conformity," *Neuron* 61 (2009): 140–151.

2. Those fish that find themselves on the outer edges of their school are more vulnerable to attack not for the classic reasons (they are slow, old, or weak) but simply because it is easiest for a predator to "isolate and prey upon those on the social perimeter." John T. Cacioppo et al., "Loneliness Across Phylogeny and a Call for Comparative Studies and Animal Models," *Perspectives on Psychological Science* 10, no. 2 (2015): 202–212.

3. Klucharev et al., "Reinforcement Learning Signal."

4. Sweta Anantharaman, *Majority Influence in Infancy* (Auckland: University of Auckland, 2017), 29–30.

5. "Social species, from Drosophila melanogaster to Homo sapiens, fare poorly when isolated. Homo sapiens, an irrepressibly meaning-making species, are, in normal circumstances, dramatically affected by perceived social isolation. Research indicates that perceived social isolation (i.e. loneliness) is a risk factor for, and may contribute to, poorer overall cognitive performance, faster cognitive decline, poorer executive functioning, increased negativity and depressive cognition, heightened sensitivity to social threats, a confirmatory bias in social cognition that is self-protective and paradoxically self-defeating, heightened anthropomorphism and contagion that threatens social cohesion." John T. Cacioppo and Louise C. Hawkley, "Perceived Social Isolation and Cognition," *Trends in Cognitive Science* 13, no. 10 (2009): 447–454.

6. Lyn Y. Abramson, Martin E. P. Seligman, and John D. Teasdale, "Learned Helplessness in Humans: Critique and Reformulation," *Journal of Abnormal Psychology* 87, no. 1 (1978): 49–74.

7. Elisabeth Noelle-Neumann, "The Spiral of Silence: A Theory of Public Opinion," *Journal of Communication* 24, no. 2 (1974): 43–51.

8. Josh Boak, "Anatomy of a Comeback: How Biden Won the Democratic Presidential Nomination," *Detroit News*, June 6, 2020, https://www.detroitnews.com/story/news/politics/2020/06/06/biden-comeback-nomination-democratic/111915566.

9. Elisabeth Noelle-Neumann, "Turbulences in the Climate of Opinion: Methodological Applications of the Spiral of Silence Theory," *Public Opinion Quarterly* 41, no. 2 (1977): 143–158; Elisabeth Noelle-Neumann, *The Spiral of Silence: Public Opinion—Our Social Skin* (Chicago: University of Chicago Press, 1993), 5.

10. Janine Stollberg et al., "Extending Control Perceptions to the Social Self: Ingroups Serve the Restoration of Control," *Current Issues in Social Psychology: Coping with Lack of Control in a Social World*, ed. Marcin Bukowski et al. (London: Routledge/Taylor & Francis Group, 2017), 133–150.

11. This was an actual ethical dilemma faced by the Annapolis Housing Authority in 1989. See Lisa Leff, "Cities Face Ethical Dilemma in Drug Wars Evict Juveniles?," *Washington Post*, August 30, 1989, https://www.washingtonpost.com/archive/local/1989/08/30/cities-face-ethical-dilemma-in-drug-wars-evict-juveniles/7d31541d-6210-46a9-9da3-94c52447d166.

12. "Ivan Beltrami," Jewish Foundation for the Righteous, accessed February 16, 2021, jfr.org/rescuer-stories/beltrami-ivan.

13. "Costly Conversations: Why the Way Employees Communicate Will Make or Break Your Bottom Line," VitalSmarts, December 6, 2016, https://www.vitalsmarts.com/press/2016/12/costly-conversations-why-the-way-employees-communicate-will-make-or-break-your-bottom-line; VitalSmarts, *Silent Danger: The Five Crucial Conversations That Drive Workplace Safety* (Provo, UT: VitalSmarts, 2013).

14. For more on the importance of psychological safety in the workplace, see the seminal work of Dr. Amy Edmondson, *The Fearless Organization: Creating Psychological Safety in the Workplace for Learning, Innovation, and Growth* (Hoboken, NJ: Wiley, 2018).

15. Joe Atkinson, "Engineer Who Opposed Challenger Launch Offers Personal Look at Tragedy," *Researcher News*, October 5, 2012, https://www.nasa.gov/centers/langley/news/researchernews/rn_Colloquium 1012.html; Howard Berkes, "Remembering Allan McDonald: He Refused to Approve Challenger Launch, Exposed Cover-Up," *NPR*, March 7, 2021, https://www.npr.org/2021/03/07/974534021/remembering-allan-mcdonald-he-refused-to-approve-challenger-launch-exposed-cover.

16. "Volkswagen Executives Describe Authoritarian Culture Under Former CEO," *The Guardian*, October 20, 2015, https://www.theguardian.com/business/2015/oct/10/volkswagen-executives-martin-winterkorn-company-culture.

17. Bobby Allyn, "Ousted Black Google Researcher: 'They Wanted to Have My Presence, but Not Me Exactly,'" *NPR*, December 17, 2020, https://www.npr.org/2020/12/17/947719354/ousted-black-google-researcher-they-wanted-to-have-my-presence-but-not-me-exactl.

18. Jessica Silver-Greenberg and Rachel Abrams, "Nursing Homes Oust Unwanted Patients with Claims of Psychosis," *New York Times*, September 19, 2020, https://www.nytimes.com/2020/09/19/business/coronavirus-nursing-homes.html.

19. Molly Gamble, "Indiana Hospital Employee Fired After Speaking to New York Times," *Becker Hospital Review*, October 1, 2020, https://www.beckershospitalreview.com/hr/indiana-hospital-employee-fired-after-speaking-to-new-york-times.html.

20. Andrew Siddons, "Miners, Fearing Retaliation, May Skip Black Lung Screenings," *Medical Xpress*, March 1, 2019, https://medicalxpress .com/news/2019-03-miners-retaliation-black-lung-screenings.html.

21. "Mine Safety and Health Research Advisory Committee Meeting Minutes," US Department of Health and Human Services, Centers for Disease Control and Prevention, May 6–7, 2019, https://www.cdc .gov/faca/committees/pdfs/mshrac/mshrac-minutes-20190506-07-508 .pdf.

22. "Author Laurie Forest Discusses The Black Witch Chronicles," video posted to YouTube by Harlequin Books, December 4, 2018, https:// www.youtube.com/watch?v=vl_Hd0GAnvw.

23. Kat Rosenfield, "The Toxic Drama on YA Twitter," *New York Magazine: Vulture*, August 2017, https://www.vulture.com/2017/08/the -toxic-drama-of-ya-twitter.html.

24. Rosenfield, "The Toxic Drama."

25. Rosenfield, "The Toxic Drama."

26. These responses were posted by Joel Adamson and Elisa, respectively. "The Black Witch, by Laurie Forest," Goodreads Q&A, accessed March 30, 2021, https://www.goodreads.com/questions /1013221-why-is-a-book-that-includes-this-text.

27. "The Black Witch, by Laurie Forest," Goodreads, accessed March 30, 2021, https://www.goodreads.com/book/show/25740412-the-black -witch. Also worth noting: although Forest prevailed, her story is sadly familiar. To take just one example, an eerily similar drama played out two years later when Amélie Wen Zhao, a young Asian immigrant, was about to publish her own debut novel, *Blood Heir*. In online comments a small group of angry readers, plus many others who hadn't read the book, accused Zhao of racism and plagiarism. When her supporters leapt into the fray to defend her, a fiery chaos ensued. Panicked and overwhelmed, the twenty-six-year-old Zhao issued an apology and cancelled the book's publication. But after months of painfully scrutinizing each plot twist and character detail, she found she disagreed with her critics. Her book was finally released, with some revisions, in November 2019. See Alexandra Alter, "She Pulled Her Debut Book When Critics Found It Racist. Now She Plans to Publish," *New York Times*, April 29, 2019, https:// www.nytimes.com/2019/04/29/books/amelie-wen-zhao-blood-heir.html.

28. Aja Romano, "Why We Can't Stop Fighting About Cancel Culture," *Vox*, August 25, 2020, https://www.vox.com/culture/2019/12/30/20879720 /what-is-cancel-culture-explained-history-debate.

29. Mark Fisher, "Exiting the Vampire Castle," Open Democracy, November 24, 2013, https://www.opendemocracy.net/en/opendemo cracyuk/exiting-vampire-castle.

30. Fisher, "Exiting the Vampire Castle."

31. Alex Hern, "Facebook and Twitter Are Being Used to Manipulate Public Opinion—Report," *The Guardian*, June 19, 2017, https:// www.theguardian.com/technology/2017/jun/19/social-media-proganda -manipulating-public-opinion-bots-accounts-facebook-twitter.

32. Noelle-Neumann, "Turbulences."

33. "Platform Manipulation and Spam Policy," Twitter, September 2020, https://help.twitter.com/en/rules-and-policies/platform-manipu lation.

34. Juan S. Morales, "Perceived Popularity and Online Political Dissent: Evidence from Twitter in Venezuela," *International Journal of Press/ Politics* 25, no. 1 (2020): 5–27.

35. Morales, "Perceived Popularity."

36. Chun Cheng, Yun Luo, and Changbin Yu, "Dynamic Mechanism of Social Bots Interfering with Public Opinion in Network," *Physica A: Statistical Mechanics and Its Applications* 551 (2020): 124163. In terms of where bots stand politically, slightly more of them appear to be conservative than liberal at the moment. See Adam Badawy, Emilio Ferrara, and Kristina Lerman, "Analyzing the Digital Traces of Political Manipulation: The 2016 Russian Interference Twitter Campaign" (paper presented at the IEEE/ACM International Conference on Advances in Social Networks Analysis and Mining [ASONAM], Barcelona, Spain, 2018), 258–265.

37. Of course, public silence in the face of a perceived majority is an old problem. As noted in the introduction, it was observed in the nineteenth century by Hans Christian Andersen.

38. Noelle-Neumann, "The Spiral of Silence"; James L. Gibson and Joseph L. Sutherland, "Keeping Your Mouth Shut: Spiraling Self-Censorship in the United States" (working paper, SSRN eLibrary, 2020), https://papers .ssrn.com/sol3/papers.cfm?abstract_id=3647099.

39. Hugo Márquez, "Persecution of Homosexuals in the McCarthy Hearings: A History of Homosexuality in Postwar America and McCarthyism," *Fairmount Folio: Journal of History* 12 (2010): 52–76.

40. Rebecca Gibian, "Hollywood Actors Who Were Blacklisted During the Red Scare," *InsideHook*, October 20, 2017, https://www.insidehook.com/article/history/hollywood-actors-blacklisted-during-the-red-scare; Jack Anderson and Dale van Atta, "Apparently, the FBI Did Not Love Lucy," *Washington Post*, December 7, 1989, https://www.washingtonpost.com/archive/business/1989/12/07/apparently-the-fbi-did-not-love-lucy/ca6ccf7b-269b-4992-abb8-26afef7bae28; "Danny Kaye," FBI Records: The Vault, accessed April 7, 2021, https://vault.fbi.gov/Danny%20Kaye%20/Danny%20Kaye%20Part%202%20of%203/view; "Einstein's Deeply Held Political Beliefs," American Museum of Natural History, accessed April 7, 2021, https://www.amnh.org/exhibitions/einstein/global-citizen; Josh Jones, "Bertolt Brecht Testifies Before the House Un-American Activities Committee (1947)," Open Culture, November 12, 2012, https://www.openculture.com/2012/11/bertolt_brecht_testifies_before_the_house_un-american_activities_committee_1947.html.

41. Gibson and Sutherland, "Keeping Your Mouth Shut."

42. Emily Ekins, "Poll: 62% of Americans Say They Have Political Views They're Afraid to Share," CATO Institute, July 22, 2020, https://www.cato.org/survey-reports/poll-62-americans-say-they-have-political-views-theyre-afraid-share.

43. In other words, "learning to keep one's mouth shut is in part a function of increasing socialization, learning what views are, and especially what views are not, appropriate to express," a process also known as "democratic learning." This pattern suggests that more education and resources may actually increase our likelihood of self-censoring. Gibson and Sutherland, "Keeping Your Mouth Shut."

44. Nathaniel Geiger and Janet K. Swim, "Climate of Silence: Pluralistic Ignorance as a Barrier to Climate Change Discussion," *Journal of Environmental Psychology* 47 (2016): 79–90.

45. Vernon L. Allen and John M. Levine, "Social Support, Dissent and Conformity," *Sociometry* 31, no. 2 (1968): 138–149.

46. It is difficult to estimate the distribution of various thresholds for speaking up, but this mix can affect how, and whether, spirals of silence play out in any given population. See Eszter Bartha and Joanna

Wolszczak-Derlacz, "Why Do People Choose to Be Silent? Simulating Electoral Behaviour" (EUI MWP Working Paper 26, European University Institute, 2008).

47. Tarana Burke, "Me Too Is a Movement, Not a Moment," TED, November 2018, https://www.ted.com/talks/tarana_burke_me_too_is_a _movement_not_a_moment.

48. According to a 2018 study by a nonprofit called Stop Street Harassment, 77 percent of women had experienced verbal sexual harassment and 51 percent had been sexually touched without their permission. About 41 percent said they had been sexually harassed online, and 27 percent said they had survived sexual assault. See Rhitu Chatterjee, "A New Survey Finds 81 Percent of Women Have Experienced Sexual Harassment," NPR, February 21, 2018, https://www.npr.org/sections /thetwo-way/2018/02/21/587671849/a-new-survey-finds-eighty-percent -of-women-have-experienced-sexual-harassment.

49. Burke, "Me Too Is a Movement."

50. Abby Ohlheiser, "The Woman Behind 'Me Too' Knew the Power of the Phrase When She Created It—10 Years Ago," Washington Post, October 19, 2017, https://www.washingtonpost.com/news/the-intersect /wp/2017/10/19/the-woman-behind-me-too-knew-the-power-of-the -phrase-when-she-created-it-10-years-ago.

51. Ohlheiser, "The Woman Behind 'Me Too.'"

52. Samantha Schmidt, "#MeToo: Harvey Weinstein Case Moves Thousands to Tell Their Own Stories of Abuse, Break Silence," Washington Post, October 16, 2017, https://www.washingtonpost.com/news /morning-mix/wp/2017/10/16/me-too-alyssa-milano-urged-assault-vic tims-to-tweet-in-solidarity-the-response-was-massive.

53. Burke, "Me Too Is a Movement."

54. Stephanie Zacharek, Eliana Dockterman, and Haley Sweetland Edwards, "Person of the Year 2017," Time, accessed April 7, 2021, https:// time.com/time-person-of-the-year-2017-silence-breakers.

CHAPTER 4

Little Chameleons

1. Solomon E. Asch, "Opinions and Social Pressure," Scientific American 193, no. 5 (1955): 31–35.

2. Asch, "Opinions."

3. Gregory S. Berns et al., "Neurobiological Correlates of Social Conformity and Independence During Mental Rotation," *Biological Psychiatry* 58 (2005): 245–253.

4. Esther Hermann et al., "Humans Have Evolved Specialized Skills of Social Cognition: The Cultural Intelligence Hypothesis," *Science* 317 (2007): 1360–1366.

5. Peter J. Richerson, *Not by Genes Alone: How Culture Transformed Human Evolution* (Chicago: University of Chicago Press, 2006); Joseph Henrich, *The Secret of Our Success: How Culture Is Driving Human Evolution, Domesticating Our Species, and Making Us Smarter* (Princeton, NJ: Princeton University Press, 2015).

6. Leslie C. Aiello and R. I. M. Dunbar, "Neocortex Size, Group Size, and the Evolution of Language," *Current Anthropology* 34, no. 2 (1993): 184–193.

7. Indeed, a dedicated area of our brain—the ventral striatum—codes social information such as other people's decisions and may hold a clue to human herd behavior. See Christopher J. Burke et al., "Striatal BOLD Response Reflects the Impact of Herd Information on Financial Decisions," *Frontiers in Human Neuroscience* 4 (2010): 48.

8. Aiello and Dunbar, "Neocortex Size, Group Size."

9. Babies who are unable to form this bond suffer lifelong problems. See Kathryn L. Hildyard and David A. Wolfe, "Child Neglect: Developmental Issues and Outcomes," *Child Abuse & Neglect* 26, no. 6–7 (2002): 679–695.

10. Marco Iacoboni, "Neural Mechanisms of Imitation," *Current Opinion in Neurobiology* 15 (2005): 632–637.

11. Jo-Marie v. d. M. Bothma, "Mirror Neurons and Baby Development," Mind Moves Institute, June 7, 2019, https://www.mindmoves.co.za/2019/06/07/mirror-neurons-and-baby-development.

12. Marco Iacoboni, "Imitation, Empathy, and Mirror Neurons," *Annual Review of Psychology* 60 (2009): 653–670; Jean Decety and Andrew N. Meltzoff, "Empathy, Imitation, and the Social Brain," in *Empathy: Philosophical and Psychological Perspectives*, ed. Amy Copland and Peter Goldie (New York: Oxford University Press, 2011), 58–81.

13. Iacoboni, "Neural Mechanisms."

14. Joni N. Saby, Andrew N. Meltzoff, and Peter J. Marshall, "Infants' Somatotopic Neural Responses to Seeing Human Actions: I've Got You

Under My Skin," *PLoS ONE* 8, no. 10 (2013): e77905; Molly McElroy, "A First Step in Learning by Imitation, Baby Brains Respond to Another's Actions," *University of Washington News*, October 30, 2013, https://www.washington.edu/news/2013/10/30/a-first-step-in-learning-by-imitation-baby-brains-respond-to-anothers-actions.

15. Marcel Brass and Cecilia Heyes, "Imitation: Is Cognitive Neuroscience Solving the Correspondence Problem?," *TRENDS in Cognitive Sciences* 9, no. 10 (2005): 489–495.

16. Tanya L. Chartrand and John A. Bargh, "The Chameleon Effect: The Perception-Behavior Link and Social Interaction," *Journal of Personality and Social Psychology* 76, no. 6 (1999): 893–910; Rod Parker-Rees, "Liking to Be Liked: Imitation, Familiarity and Pedagogy in the First Years of Life," *Early Years* 27, no. 1 (2007): 3–17.

17. Chartrand and Bargh, "The Chameleon Effect," 894–895.

18. Malia F. Mason, Rebecca Dyer, and Michael I. Norton, "Neural Mechanisms of Social Influence," *Organizational Behavior and Human Decision Processes* 110 (2009): 152–159.

19. Jean-Pierre Dupuy, "Naturalizing Mimetic Theory," in *Mimesis and Science: Empirical Research on Imitation and the Mimetic Theory of Culture and Religion*, ed. Scott R. Garrels (East Lansing: Michigan State University Press, 2011), 193–214. Or, as Girard noted, "Every desire redoubles when it is seen to be shared." See Maël Lebreton et al., "Your Goal Is Mine: Unraveling Mimetic Desires in the Human Brain," *Journal of Neuroscience* 32, no. 21 (2012): 7146–7157.

20. René Girard, *Deceit, Desire, and the Novel* (Baltimore: Johns Hopkins University Press, 1966), 99.

21. Vittorio Gallese, "The Two Sides of Mimesis: Girard's Mimetic Theory, Embodied Simulation and Social Identification," *Journal of Consciousness Studies* 16, no. 4 (2009): 21–44.

22. The only way out of this Chinese finger-trap, Girard argues, is a mutually agreed upon sacrifice: a scapegoat. A scapegoat is an innocent (in ancient Western civilization, a bull, goat, or even a human to be sacrificed to the gods) who gets blamed for the problems of the larger community, allowing people to unite against a common enemy. Often the scapegoat is an outsider. The history of humanity is rife with instances of scapegoating based on social groupings, from slavery and intertribal warfare to Nazism, China's internment of the Uygur, and American

identity politics. One particularly sad contemporary example can be found in the mountains of Papua New Guinea, where accusations of *sanguma*, or a kind of sorcery based on supernatural powers and the ability to cause death, have led to repeated tragedy as innocent people are tortured and even murdered. In *sanguma* accusations, the strength of the clan often overrides even the closest kin bonds, and the persecution of a witch is viewed as legitimate, reasonable, and even moral. Indeed, even a witch's murder is a justifiable act in defense of one's clan, especially when the accused are either "strangers on the inside," such as women who have married into the community, or "insiders who have become strangers" due to social isolation. See Philip Gibbs, "Engendered Violence and Witch-Killing in Simbu," in *Engendering Violence in Papua New Guinea*, ed. Margaret Jolly, Christine Stewart, and Carolyn Brewer (Canberra: Australian National University, 2012), 107–135; Miranda Forsyth, "Summary of Main Themes Emerging from the Conference on Sorcery and Witchcraft-Related Killings in Melanesia, 5–7 June 2013, ANU, Canberra," *Outrigger: Blog of the Pacific Institute*, June 18, 2013, http://pacificinstitute.anu.edu.au/outrigger/2013/06/18/summary -sorcery-witchcraft-related-killings-in-melanesia-5-7-june-2013.

23. "Weber State University," *U.S. News & World Report*, accessed March 11, 2021, https://www.usnews.com/best-colleges/weber-state -university-3680.

24. Abraham P. Buunk and Frederick X. Gibbons, "Social Comparison: The End of a Theory and the Emergence of a Field," *Organizational Behavior and Human Decision Processes* 102 (2007): 3–21.

25. Gayannée Kedia, Thomas Mussweiler, and David E. J. Linden, "Brain Mechanisms of Social Comparison and Their Influence on the Reward System," *NeuroReport* 25, no. 16 (2014): 1255–1265.

26. Brent McFerran et al., "I'll Have What She's Having: Effects of Social Influence and Body Type on the Food Choices of Others," *Journal of Consumer Research* 36 (2010): 915–929.

27. Lauren E. Sherman et al., "What the Brain 'Likes': Neural Correlates of Providing Feedback on Social Media," *Social Cognitive and Affective Neuroscience* 13, no. 7 (2018): 699–707.

28. David T. Hsu et al., "Response of the μ-Opioid System to Social Rejection and Acceptance," *Molecular Psychiatry* 18, no. 11 (2013): 1211–1217.

29. Yi Luo et al., "Social Comparison in the Brain: A Coordinate-Based Meta-analysis of Functional Brain Imaging Studies on the Downward and Upward Comparisons," *Human Brain Mapping* 39 (2018): 440–458.

30. Sara J. Solnick and David Hemenway, "Is More Always Better? A Survey on Positional Concerns," *Journal of Economic Behavior & Organization* 37, no. 3 (1998): 373–383.

31. Bill D. Moyers, "What a Real President Was Like," *Washington Post*, November 13, 1988, https://www.washingtonpost.com/archive/opinions/1988/11/13/what-a-real-president-was-like/d483c1be-d0da-43b7-bde6-04e10106ff6c.

32. Erik C. Nook and Jamil Zaki, "Social Norms Shift Behavioral and Neural Responses to Foods," *Journal of Cognitive Neuroscience* 27, no. 7 (2015): 1412–1426.

33. Social psychologist Henri Tajfel and his colleagues also explored this weird bias toward the majority in the 1970s. They found that people will form two "minimal groups" even over the most meaningless superficialities such as the toss of a coin, the arrangement of dots on a page, or their interest in two kinds of abstract art. In the 1970s, Tajfel tested this propensity by studying how fourteen- and fifteen-year-old schoolboys would respond when given the chance to advance their own group's interests at the expense of another's. The groupings themselves were trivial (based on the color of the boys' shirts), and none of the study participants were allowed to interact with each other face-to-face. Yet participants still cared most about advancing their own group's share of a reward, either fairly or unfairly. This was true even when that reward required the sacrifice of other, more objective advantages their group might have. Moreover, the boys chose to advance their own group's interests even when it had little to do with their own personal gain and when it would have cost little to themselves or their group to reward everyone from both groups equally. See Henri Tajfel et al., "Social Categorization and Intergroup Behavior," *European Journal of Social Psychology* 1, no. 2 (1977): 149–178; see also Henri Tajfel, "Experiments in Intergroup Discrimination," *Scientific American* 223, no. 5 (1970): 96–103.

34. Jessica M. Perkins et al., "Social Norms, Misperceptions, and Mosquito Net Use: A Population-Based, Cross-Sectional Study in Rural Uganda," *Malaria Journal* 18, no. 1 (2019): 189.

35. "2 Billion Mosquito Nets Delivered Worldwide Since 2004," RBM Partnership to End Malaria, January 16, 2020, https://endmalaria.org /news/2-billion-mosquito-nets-delivered-worldwide-2004.

CHAPTER 5

Chasing Ghosts

1. The ancient Egyptians, Greeks, and Romans all used forks of various kinds for spearing and carving things but not for eating. The first known dining forks were used in the seventh century by nobles of the Middle East and the Byzantine Empire. When the Greek niece of Byzantine emperor Basil II brought a set of golden forks to her wedding in Venice in 1004, she was openly mocked. After she died of the plague two years later, Saint Peter Damian blamed her demise on her aristocratic airs and the "golden instrument with two prongs" with which she insisted on eating her meals. See Chad Ward, "Origins of the Common Fork," *Culinaria*, May 6, 2009, https://leitesculinaria.com/1157/writings-origins-fork.html.

2. Sara Goldsmith, "The Rise of the Fork," *Slate*, June 20, 2012, http:// www.slate.com/articles/arts/design/2012/06/the_history_of_the_fork _when_we_started_using_forks_and_how_their_design_changed _over_time_.html.

3. Stephanie Butler, "Of Knives and Forks," *History*, May 23, 2019, https://www.history.com/news/of-knives-and-forks.

4. See Pascal Tréguer, "Origin of the Phrase, 'To Sit Below the Salt,'" Word Histories, accessed March 17, 2021, https://wordhistories .net/2017/12/20/below-salt-origin.

5. "Online Course: Dining Etiquette—CreativeLive," Emily Post Institute, accessed March 3, 2021, https://emilypost.com/lifestyle /online-dining-etiquette.

6. See Norbert Elias, *The Civilizing Process*, vol. 1: *The History of Manners*, trans. Edmund Jephcott (New York: Urizen Books, 1978).

7. Audie Cornish and Mark Vanhoenacker, "Americans' Dining Technique Was Long-Abandoned by French," *NPR*, July 5, 2013, https:// www.npr.org/templates/story/story.php?storyId=199114108.

8. Mimsie Ladner, "10 Superstitions That Koreans Still Believe Today," Culture Trip, May 24, 2018, https://theculturetrip.com/asia/south-korea /articles/10-superstitions-that-koreans-still-believe-today.

9. Jeffrey Rifkin, "Ethnography and Ethnocide: A Case Study of the Yanomami," *Dialectical Anthropology* 19, no. 2/3 (1994): 295–327.

10. Denise Winterman, "Queuing: Is It Really the British Way?," *BBC*, July 4, 2013, https://www.bbc.com/news/magazine-23087024.

11. Yes, Melissa got her TV!

12. Jonathan Haidt et al., "Body, Psyche, and Culture: The Relationship Between Disgust and Morality," *Psychology and Developing Societies* 9, no. 1 (1997): 107–131

13. R. N. Rossier, "The Lessons We Forget—Distraction, Disorientation, and Illusions," *Business and Commercial Aviation* 95, no. 3 (2004): 50–55.

14. Michele Rucci and Martina Poletti, "Control and Functions of Fixational Eye Movements," *Annual Review of Vision Science* 1 (2015): 499–518.

15. H. R. Everett, *Unmanned Systems of World Wars I and II* (Cambridge, MA: MIT Press, 2015), 401; Zoe Krasney, "What Were the Mysterious 'Foo Fighters' Sighted by WWII Night Flyers?," *Air and Space Magazine*, August 2016, https://www.airspacemag.com/history-of-flight/what-were-mysterious-foo-fighters-sighted-ww2-night-flyers-180959847.

16. Muzafer Sherif, "A Study of Some Social Factors in Perception," *Archives of Psychology* 27, no. 187 (1935): 1–60.

17. Muzafer Sherif, "An Experimental Approach to the Study of Attitudes," *Sociometry* 1, no. 1/2 (1937): 90–98.

18. Muzafer Sherif, *The Psychology of Social Norms* (New York: Harper & Row, 1936).

19. Sherif, "A Study of Some Social Factors in Perception."

20. Markham Heid, "Does Thinking Burn Calories? Here's What the Science Says," *Time*, September 19, 2018, https://time.com/5400025/does-thinking-burn-calories.

21. Bo-Rin Kim et al., "Social Deviance Activates the Brain's Error-Monitoring System," *Cognitive, Affective and Behavioral Neuroscience* 12, no. 1 (2012): 65–73.

22. In some places, the convention against eating tomatoes took on a religious edge: like other fruits and vegetables in the nightshade family, the tomato was thought to be helpful to witches, so it was deemed a source of devilish temptation. See K. Annabelle Smith, "Why the Tomato Was Feared in Europe for More Than 200 Years," *Smithsonian Magazine*, June 18, 2013, https://www.smithsonianmag.com/arts-culture

/why-the-tomato-was-feared-in-europe-for-more-than-200-years-863735; Romie Stott, "When Tomatoes Were Blamed for Witchcraft and Were- wolves," *Atlas Obscura*, October 24, 2016, https://www.atlasobscura.com /articles/when-tomatoes-were-blamed-for-witchcraft-and-werewolves.

23. Gayle Turim, "Who Invented Pizza?," *History*, July 27, 2012, https:// www.history.com/news/a-slice-of-history-pizza-through-the-ages.

24. In *Candide*, Voltaire makes fun of the philosophy of Gottfried Leibniz, who believed the existing world is the best world that God could have created. Leibniz's argument for the doctrine of what is now called Leibnizian optimism defended the justness of God despite the obvious problems of evil in the world. See "Best of All Possible Worlds," *Encyclo- pedia Britannica*, accessed March 5, 2021, https://www.britannica.com /topic/best-of-all-possible-worlds.

25. Voltaire, *Candide: or Optimism*, trans. Burton Raffel (New Haven, CT: Yale University Press, 2005).

26. Voltaire, *Candide*.

27. Elizabeth Flock, "Dagen H: The Day Sweden Switched Sides of the Road (Photo)," *Washington Post*, February 17, 2012, https://www .washingtonpost.com/blogs/blogpost/post/dagen-h-the-day-sweden -switched-sides-of-the-road-photo/2012/02/17/gIQAOwFVKR_blog.html; Maddy Savage, "A 'Thrilling' Mission to Get the Swedish to Change Overnight," *BBC*, April 17, 2018, https://www.bbc.com/worklife/arti cle/20180417-a-thrilling-mission-to-get-the-swedish-to-change-over night.

28. Doug Bierend, "Throwback Thursday: Hilarity Ensues as Sweden Starts Driving on the Right," *Wired*, February 6, 2014, https://www.wired .com/2014/02/throwback-thursday-sweden.

29. Evan Andrews, "The History of the Handshake," *History*, August 9, 2016, https://www.history.com/news/what-is-the-origin-of-the-handshake.

30. Theodore G. Obenchain, *Genius Belabored: Childbed Fever and the Tragic Life of Ignaz Semmelweis* (Tuscaloosa: University of Alabama Press, 2016), 32.

31. The deadly difference between these two wards was so stark that it was obvious, even to the public. Semmelweis noted how women randomly assigned to the doctors' ward would kneel and wring their hands, begging to be released so they could be readmitted and sent to the midwives' ward. Obenchain, *Genius Belabored*, 68.

32. Obenchain, *Genius Belabored*, 103, 174; Irvine Loudon, "Ignaz Phillip Semmelweis' Studies of Death in Childbirth," *Journal of the Royal Society of Medicine* 106, no. 11 (2013): 461–463.

33. Ignaz Semmelweis, *Etiology, Concept and Prophylaxis of Childbed Fever*, trans. K. Codell Carter (Madison: University of Wisconsin Press, 1983 [1861]), 142–143.

CHAPTER 6

The Reign of Error

1. David DiSalvo, "Your Brain Sees Even When You Don't," *Forbes*, June 22, 2013, https://www.forbes.com/sites/daviddisalvo/2013/06/22 /your-brain-sees-even-when-you-dont.

2. Karl Friston, "Prediction, Perception and Agency," *International Journal of Psychophysiology* 83, no. 2 (2012): 248–252; see also Jordana Cepelewicz, "To Make Sense of the Present, Brains May Predict the Future," *Quanta Magazine*, July 10, 2018, https://www.quantamagazine .org/to-make-sense-of-the-present-brains-may-predict-the-future -20180710.

3. Dale T. Miller and Cathy McFarland, "Pluralistic Ignorance: When Similarity Is Interpreted as Dissimilarity," *Journal of Personality and Social Psychology* 53, no. 2 (1987): 298–305.

4. Juan Manuel Contreras et al., "Common Brain Regions with Distinct Patterns of Neural Responses During Mentalizing About Groups and Individuals," *Journal of Cognitive Neuroscience* 25, no. 9 (2013): 1406–1417.

5. Miller and McFarland, "Pluralistic Ignorance."

6. Lee Ross, David Greene, and Pamela House, "The 'False Consensus Effect': An Egocentric Bias in Social Perception and Attribution Processes," *Journal of Experimental Social Psychology* 13 (1976): 219–301. Populace and Gallup, "The Success Index," Populace.org, 2019, https:// static1.squarespace.com/static/59153bc0e6f2e109b2a85cbc/t/5d939cc86 670c5214abe4b50/1569955251457/Populace+Success+Index.pdf.

7. Emily Ekins, "Poll: 62% of Americans Say They Have Political Views They're Afraid to Share," CATO Institute, July 22, 2020, https:// www.cato.org/survey-reports/poll-62-americans-say-they-have-political -views-theyre-afraid-share; Populace and Gallup, "The Success Index."

8. Sarah K. Cowan and Delia Baldassarri, " 'It Could Turn Ugly': Selective Disclosure of Attitudes in Political Discussion Networks," *Social Networks* 52 (2018): 1–17.

9. "Historical Estimates of World Population," US Census Bureau, accessed March 19, 2021, https://www.census.gov/data/tables/time-series /demo/international-programs/historical-est-worldpop.html; Population Estimates Program, Population Division, US Census Bureau, "Historical National Population Estimates: July 1, 1900, to July 1, 1999," United States Census Bureau, April 11, 2000, https://www2.census.gov/programs -surveys/popest/tables/1900-1980/national/totals/popclockest.txt.

10. "Life Expectancy for Social Security," Social Security Administration, accessed March 22, 2012, https://www.ssa.gov/history/lifeexpect .html.

11. Robin I. M. Dunbar, "Neocortex Size as a Constraint on Group Size in Primates," *Journal of Human Evolution* 22, no. 6 (1992): 469–493.

12. Dunbar, "Neocortex Size."

13. Abby Ohlheiser, "Did Drake Die? No, That Was—Yawn—a 4chan Hoax," *Washington Post*, November 24, 2015, https://www .washingtonpost.com/news/the-intersect/wp/2015/11/24/did-drake -die-no-that-was-yawn-a-4chan-hoax.

14. Alex Kaplan, "A Fake CNN Site Started a Viral Hoax. Radio Stations Blamed CNN," Media Matters for America, April 17, 2018, https://www .mediamatters.org/fake-news/fake-cnn-site-started-viral-hoax-radio -stations-blamed-cnn; "Former First Lady Barbara Bush Dies at 92," Archive.today, accessed March 11, 2021, http://archive.li/EGhsB.

15. See Craig Silverman, Jane Lytvynenko, and Scott Pham, "These Are 50 of the Biggest Fake News Hits on Facebook in 2017," *Buzz-feed News*, December 28, 2017, https://www.buzzfeednews.com/article /craigsilverman/these-are-50-of-the-biggest-fake-news-hits-on-face book-in; Kim LaCapria, "Did President Trump Reverse President Obama's Turkey Pardons?," Snopes, January 25, 2017, https://www .snopes.com/fact-check/trump-turkey-pardons-reversed; Bethania Palma, "Did an Elderly Woman Train 65 Cats to Steal from Her Neighbors?," Snopes, November 9, 2017, https://www.snopes.com/fact-check /did-elderly-woman-train-cats-to-steal.

16. Christo Petrov, "25+ Impressive Big Data Statistics for 2020," *Techjury* (blog), February 5, 2021, https://techjury.net/blog/big-data-statistics.

17. Jacquelyn Bulao, "How Much Data Is Created Every Day in 2020?," *Techjury* (blog), May 18, 2021, https://techjury.net/blog /how-much-data-is-created-every-day.

18. Bernard Marr, "How Much Data Do We Create Every Day? The Mind-Blowing Stats Everyone Should Read," *Forbes*, May 21, 2018, https://www.forbes.com/sites/bernardmarr/2018/05/21/how-much -data-do-we-create-every-day-the-mind-blowing-stats-everyone-should -read.

19. Steve James, "The George Washington Bridge Can Be a Motorist's Nightmare," CNBC, January 9, 2014, https://www.cnbc.com/2014/01/09 /the-george-washington-bridge-can-be-a-motorists-nightmare.html.

20. Daniel J. Levitin, "Why It's So Hard to Pay Attention, Explained by Science," *Fast Company*, September 23, 2015, https://www.fast company.com/3051417/why-its-so-hard-to-pay-attention-explained -by-science.

21. Here's another mind-blowing set of facts: one byte of digital data (7.5 bits) is enough to store a single character of text. If each star in our Milky Way (as many as four hundred billion) were a byte of digital data, we would have about four hundred gigabytes. Multiply that by 750 million, and you arrive at the total amount of information we have today. If, for some reason, you wanted to download all the data on the internet, it would take you 181 million years to do so. See Maggie Masetti, "How Many Stars in the Milky Way?," *Blueshift*, July 22, 2015, https://asd.gsfc .nasa.gov/blueshift/index.php/2015/07/22/how-many-stars-in-the-milky -way; Petrov, "25+ Impressive Big Data Statistics."

22. At its worst, this process can have damaging mental and physical consequences. An overloaded brain leads to feelings of stress, anxiety, powerlessness, and exhaustion. Adrenaline and the stress hormone cortisol flood our systems, keeping us on perpetual high alert and feeding our addiction to the source of the stress. We lose sleep and gain weight. Eventually the brain begins to shut down, like a circuit breaker, to protect itself from becoming completely overwhelmed. Daniel J. Levitin, "Why the Modern World Is Bad for Your Brain," *The Guardian*, January 18, 2015, https://www.theguardian.com/science/2015/jan/18/modern-world -bad-for-brain-daniel-j-levitin-organized-mind-information-overload; Daniel J. Levitin, *The Organized Mind: Thinking Straight in the Age of Information Overload* (New York: Penguin, 2015).

23. Gordon Pennycook, Tyrone D. Cannon, and David G. Rand, "Prior Exposure Increases Perceived Accuracy of Fake News," *Journal of Experimental Psychology: General* 147, no. 12 (2018): 1865–1880.

24. Ian Maynard Begg, Ann Anas, and Suzanne Farinacci, "Dissociation of Processes in Belief: Source Recollection, Statement Familiarity, and the Illusion of Truth," *Journal of Experimental Psychology: General* 121, no. 4 (1992): 446–458.

25. Anthony Kenny, *Wittgenstein* (Cambridge, MA: Harvard University Press, 1973).

26. Garth S. Jowett and Victoria O'Donnell, *Propaganda and Persuasion* (London: Sage Publications, 2006), 230. Still, there is a limit to how much repetition works. Scientists have found that information repeated too many times, or pressed upon us, raises our suspicions and leads us to mistrust the source. See Thomas Koch and Thomas Zerback, "Helpful or Harmful? How Frequent Repetition Affects Perceived Statement Credibility," *Journal of Communication* 63, no. 6 (2013): 993–1010.

27. Stefan Wojcik and Adam Hughes, "Sizing Up Twitter Users," Pew Research Center, April 24, 2019, https://www.pewresearch.org/internet/2019/04/24/sizing-up-twitter-users.

28. Tony Bartelme, "Troll Hunters: 2 Clemson Professors Race to Expose a Shadowy Force of Russian Internet Soldiers," *Post and Courier*, January 16, 2020, https://www.postandcourier.com/news/2-clemson-professors-race-to-expose-a-shadowy-force-of-russian-internet-soldiers/article_ebdaa49e-0569-11ea-865a-7f0b0aef77e6.

29. Scott Shane, "The Fake Americans Russia Created to Influence the Election," *New York Times*, September 7, 2017, https://www.nytimes.com/2017/09/07/us/politics/russia-facebook-twitter-election.html.

30. US Senate, "Report of the Select Committee on Intelligence, United States Senate, on Russian Active Measures Campaigns and Interference in the 2016 U.S. Election," Vol. 2, 116th Congress, accessed April 26, 2021, https://www.intelligence.senate.gov/sites/default/files/documents/Report_Volume2.pdf.

31. Darren L. Linvill and Patrick L. Warren, "Troll Factories: Manufacturing Specialized Disinformation on Twitter," *Political Communication* 37, no. 4 (2020): 447–467

32. Bartelme, "Troll Hunters."

33. Bartelme, "Troll Hunters."

34. US Senate, "Report of the Select Committee."

35. Emerging Technology from the arXiv, "How the Friendship Paradox Makes Your Friends Better Than You Are," *MIT Technology Review*, January 14, 2014, https://www.technologyreview.com/2014/01/14/174587/how-the-friendship-paradox-makes-your-friends-better-than-you-are.

36. Populace and Gallup, "The Success Index."

37. Populace and Gallup, "The Success Index."

38. Yalda T. Uhls and Patricia M. Greenfield, "The Rise of Fame: An Historical Content Analysis," *Cyberpsychology* 5, no. 1 (2011): 1.

39. "Internet Growth Statistics," Internet World Stats, accessed March 11, 2021, https://www.internetworldstats.com/emarketing.htm.

40. Monica Anderson and Jingjing Jiang, "Teens' Social Media Habits and Experiences," Pew Research Center, November 28, 2018, https://www.pewresearch.org/internet/2018/11/28/teens-social-media-habits-and-experiences.

41. Yalda T. Uhls, "Kids Want Fame More Than Anything," *HuffPost*, January 19, 2012, https://www.huffpost.com/entry/kids-want-fame_b_1201935.

CHAPTER 7

The Virtue of Congruence

1. Bob Delaney, Dave Scheiber, and Bill Walton, *Covert: My Years Infiltrating the Mob* (New York: Union Square Press, 2009).

2. Bob Delaney, interviewed by Todd Rose and Bronwyn Fryer, January 11, 2021. "Dudley Do-Right" was the do-gooder Canadian Mountie character in *The Adventures of Rocky and Bullwinkle*, a cartoon show in the early 1960s.

3. Delaney, Scheiber, and Walton, *Covert*.

4. Delaney, Scheiber, and Walton, *Covert*.

5. Delaney, Scheiber, and Walton, *Covert*.

6. Delaney, Scheiber, and Walton, *Covert*.

7. Bob Delaney, interviewed by Todd Rose and Bronwyn Fryer, January 11, 2021.

8. Rogers was also a disciple of Abraham Maslow, who is best known for his hierarchy of needs. See Saul McLeod, "Maslow's Hierarchy of

Needs," *Simply Psychology*, December 29, 2020, https://www.simply psychology.org/maslow.html.

9. Carl R. Rogers, "The Necessary and Sufficient Conditions of Therapeutic Personality Change," *Psychotherapy: Theory, Research, Practice, Training* 44, no. 3 (2007): 240–248.

10. Eddie Harmon-Jones and Judson Mills, "An Introduction to Cognitive Dissonance Theory and an Overview of Current Perspectives on the Theory," in *Cognitive Dissonance: Reexamining a Pivotal Theory in Psychology*, ed. Eddie Harmon-Jones, 2nd ed. (Washington, DC: American Psychological Association, 2019), 1–24; see also Dan Ariely, *The (Honest) Truth About Dishonesty: How We Lie to Everyone—Especially Ourselves* (New York: HarperCollins, 2012).

11. Henry David Thoreau, *Walden* (New York: Thomas Y. Crowell & Co., 1910), 8.

12. Harmon-Jones and Mills, "An Introduction to Cognitive Dissonance Theory."

13. Liane Young, Alek Chakroff, and Jessica Tom, "Doing Good Leads to More Good: The Reinforcing Power of a Moral Self-Concept," *Review of Philosophy and Psychology* 3 (2012): 325–334.

14. "Plagiarism: Stopping Word Thieves," CBS News, October 21, 2012, https://www.cbsnews.com/news/plagiarism-stopping-word-thieves.

15. David T. Welsh et al., "The Slippery Slope: How Small Ethical Transgressions Pave the Way for Larger Future Transgressions," *Journal of Applied Psychology* 100, no. 1 (2014): 114–127.

16. Leon Festinger, "Cognitive Dissonance," *Scientific American* 207, no. 4 (1962): 93–106.

17. Maxim Kireev et al., "Possible Role of an Error Detection Mechanism in Brain Processing of Deception: PET-fMRI Study," *International Journal of Psychophysiology* 90 (2013): 291–299.

18. Theodor Schaarschmidt, "The Art of Lying," *Scientific American*, July 11, 2018, https://www.scientificamerican.com/article/the-art-of-lying.

19. Nobuhito Abe et al., "Deceiving Others: Distinct Neural Responses of the Prefrontal Cortex and Amygdala in Simple Fabrication and Deception with Social Interactions," *Journal of Cognitive Neuroscience* 19, no. 2 (2007): 287–295.

20. Abe et al., "Deceiving Others."

21. When the subjects of one study misled others about what they truly believed, they felt dirty and immoral. Distressed, they sought ways to physically cleanse themselves and engage positively with others, to compensate for their violation of the truth. See Francesca Gino, Maryam Kouchaki, and Adam D. Galinsky, "The Moral Virtue of Authenticity: How Inauthenticity Produces Feelings of Immorality and Impurity," *Psychological Science* 26, no. 7 (2015): 983–996.

22. Steve Silberman, "Don't Even Think About Lying: How Brain Scans Are Reinventing the Science of Lie Detection," *Wired*, January 1, 2006, https://www.wired.com/2006/01/lying.

23. Li Bel, "The Neuroscience of Lying," *BrainWorld*, June 26, 2020, https://brainworldmagazine.com/the-neuroscience-of-lying.

24. Scientists have found that those with damage to their lateral prefrontal cortex are more likely to lie in order to earn more money. Thus, input from the lateral prefrontal cortex can help us to do the right thing even when it's in our own interest to lie. See Adrianna Jenkins, Lusha Zhu, and Ming Hsu, "Cognitive Neuroscience of Honesty and Deception: A Signaling Framework," *Current Opinion in Behavioral Sciences* 11 (2016): 130–137.

25. Delaney, Scheiber, and Walton, *Covert*.

26. Studies of self-esteem show how people with higher self-esteem who receive positive feedback consistent with their own self-image view it as an affirmation of their value and social standing and a positive reflection of the person giving the feedback. By contrast, even when given compliments that correlate with their own vision of themselves, those with low self-esteem tend not to feel the same social affirmation or affinity for the person giving the feedback. See Charlotte C. Van Schie et al., "When Compliments Do Not Hit but Critiques Do: An fMRI Study into Self-Esteem and Self-Knowledge in Processing Social Feedback," *Social Cognitive and Affective Neuroscience* 13, no. 4 (2018): 404–417.

27. Brain scans show how this process occurs in real time. Social rejection prompts less regulation of emotions and more social pain (in the medial prefrontal cortex and ventral anterior cingulate cortex) in the brains of people with lower self-esteem. Meanwhile, the same rejection triggers less distress, for a shorter period, in those with higher self-esteem. See Van Schie et al., "When Compliments Do Not Hit."

28. Though I disagree with some of Branden's political leanings, the book helped me enormously at the time.

29. Nathaniel Branden, *The Six Pillars of Self-Esteem* (London: Bantam, 1994).

30. People with low self-esteem experience more negative feelings, including anxiety and depression. They tend to engage in more hazardous behaviors and often slip into unhealthy habits such as smoking or drug or alcohol abuse, activities that put them at higher risk for heart disease, cancer, and other illnesses. See Huanhua Lu et al., "The Hippocampus Underlies the Association Between Self-Esteem and Physical Health," *Scientific Reports* 8 (2018): 17141.

31. Therapists have found that having people write about their core personal values expands their perception of themselves and the resources at their disposal, strengthening their sense of integrity and connection to self. As the results of this exercise play out in behaviors, self-reflection, and social interactions over time, psychologists say, self-esteem increases. See Geoffrey L. Cohen and David K. Sherman, "The Psychology of Change: Self-Affirmation and Social Psychological Intervention," *Annual Review of Psychology* 65 (2014): 333–371.

32. Those with lower self-esteem will avoid conflict even when doing so requires behaviors that contradict their view of themselves. This incongruence, in turn, compounds the internal conflict between a person's understanding of their self-worth and their behavior, making them even less likely to resist future social influence. See Katharine L. Cimini, "The Effect of Self-Esteem on Attitude-Behavior Consistency" (undergraduate honors thesis, Lycoming College, 1990).

33. McLeod, "Maslow's Hierarchy."

34. Populace and Gallup, "The Success Index," Populace.org, 2019, https://static1.squarespace.com/static/59153bc0e6f2e109b2a85cbc/t /5d939cc86670c5214abe4b50/1569955251457/Populace+Success+Index .pdf.

35. Rogers, "The Necessary and Sufficient."

36. Populace and Gallup, "The Success Index."

37. Jiménez and Mesoudi, "Prestige-Biased Social Learning."

38. Stefania Innocenti and Robin Cowan, "Self-Efficacy Beliefs and Imitation: A Two-Armed Bandit Experiment," *European Economic Review* 113 (2019): 156–172.

39. Van Schie et al., "When Compliments Do Not Hit"; Cimini, "The Effect of Self-Esteem."

40. Johannes Klacki, Eva Jonas, and Martin Kronbichler, "Existential Neuroscience: Self-Esteem Moderates Neuronal Responses to Mortality-Related Stimuli," *Social Cognitive and Affective Neuroscience* 9, no. 11 (2014): 1754–1761; Branden, *The Six Pillars*. At a neurological level, greater self-esteem strengthens our ability to both detect and manage anxiety and mortal threats. Studies have shown how a particular area of the brain (the bilateral insula) dampens the impact of unpleasant or death-related information, whereas heightened activity in the brains of people with lower self-esteem (in the bilateral ventrolateral prefrontal and medial orbitofrontal cortex) showed how they had to expend more effort to handle thoughts relating to death. See Klacki, Jonas, and Kronbichler, "Existential Neuroscience."

41. Johannes Abeler, Anke Becker, and Armin Falk, "Truth-Telling: A Representative Assessment" (CeDEx Discussion Paper Series No. 2012-15, University of Nottingham, Centre for Decision Research and Experimental Economics, 2012).

42. Diana I. Tamir and Jason P. Mitchell, "Disclosing Information About the Self Is Intrinsically Rewarding," *PNAS* 109, no. 21 (2012): 8038–8043; Kevan Lee, "Your Brain on Dopamine: The Science of Motivation," *I Done This Blog*, April 9, 2019, http://blog.idonethis.com/the-science-of-motivation-your-brain-on-dopamine. Our relationship to lying also responds to the situation we are in and how it might impact others. For example, we are more likely to lie the more we can gain from it but less likely to do so the more others appear to lose from it. Our natural aversion to lying grows the less true a lie is and the more we have riding on it. See Tobias Lundquist et al., "The Aversion to Lying," *Journal of Economic Behavior & Organization* 70, nos. 1–2 (2009): 81–92.

43. Robin I. M. Dunbar, "Breaking Bread: The Functions of Social Eating," *Adaptive Human Behavior and Physiology* 3 (2017): 198–211.

44. J. Kiley Hamlin, "The Origins of Human Morality: Complex Socio-moral Evaluations by Preverbal Infants," in *New Frontiers in Social Neuroscience*, ed. Jean Decety and Yves Christen (New York: Springer, 2014), 165–188.

45. Young, Chakroff, and Tom, "Doing Good Leads to More Good."

46. Young, Chakroff, and Tom, "Doing Good Leads to More Good."

47. Aristotle was born in 384 BC.

48. Laura Kipnis, "I Mean It," *New York Times*, August 10, 2012, https://www.nytimes.com/2012/08/12/books/review/sincerity-by-r-jay-magill-jr.html.

49. Michel de Montaigne, *The Essays of Montaigne, Complete*, trans. Charles Cotton, ed. William Carew Hazlitt (Salt Lake City, UT: Project Gutenberg, 1877), https://www.gutenberg.org/files/3600/3600-h/3600-h.htm.

50. Edward Muir, *Ritual in Early Modern Europe* (Cambridge: Cambridge University Press, 2005), 281.

51. Voltaire, *Candide: or Optimism*, trans. Burton Raffel (New Haven, CT: Yale University Press, 2005).

52. Kipnis, "I Mean It."

53. Bill George, author of the seminal book on authentic leadership, says authentic leaders do the following: understand their purpose, practice solid values, lead with heart, establish connected relationships, and demonstrate self-discipline. See Bill George, "Authentic Leadership Rediscovered," *Harvard Business School Working Knowledge*, November 10, 2015, https://hbswk.hbs.edu/item/authentic-leadership-rediscovered.

54. Charles Dickens, *A Christmas Carol* (London: Chapman & Hall, 1843), 8.

55. Yanming An, "Western 'Sincerity' and Confucian 'Cheng,'" *Asian Philosophy* 14, no. 2 (2004): 155–169.

56. An, "Western 'Sincerity'" (my emphasis).

57. Benjamin Franklin, *The Art of Virtue: Ben Franklin's Formula for Successful Living* (New York: Skyhorse Publishing, 2012), 15.

58. Delaney, Scheiber, and Walton, *Covert*.

59. Bob Delaney, interviewed by Todd Rose and Bronwyn Fryer, January 11, 2021.

60. Brain scans have revealed an association between higher self-esteem and increased neural activity in the zone connecting the areas responsible for self-knowledge (the medial prefrontal cortex) and motivation and reward (ventral striatum). The size of this zone, known as the frontostriatal pathway, and the amount of neural activity along it correlate directly to a person's self-esteem. See Robert S. Chavez and Todd F. Heatherton, "Multimodal Frontostriatal Connectivity Underlies Individual Differences in Self-Esteem," *Social Cognitive and Affective Neuroscience* 10, no. 3 (2015): 364–370.

61. Delaney, Scheiber, and Walton, *Covert*.
62. Delaney, Scheiber, and Walton, *Covert*.

CHAPTER 8

Trusting Strangers

1. His words stuck with me: I have since paid back a few lifetimes' worth.

2. During the pandemic, some mothers and children went without food because the discounted foods they are allowed to buy through the Special Supplemental Nutrition Program for Women, Infants, and Children (aka WIC) weren't available. This forced them to visit several different stores in search of the items they could buy—all during a pandemic when you've been laid off and are supposed to be teaching your kids remotely and your hungry toddler is screaming in the backseat. How frustrating and infuriating would that be? See Mike Stunson, "As Shoppers Stockpile Groceries, Moms Have Trouble Finding WIC Items amid Coronavirus," *Sacramento Bee*, March 24, 2020, https://www.sacbee.com/news/coronavirus/article241456946.html.

3. Of course, the federal food stamp supervisors take home six-figure salaries from the administrative fees they earn overseeing dozens of overlapping welfare programs. One US Department of Agriculture report written by a Brookings Institution fellow noted that the Food Stamp Program spends roughly sixteen cents per dollar on the food stamps it issues. See Julia Isaacs, "The Costs of Benefit Delivery in the Food Stamp Program: Lessons from a Cross-Program Analysis," Contractor and Cooperator Report 39 (Washington, DC: USDA, 2008).

4. According to the Urban Institute, 96 percent of the $361 billion spent on welfare programs in 2017 went toward operational costs, including program administration and payments to Medicaid providers, nonprofits, and other private providers of public services for low-income beneficiaries. Federal programs include the refundable portions of the Earned Income Tax Credit and Child Tax Credit, which assist low- and moderate-income working families; programs that provide cash payments to eligible individuals or households, including Supplemental Security Income for the elderly or disabled poor and unemployment insurance; various forms of in-kind assistance for low-income people, including

the Supplemental Nutrition Assistance Program (food stamps), school meals, low-income housing assistance, child care assistance, and help meeting home energy bills; and various other programs such as those that aid abused or neglected children. The largest slice of operational costs (81 percent) were vendor payments for medical care. See "Policy Basics: Where Do Our Federal Tax Dollars Go?," Center on Budget and Policy Priorities, April 9, 2020, https://www.cbpp.org/research/federal -budget/policy-basics-where-do-our-federal-tax-dollars-go. That doesn't include the roughly $700 billion that state and local governments spend on programs such as cash assistance through Temporary Assistance for Needy Families, Supplementary Security Income, the Federal Low Income Home Energy Assistance Program, the Supplemental Nutrition Program for Women and Children (WIC), "and other payments made directly to individuals as well as payments to physicians and other service providers under programs like Medicaid." See "Public Welfare Expenditures," Urban Institute, accessed February 18, 2021, https://www.urban.org /policy-centers/cross-center-initiatives/state-and-local-finance-initiative /state-and-local-backgrounders/public-welfare-expenditures.

5. Lindsay J. Thompson, "Paternalism," *Britannica*, accessed March 12, 2021, https://www.britannica.com/topic/paternalism.

6. "Paternalism," *New World Encyclopedia*, accessed March 10, 2021, https://www.newworldencyclopedia.org/entry/Paternalism.

7. Only in the nineteenth century, when the English philosopher John Stuart Mill questioned whether paternalism caused more harm than good, did people begin to see paternalism as a justification for silencing the powerless. In his classic treatise "On Liberty," Mill wrote, "The disposition of mankind, whether as rulers or as fellow-citizens, to impose their own opinions and inclinations as a rule of conduct on others, is so energetically supported by some of the best and by some of the worst feelings incident to human nature, that it is hardly ever kept under restraint by anything but want of power." Mill argued that individuals know their own interests better than those seeking to impose paternalism on them. Apparently Taylor neither read Mill nor cared. See John Stuart Mill, *On Liberty* (London: John W. Parker and Son, 1859), 29.

8. Arthur G. Bedeian and Daniel A. Wren, "Most Influential Management Books of the 20th Century," *Organizational Dynamics* 29, no. 3 (2001): 221–225.

9. Debbie Sniderman, "Frederick Winslow Taylor," American Society of Mechanical Engineers, June 22, 2012, https://www.asme.org/topics-resources/content/frederick-winslow-taylor; "Frederick Winslow Taylor," *Dictionary of American Biography* (New York: Charles Scribner & Sons, 1936).

10. "Frederick Winslow Taylor," *PBS: Who Made America?*, accessed January 27, 2021, http://www.pbs.org/wgbh/theymadeamerica/whomade/taylor_hi.html.

11. Meagan Day, "We Are All Charlie Chaplin on the Assembly Line," *Jacobin*, June 17, 2019, https://jacobinmag.com/2019/06/taylorism-scientific-management-worker-power.

12. Frederick Winslow Taylor, *The Principles of Scientific Management* (New York: Harper & Brothers Publishers, 1919), 59.

13. Charlie Chaplin, dir., *Modern Times* (Los Angeles: United Artists, 1936).

14. "Company Overview," *Harvard Business Review*, accessed March 10, 2021, https://hbr.org/corporate/about; see also Justin Fox, "The Bedraggled Return of the Organization Man," *Harvard Business Review*, June 5, 2013, https://hbr.org/2013/06/the-bedraggled-return-of-the-orga.

15. Alex Tabarrok, "Regulation and Distrust—The Ominous Update," *Marginal Revolution*, August 16, 2016, https://marginalrevolution.com/marginalrevolution/2016/08/regulation-and-distrust-revisited.html.

16. Philippe Aghion et al., "Regulation and Distrust," *Quarterly Journal of Economics* 125, no. 3 (2010): 1015–1049.

17. Lindsey M. Rodriguez et al., "The Price of Distrust: Trust, Anxious Attachment, Jealousy, and Partner Abuse," *Partner Abuse* 6, no. 3 (2015): 298–319; Judith E. Glaser, "Your Brain Is Hooked on Being Right," *Harvard Business Review*, February 28, 2013, https://hbr.org/2013/02/break-your-addiction-to-being.

18. See Robert V. Robinson and Elton F. Jackson, "Is Trust in Others Declining in America? An Age-Period-Cohort Analysis," *Social Science Research* 30 (2001): 117–145; Robert D. Putnam, *Bowling Alone: The Collapse and Revival of American Community* (New York: Simon & Schuster, 2000).

19. Survey responses over time have revealed how Americans have become increasingly distrustful. Today's youngest Americans are also the least trusting of others. This is due, in part, to how a person changes

as they age, as well as the events, social formation, and historical context they share with others in the same generation. Americans, in general, become more trusting of others as we get older. See Robinson and Jackson, "Is Trust in Others Declining."

20. In addition, according to the General Social Survey, which periodically assesses the moods and values of Americans, the number of respondents who believed others could generally be trusted dropped by an average of ten points from 1976 to 2006. Lee Rainie, Scott Keeter, and Andrew Perrin, "Trust and Distrust in America," Pew Research Center, July 22, 2019, https://www.pewresearch.org/politics/2019/07/22 /trust-and-distrust-in-america.

21. David Brooks, "America Is Having a Moral Convulsion," *The Atlantic*, October 5, 2020, https://www.theatlantic.com/ideas/archive/2020/10 /collapsing-levels-trust-are-devastating-america/616581.

22. Megan Brenan, "U.S. National Pride Falls to Record Low," Gallup, June 15, 2020, https://news.gallup.com/poll/312644/national-pride-falls -record-low.aspx.

23. Mark Murray, "Poll: 80 Percent of Voters Say Things Are Out of Control in the U.S.," NBC News, June 7, 2020, https://www .nbcnews.com/politics/meet-the-press/poll-80-percent-voters-say -things-are-out-control-u-n1226276.

24. Brooks, "America Is Having." Right after the January 20, 2021, inauguration of President Joe Biden, Populace confirmed the bad news. Our surveys showed that 82 percent of the country thinks Americans are more divided than united (and 41 percent said we are extremely divided). See Populace, "The American Aspirations Index," Populace, 2021, https:// static1.squarespace.com/static/59153bc0e6f2e109b2a85cbc/t/603d422cc fad7f5152ab9a40/1614627374630/Populace+Aspirations+Index.pdf.

25. See "BU Historian Answers: Are We Headed for Another Civil War?," *BU Today*, March 27, 2019, http://www.bu.edu/articles/2019 /are-we-headed-for-another-civil-war.

26. Eric Rosales, "Man Finds $125,000 in Cash & Gives It Back, Gets Reward!," *Fox26News*, May 29, 2014, https://kmph.com/archive /man-finds-125000-in-cash-gives-it-back-gets-reward.

27. Alain Cohn et al., "Civic Honesty Around the Globe," *Science* 365, no. 6448 (2019): 70–73.

28. Jill Suttie, "Why People May Be More Honest Than You Think," *Greater Good Magazine*, August 13, 2019, https://greatergood.berkeley .edu/article/item/why_people_may_be_more_honest_than_you_think.

29. Populace and Gallup, "The Success Index," Populace.org, 2019, https://static1.squarespace.com/static/59153bc0e6f2e109b2a85cbc/t/5d 939cc86670c5214abe4b50/1569955251457/Populace+Success+Index.pdf.

30. In 2019, a survey found that Republican respondents believed Democrats to be 55 percent more immoral than other Americans, while Democrat respondents said Republicans were 47 percent more immoral than others. See "Partisan Antipathy: More Intense, More Personal," Pew Research Center, October 10, 2019, https://www.pewresearch.org /politics/2019/10/10/how-partisans-view-each-other.

31. Populace, "The American Aspirations Index."

32. Populace, "The American Aspirations Index."

33. Paul Ekman, Eve Ekman, and Jason Marsh, "Can I Trust You?," *Greater Good Magazine*, September 1, 2008, https://greatergood.berkeley .edu/article/item/can_i_trust_you; see also Paul Ekman, *Why Kids Lie: How Parents Can Encourage Truthfulness* (London: Penguin Books, 1991).

34. Paul J. Zak, "The Neuroscience of Trust," *Harvard Business Review*, January–February 2017, https://hbr.org/2017/01/the-neuroscience-of-trust.

35. Zak, "The Neuroscience of Trust."

36. Marc A. Cohen and Mathew S. Isaac, "Trust *Does* Beget Trustworthiness and Also Begets Trust in Others," *Social Psychology Quarterly*, December 8, 2020, https://doi.org/10.25384/SAGE.c.5236125.v1.

37. Brooks, "America Is Having."

38. Brooks, "America Is Having."

39. Though most of us trim the occasional corner. See Dan Ariely, *The (Honest) Truth About Dishonesty: How We Lie to Everyone—Especially Ourselves* (New York: HarperCollins, 2012).

40. Terence Burnham, Kevin McCabe, and Vernon L. Smith, "Friend-or-Foe Intentionality Priming in an Extensive Form Trust Game," *Journal of Economic Behavior & Organization* 43 (2000): 57–73.

41. Nancy L. Carter and J. Mark Weber, "Not Pollyannas: Higher Generalized Trust Predicts Lie Detection Ability," *Social Psychological and Personality Science* 1, no. 3 (2010): 274–279.

42. See Zak, "The Neuroscience of Trust."

43. "Hometown Hero: Oakland's Mauricio Miller Forges New Path Out of Poverty for Clients," *East Bay Times*, March 16, 2015, https://www.eastbaytimes.com/2015/03/16/hometown-hero-oaklands-mauricio-miller-forges-new-path-out-of-poverty-for-clients.

44. Anne Stuhldreher and Rourke O'Brien, "The Family Independence Initiative: A New Approach to Help Families Exit Poverty" (Washington, DC: New America Foundation, 2011).

45. Stuhldreher and O'Brien, "The Family Independence Initiative."

46. "Partner: UpTogether Is Not a Program," UpTogether, accessed June 28, 2021, https://www.uptogether.org/partner.

47. "A Community-Centered Approach to Socioeconomic Mobility," UpTogether, accessed June 28, 2021, https://www.uptogether.org/approach.

48. "A Community-Centered Approach"; Stuhldreher and O'Brien, "The Family Independence Initiative."

49. "Lunch with a Genius," *Nonprofit Chronicles*, October 19, 2016, https://nonprofitchronicles.com/2016/10/19/lunch-with-a-genius; "Our Story," UpTogether, accessed June 28, 2021, https://www.uptogether.org/our-story.

50. "UpTogether: Trusting and Investing in Families," video posted to YouTube by UpTogether, May 4, 2021, https://www.youtube.com/watch?v=dUXwFGyozzA&t=43s.

51. Family Independence Initiative, "COVID-19 Impact Report," UpTogether, August 2020, https://www.uptogether.org/wp-content/uploads/2021/05/FII_COVID_ImpactReport.pdf.

52. "Our Story"; Family Independence Initiative, "COVID-19 Impact Report."

53. "Investing in People Has Huge Returns," UpTogether, accessed June 28, 2021, https://www.uptogether.org/impact.

54. "Lunch with a Genius."

55. "Donate," UpTogether, accessed June 28, 2021, https://www.uptogether.org/donate.

56. "Californians on Universal Basic Income Paid Off Debt and Got Full-Time Jobs," *The Guardian*, March 4, 2021, https://www.theguardian.com/us-news/2021/mar/03/california-universal-basic-income-study; Amy Castro Baker et al., "Mitigating Loss of Health Insurance and Means Tested Benefits in an Unconditional Cash Transfer Experiment:

Implementation Lessons from Stockton's Guaranteed Income Pilot," *SSM—Population Health* 11 (August 2020): 100578.

57. Jesse M. Cunha, Giacomo De Giorgi, and Seema Jayachandran, "The Price Effects of Cash Versus In-Kind Transfers" (NBER Working Paper 17456, National Bureau of Economic Research, 2011).

58. Francesca Giuliani-Hoffman, "Researchers Gave Thousands of Dollars to Homeless People. The Results Defied Stereotypes," CNN, October 9, 2020, https://www.cnn.com/2020/10/09/americas/direct -giving-homeless-people-vancouver-trnd/index.html.

59. "Aseptic/Packaging Mechanic, Morning Star Company," SmartRecruiters, accessed January 25, 2021, https://jobs.smartrecruiters .com/TheMorningStarCompany/743999724783626-aseptic-packaging -mechanic; Gary Hamel, "First, Let's Fire All the Managers," *Harvard Business Review*, December 2011, https://hbr.org/2011/12/first -lets-fire-all-the-managers.

60. "Morning Star Videos," Morning Star, accessed March 10, 2021, https://www.morningstarco.com/resources/morning-star-videos; Hamel, "First, Let's Fire All the Managers"; "Join Our Team," Morning Star, accessed March 10, 2021, https://www.morningstarco.com/careers.

61. Hamel, "First, Let's Fire All the Managers."

62. Zak, "The Neuroscience of Trust."

63. In the context of the Covid-19 pandemic, greater trust in Scandinavia's government health care systems contributed to an extremely high rate of compliance with personal measures to prevent infection (over 98 percent in both Norway and Sweden). See Lisa M. Helsingen et al., "The COVID-19 Pandemic in Norway and Sweden—Threats, Trust, and Impact on Daily Life: A Comparative Survey," *BioMed Central Public Health* 20, no. 1 (2020): 1597.

64. Halden was designed by Danish group Erik Moller Architects and the Norwegian HLM Arkitekur AS. In 2010, Halden received the Arnstein Arneberg Award for interior design. See Knut Egil Wang, "Inside Norway's Halden Prison," The Story Institute, accessed March 12, 2021, https://www.thestoryinstitute.com/halden.

65. Christina Sterbenz and Pamela Engel, "A Norwegian Who Killed 77 People Is Suing over Prison Conditions—These Photos Show How Luxurious Norwegian Prisons Are," *Insider*, March 19, 2016, https:// www.businessinsider.com/what-are-norway-prisons-like.

66. Jeffrey Kofman, "In Norway, a Prison Built on Second Chances," *NPR*, May 31, 2015, https://www.npr.org/sections/parallels/2015/05/31/410532066 /in-norway-a-prison-built-on-second-chances; Wang, "Inside Norway's Halden Prison." Research consistently shows that time spent in solitary confinement elevates emotional trauma. "Isolation syndrome" is the term used for the severe and long-lasting effects of this type of disciplinary action in prisons. See Stuart Grassian, "Psychiatric Effects of Solitary Confinement," *Journal of Law and Policy* 22 (2006): 325–383.

67. "About the Norwegian Correctional Service," Norwegian Correctional Service, accessed February 19, 2021, https://www.kriminalom sorgen.no/?cat=536003.

68. A growing number of American prison and criminal justice professionals are embracing Norway's methods. "I think you have to see it to believe it," said North Dakota corrections director Leann Bertsch, who has twice visited Halden and has adopted reforms based on the Norwegian model. Taylorist critics note that Norway spent $129,222 per prisoner in 2018, compared with $38,051 per prisoner in Michigan. Skeptics also argue that Norwegian methods could not work in the United States because Norway is more racially homogeneous. See "Is Norway a Model for Better Prison Practices?," *The Crime Report*, October 10, 2019, https://thecrimereport.org/2019/10/10/is-norway-a-model-for -better-prison-practices; on the North Dakota experiment, see Dashka Slater, "North Dakota's Norway Experiment," *Mother Jones*, July/ August 2017, https://www.motherjones.com/crime-justice/2017/07 /north-dakota-norway-prisons-experiment.

69. Wendy Sawyer and Peter Wagner, "Mass Incarceration: The Whole Pie 2020," Prison Policy Initiative, March 24, 2020, https:// www.prisonpolicy.org/reports/pie2020.html; "Mass Incarceration Costs $182 Billion Every Year, Without Adding Much to Public Safety," Equal Justice Initiative, February 6, 2017, https://eji.org/news /mass-incarceration-costs-182-billion-annually.

CHAPTER 9

Living in Truth

1. See Václav Havel, "The Power of the Powerless," in *The Power of the Powerless: Citizens Against the State in Central-Eastern Europe*, ed. John

Keane (London: Hutchinson, 1985). In 1993 Czechoslovakia peacefully split into two countries, the Czech Republic and Slovakia.

2. Havel, "The Power of the Powerless."

3. M. Mark Stolarik, *The Czech and Slovak Republics: Twenty Years of Independence, 1993–2013* (Budapest: Central European University Press, 2016).

4. Václav Havel, *The Garden Party: and Other Plays* (New York: Grove Press, 1994).

5. Michael Zantovsky, *Havel: A Life* (New York: Grove Press, 2014), 128.

6. Zantovsky, *Havel*.

7. See Havel, "The Power of the Powerless."

8. Havel, "The Power of the Powerless."

9. David Dorsey, "Positive Deviant," *Fast Company*, November 30, 2000, https://www.fastcompany.com/42075/positive-deviant.

10. Richard Pascale, Jerry Sternin, and Monique Sternin, *The Power of Positive Deviance: How Unlikely Innovators Solve the World's Toughest Problems* (Cambridge, MA: Harvard Business Review Press, 2010), 27.

11. Pascale, Sternin, and Sternin, *The Power of Positive Deviance*, 34, 38.

12. Monique Sternin, "To Solve Hard Challenges, We Must Look for the Positive Deviants | Monique Sternin | TEDxMidAtlantic," video posted to YouTube by TEDx Talks on October 24, 2014, https://www.youtube.com/watch?v=B8J4fc3XyV4.

13. Pascale, Sternin, and Sternin, *The Power of Positive Deviance*, 5.

14. Pascale, Sternin, and Sternin, *The Power of Positive Deviance*, 43.

15. The term was invented by Tufts University nutritionist Marian Zeitlin. See Pascale, Sternin, and Sternin, *The Power of Positive Deviance*, 23.

16. Pascale, Sternin, and Sternin, *The Power of Positive Deviance*, 7.

17. "Positive Deviance Approach by Jerry Sternin," video uploaded to YouTube by Positive Deviance approach, April 30, 2015, https://www.youtube.com/watch?v=9Pj4egHN0-E.

18. Stella Babalola, David Awasum, and Brigitte Quenum-Renaud, "The Correlates of Safe Sex Practices Among Rwandan Youth: A Positive Deviance Approach," *African Journal of AIDS Research* 1, no. 1 (2002): 11–21; Samir S. Awad et al., "Implementation of a Methicillin-Resistant *Staphylococcus aureus* (MRSA) Prevention Bundle Results in Decreased

MRSA Surgical Site Infections," *American Journal of Surgery* 198, no. 5 (2009): 607–610; Pascale, Sternin, and Sternin, *The Power of Positive Deviance*, 156; Gretchen M. Spreitzer and Scott Sonenshein, "Toward the Construct Definition of Positive Deviance," *American Behavioral Scientist* 47, no. 6 (2004): 828–847.

19. United Nations Children's Fund (UNICEF), *Female Genital Mutilation/Cutting: A Statistical Overview and Exploration of the Dynamics of Change* (New York: UNICEF, 2013).

20. Ronan Van Rossem and Dominique Meekers, "The Decline of FGM in Egypt Since 1987: A Cohort Analysis of the Egypt Demographic and Health Surveys," *BMC Women's Health* 20, no. 1 (2020): 100; UNICEF, *Female Genital Mutilation*; Ronan Van Rossem, Dominique Meekers, and Anastasia J. Gage, "Women's Position and Attitudes Towards Female Genital Mutilation in Egypt: A Secondary Analysis of the Egypt Demographic and Health Surveys, 1995–2014," *BMC Public Health* 15 (2015): 874.

21. *The Guardian* shared the horrifying story of one seven-year-old girl. See Maryum Saifee, "I'm a Survivor of Female Genital Cutting and I'm Speaking Out—as Others Must Too," *The Guardian*, February 8, 2016, https://www.theguardian.com/commentisfree/2016/feb/08/victim-fgm -speaking-out-cut-genitals-culture-of-silence. In 2020, one Egyptian father tricked his daughters into circumcision by telling them they were going to get a Covid-19 vaccine. See "Egyptian Girls 'Tricked into FGM' with COVID-19 Vaccine," Aljazeera, June 5, 2020, https://www.aljazeera .com/news/2020/6/5/egyptian-girls-tricked-into-fgm-with-covid-19 -vaccine.

22. Peggy Mulongo, Sue McAndrew, and Caroline Hollins Martin, "Crossing Borders: Discussing the Evidence Relating to the Mental Health Needs of Women Exposed to Female Genital Mutilation," *International Journal of Mental Health Nursing* 23, no. 4 (2014): 296–305; Jeroen Knipscheer et al., "Mental Health Problems Associated with Female Genital Mutilation," *BJPsych Bulletin* 39, no. 6 (2015): 273–277; "Health Risks of Female Genital Mutilation (FGM)," World Health Organization, accessed April 12, 2021, https://www.who.int/teams/sexual-and-repro ductive-health-and-research/areas-of-work/female-genital-mutilation /health-risks-of-female-genital-mutilation.

23. The FGM numbers for Egypt are similar to those seen in Burkina Faso: over 95 percent of Egyptian women between the ages of fifteen

and forty-nine are circumcised, while 37 percent think the practice should be discontinued. "Female Genital Mutilation (FGM)," UNICEF, February 2020, https://data.unicef.org/topic/child-protection/female-genital-mutilation. Only Somalia, Guinea, Djibouti, Sierra Leone, and Mali surpass Egypt in the prevalence of FGM. Van Rossem and Meekers, "The Decline of FGM."

24. Pascale, Sternin, and Sternin, *The Power of Positive Deviance*, 62.

25. Pascale, Sternin, and Sternin, *The Power of Positive Deviance*, 73.

26. Pascale, Sternin, and Sternin, *The Power of Positive Deviance*, 75. See also "As More Families Report FGM Incidents in Egypt, Advocacy Intensifies, and a New Bill Seeks to Increase Penalties," UN Women, February 5, 2021, https://www.unwomen.org/en/news/stories/2021/2/feature--families-report-fgm-in-egypt-and-advocacy-intensifies.

27. Van Rossem and Meekers, "The Decline of FGM."

28. Havel, "The Power of the Powerless."

29. Havel, "The Power of the Powerless."

INDEX

INDEX

INDEX

INDEX

INDEX

271

INDEX

INDEX

INDEX

INDEX